The Fallen Leaf Anthology
"The Write Retreat"
Stanford Sierra Camp 2010

Edited by Jerry Thrush, MD

The Fallen Leaf Anthology (as a whole) Copyright ©2011 Jerry Thrush, MD.

Each individual work, including cover photography, is Copyright ©2010, 2011 by its respective author, per Table of Contents.

ISBN 978-1-60910-596-9

All rights reserved. No part of this publication may be reproduced, stored in a retrieval system, or transmitted in any form or by any means, electronic, mechanical, recording or otherwise, without the prior written permission of the author(s). For use permissions or discussions of additional opportunities, contact the Editor or Author(s) directly, as listed in the Biography at the end of this book.

Printed in the United States of America.

Stories within are both fictional and non-fictional. Names may have been changed and works that were non-fictionally based may have been embellished with fictional material. Each author is fully credited with and completely responsible for his or her content.

As authors striving to improve our craft, we welcome your comments and suggestions. You may send work-specific comments directly to the contact info listed in the Biography section. We further encourage you to make general comments on our associated blog. Please find us at: http://fallenleafanthology.blogspot.com

Booklocker.com, Inc.
2011

For copies of this book, please go to www.booklocker.com or request a copy from your local bookseller.

Photography and Art Credits

Front Cover Photo .... Lynette Kent
Leaf Logo .... Karen Paluska
Rear Cover Photo... Karen Paluska
Rear Cover Photo... James Chandler

THE FALLEN LEAF ANTHOLOGY

"The Write Retreat"
Stanford Sierra Camp 2010

Editor

Jerry Thrush, MD

Introduction

The Write Retreat is a workshop at the Stanford Sierra Camp designed for writers of all levels to assemble and perfect their technique. In 2007 the first Write Retreat was held and since has become a Sierra Camp tradition. The Stanford Sierra Camp is located at the southern end of Fallen Leaf Lake in South Lake Tahoe, California, and is operated by the Stanford Alumni Association Sierra Programs, LLC.

Last year, at the third Write Retreat I sat staring at a fire in the Lodge chatting with James Chandler, a fellow attendee. In a flash of inspiration a spark leapt between us as I mentioned an idea that I had been mulling during the day, "What if we were to get a group of authors who wish to publish stories and collect them and publish them together?" I asked.

As fate would have it the heat of the idea fell on the ideal person and soon James was ablaze with the concept. He and I worked together during the 2009 Write Retreat to establish guidelines for submission, and develop the algorithm for a review panel to sift through the submissions. At the same time we began to recruit both reviewers and writers in earnest. As a result The Fallen Leaf Anthology 2009 was born. The Fallen Leaf Anthology 2010 continues that tradition.

Jerry Thrush, MD
Editor

Collator's Notes

This anthology is not only about "words." It's about the group of people it represents. We came together at the Stanford Sierra Camp to learn more about writing, to be inspired, to share our dreams, express ourselves to others, and be stimulated by the interactions. This anthology has allowed many of us to experience ourselves as "published authors" for the first time. It is not, however, only about that.

It's about *how* we made it happen as a group. This work has all been done by volunteers and all through emails. This has been a networked project that has depended on the benefits of technology and our ability to overcome its snags. We have relied on mutual trust, cooperation, attention to detail, willingness to learn more about software and email features, and most of all, perhaps, to accept the word "deadline" in red that headed many of my communications as Collator! We are now benefiting from a cooperative experience that has taken our Write Retreat to a new level of productivity.

I hope all of those involved realize how we as a group are learning still, being inspired anew, and finding our own voices. I hope all have had fun working through cyberspace to make this anthology we can now hold in our own hands. Perhaps it will encourage others attending the Write Retreat to contribute to future anthologies. Perhaps all other aspiring writers will realize by our example that they, too, can fulfill their writing dreams.

Betty Luceigh, Ph.D.
Collator

Special Thanks

I wish to thank the many individuals who made the Fallen Leaf Anthology 2010 possible. First of all, I wish to thank the twenty-five authors whose creative works constitute the heart of this anthology. Betty Luceigh was invaluable as Collator and spent innumerable hours collecting stories and emailing authors and myself. Petra LaVictoire provided exemplary services as Copy Editor. James Chandler was also a valuable resource as Editor Emeritus. He served as a sounding board for many of the issues we faced. Karen Paluska did an incredible job of developing the concept of the leaf logo and creating it. She also made many recommendations with respect to cover art, as did Lynette Kent. In addition, the seven reviewers were nothing short of amazing! None of us claim perfection, but we do claim our extraordinary best!

Jerry Thrush, MD
Editor

The Fallen Leaf Anthology 2010 Panel
Jerry Thrush, MD, Editor
James Chandler, Editor Emeritus
Betty Luceigh, Collator
Petra LaVictoire, Copy Editor
Karen Paluska, Graphic Artist, Leaf Logo
Lynette Kent, Front Cover Art
Reviewers, Anonymous

Prologue: Editor's Notes

This year's submissions ran the spectrum from romantic fantasy to musings over difficulties of relationships and divorce, reminisces of childhood, adventures and danger, and contemplations of social ills and physical ailments, not to mention expressions of love of the pets we cannot live without. There were many stories and poems that emphasize the human condition and raise consciousness of difficult issues that are foremost in our minds at our unique juncture in the history of the world. Such considerations stirred my interest and incited my innermost curiosity as I hope they do yours.

As a physician, as well as an editor, I noticed that there were stories that raised questions–many of them epidemiologic, that I was curious enough to explore. I have spent more than two decades in emergency departments and have walked patients through the tragedy described in the excellent story **"*Only a BB Gun*"** by Fred Michaud, and experienced the misfortune of the loss of dementia so eloquently depicted in the evocative works, ***The Swivel Chair*** by Neil McCabe, and ***The Hawk*** by Lila Perdue Naimark. Given my viewpoint as an editor who is also an Emergency Physician I wish to share some of my own considerations here. Please bear in mind that I am not an editor by profession, I was never an English or literature major, and, that the following represent my own opinions, reflections and research, and may not constitute those of the authors, Stanford University, Fallen Leaf Lake Camp or the Stanford Sierra Camps, LLC.

Taban by Will Harrison, MD is an outstanding work that personifies a child displaced by factors beyond his control while living in a war torn country. His story evoked vivid recollections of a time when I did some surgical work in a mountain "clinic" in the state of Chiapas, Mexico in the 1980's. During the period I was there, armed conflicts raged in the mountains nearby as we chased frogs and snakes out of the operating room before we could start our day. I recall operating on a small boy of about eight or nine years old who was caught in the crossfire and shot in the abdomen. We repaired nine perforations of his intestine one night *without true general anesthesia* (we only had Ketamine). The plight of the young man I described, and that of ***Taban***, is shared by millions of children around the world.

The United Nations Children's Fund (UNICEF) estimates that 20 million children have been forced to flee their homes because of conflict and human rights violations. They also estimate that 2 million children have died as a result of skirmishes and war over the last decade and that another 6 million children have been seriously injured or permanently disabled. Furthermore, according to UNICEF, in recent decades the proportion of civilian casualties in armed conflicts has increased dramatically.[1]

Stories such as ***Taban*** make us ever mindful of man's inhumanity to man and ultimately my hope remains that this increased awareness may someday lead to mitigation of this problem which is as old as mankind.

Hark the Herald Angels Sing by Bernd Kutzscher, MD is a well-written and exciting story that describes in white-knuckling detail the dangers of whitewater rafting. This is also an issue close to my own heart, as I have lost two personal friends to the wrath of rivers. I have had the honor of taking river trips with each of them. Bill Ingram and I shared a trip down the Rogue River in Oregon with his daughter and son-in-law. He sustained a sudden cardiopulmonary arrest shortly after making it to shore from an overturned inflatable on the Selway River. Joel Fegarido and I canoed down the Colorado several times together as youths. He was lost on the Snake River this year. Although he wasn't rafting at the time, he died a hero on a river while rescuing his ten-year-old son. According to my findings, fatalities as a result of river rafting are actually statistically uncommon. Information provided by an article in the official journal of the Wilderness Medical Society indicates that rafting fatalities occur at a rate of 0.55 per 100,000 user days. Kayaking fatalities are more common at 2.9 per 100,000 user days. Non-fatal rafting injuries ranged from 0.26 to 2.1 per 100,000 rafting days, while kayaking injuries ranged from 3 to 6 per 100,000 paddling days.[2] Per

---

[1] http://www.unicef.org/protection/index_armedconflict.html
[2] Winter; Wilderness Environ Med. 2003 14(4):255-60.

information from another source, **America Outdoors**, the number of deaths caused by river rafting ranges between 6 and 10 per year for an estimated 2.5 million user days on *guided* trips which gives a range of one death per 250,000 to 400,000 days of rafting. I found a reference to a CNN story about fatalities on whitewater trips and there was some concern voiced from that source that the CNN statistics did not separate *private* tours – where there are no requirements to wear a life jacket, from the *guided* tours where safety equipment is mandated.[3] It seems apparent that underlying health of the participant with respect to cardiovascular disease, life jackets use and first aid training are of critical importance to stave off the specter of the reaper while rafting.

The Swivel Chair by Neil McCabe provides a stupendous and emotional description of the evolution of dementia and its impact on family members. *The Hawk* by Lila Naimark, also marvelously constructed, goes a step further and depicts the effects of the later stages of the disease. It is well known that the incidence of dementia is increasing. What may not be appreciated by most, however, is the tremendous cost of dementia care to society. According to a report in the April 2007 issue of Alzheimer's & Dementia: The Journal of the Alzheimer's Association, entitled "An Estimate of the Total Worldwide Societal Costs of Dementia in 2005," the worldwide cost of dementia care was estimated at $315 billion U.S. dollars. The United States led the way, spending $76 billion, with Japan and China following at $34 and $28 billion respectively.[4]

It is estimated that worldwide more than 24 million people have dementia, with 4-6 million new cases presenting every year. These numbers indicate that one new case is diagnosed on our globe every seven seconds. It is also estimated that the total number of those affected with the disease will double within twenty years, and, that as lifespan increases in developing countries the forecast suggests that the

---

[3] http://www.americanwhitewater.org/content/Article/view/articleid/29824/display/full/

[4] Wimo, A, Winblad, B, Jönsson, L; "An estimate of the total worldwide societal costs of dementia in 2005." Alzheimer's & Dementia: The Journal of the Alzheimer's Association," p81-91 April 2007.

case load will increase by 100% overall, and in some countries such as India, by 300%.[5]

From my perspective as an Emergency Physician it seems clear that prevention and treatment may diminish these staggering costs, but, by the same token, society must also come to terms with what levels of care are appropriate for the patients with end-stage dementia who do not recognize those around them and cannot understand why people are doing painful procedures to them. Every day in hospitals in the United States, usually at the request of family members, people with end-stage dementia are given heroic care identified prospectively by their physicians as futile.

"Only a BB Gun" by Fred Michaud provides a fascinating insight into the whims of childhood and their disastrous consequences. Over the decades in the ER I have personally managed countless similar injuries that caused permanent disability. Three percent of visits to emergency departments nationwide in the United States are from eye related injuries.[6] More than 2 million eye injuries occur in the United States annually, with more than 40,000 resulting in some degree of permanent visual impairment.[7] Sadly, a recent study published in 2009 indicated that in spite of medical and surgical advances there were no significant changes in final visual outcome and surgical eye removal rates when a recently presenting cohort of patients were compared with a group presenting with similar injuries thirty years ago.[8]

On a humorous personal note--when I was about five years old, and my brother about thirteen, I recall him pressing me to stand still with a can on my head so he could shoot it off with a BB gun. After much argument I finally let him do it--but it had to be done MY way. I wore a full motorcycle helmet and a leather jacket. To protect myself even

---

[5] Ferri, Prince, et al; "Global prevalence of dementia: A Delphi consensus study," Lancet 2005; 366:2112-2117.

[6] Bord SP, Linden J; "Trauma to the globe and orbit." *Emerg Med Clin North Am.* Feb 2008; 26(1): 97-123

[7] Golden, DJ, MD, Acerra, JR, MD; "Globe rupture," http://emedicine.medscape.com/article/798223-overview

more I turned around and faced away from him. Better, but still not advisable! Kids--don't try that at home either!

A Change of Plans by Neil McCabe is another exceptionally well-written piece that caused me to query the frequency of arson-associated fires and numbers of lives lost as a result. I was astounded when I found the raw figures associated with loss of life and damage caused by intentionally set fires. The U.S. Fire Administration (USFA) is an entity of the Department of Homeland Security that gathers statistical information on fires in the United States. Considering structure fires alone, in 2008 there were 30,500 intentionally set structure fires that resulted in 315 civilian deaths and $866 million in property loss.[9]

My own story, **The Good Driver**, was conceived one day when I was trying to get to the hospital and found that en route there was a driver going substantially below the speed limit who blocked my every effort to pass. I do not have any statistics on those killed or injured by *good* drivers. Certainly not many, no matter how much they seem to raise the blood pressures of other drivers around them.

The numbers of persons killed in motor vehicle crashes remains staggering but continues to improve in recent years. I believe this is not as a direct result of better medical or surgical care as much it is from beneficial legislation, law enforcement, and improvements in automotive and highway engineering. According to the National Highway and Traffic Administration, fatalities in motor vehicle traffic crashes fell to 37,261 in 2008 from a recent high of 43,510 in 2005. It is exciting to note that this is the lowest level reported since 1961.[10] On September 9, 2010 the U.S. Transportation Secretary Ray LaHood released updated 2009 data indicating that national highway deaths fell to 33,208. This represents the lowest level reported since 1950.[11]

Finally, the interesting story of which I suspect Rod Sterling would have been proud to produce in a Twilight Zone episode, **The Root of All Evil Trilogy** by Petra LaVictoire, stimulated my interest in

---

[9] http://www.usfa.dhs.gov/statistics/arson/
[10] DOT HS 811 346 June 2010 National Highway and Traffic Administration: An Analysis of the Significant Decline in Motor Vehicle Traffic Fatalities in 2008.
[11] http://www.nhtsa.gov/PR/DOT-165-10

endangered plant species. In this strange tale, the author cleverly weaves a story which, although fantasy, involves a very real plant which exists securely enthroned, in all of its regal glory, on the endangered plant list. We are constantly bombarded by information about endangered animal species, but there seems less societal concern over endangered plants. We must recall however, that life as we know it on this planet depends on plants. According to scientists, plants are more fundamental to the functioning of nature than their animal counterparts. The findings of the first global plant inventory released in 1998 indicated that of the then 270,000 known species of plants, 12.5 percent were at risk of extinction.[12][13]

According to an updated study released this month, a more recent global analysis of extinction risk for the world's plants, conducted by Kew Botanical Gardens in the United Kingdom, together with the Natural History Museum, London and the International Union for Conservation of Nature (IUCN), has revealed that fully 20 percent of the world's now 380,000 known plant species are threatened with extinction.[14]

It is my hope that this year's anthology stimulates your interest, piques your curiosity, excites your imagination and creates in you a desire to read more, and write more eloquently.

Jerry Thrush, MD
Editor

---

[12] http://www.well.com/~davidu/plantextinction.html   The New York Times April 9, 1998 Page A-1 Plant Survey Reveals Many Species Threatened With Extinction. William Stevens.
[13] Science/AAAS | Random Samples: 17 April 1998; 280 (5362).
[14] http://www.kew.org/news/one-fifth-of-plants-under-threat-of-extinction.html

About Stanford Sierra Camp

Stanford Sierra Camp is located on Fallen Leaf Lake near Desolation Wilderness in the Lake Tahoe Basin. During the summer, Stanford alumni and their families come to the Camp for a week full of outdoor activities and educational opportunities coordinated by the Camp's energetic Stanford Student counselors.

During the spring, the Camp hosts a few alumni programs including the Write Retreat, a three-day golden opportunity to hone writing skills, jump-start long-imagined writing projects and collaborate with learned faculty and fellow writers in the serenity of Fallen Leaf Lake.

Stanford Sierra Camp was established in 1953 and purchased by the Stanford Alumni Association in 1959. In 1998, the Stanford Alumni Association merged with Stanford University to become Stanford Alumni Association Sierra Programs, LLC.

For more information on the Camp and/or spring programs, go to:
http://alumni.stanford.edu/get/page/sierra/family-camp
http://alumni.stanford.edu/get/page/sierra/spring

James Chandler
Editor Emeritus

Table of Contents

Section I: From the Pleasure of Words to the Ruminations of Romance 1
A Room of Words by *Betty Luceigh* 3
Memory in a Music Box by *Jerry Thrush, MD* 6
Á la Carte by *James Chandler* 20

Section II: The Drama of Relationships 23
Half Awake by *Karen Paluska* 25
Ensenada by *Kathy Nakamatsu* 38
The Runner by *Gregg Garmisa* 54
The First Step by *Jeanne Verville* 60
The Photo Gallery by *Tori Ritchie* 68
1492# by *Kathleen O'Hanlon Peterson* 75

Section III: Family Reminiscences 81
A Fine Way to Treat a Steinway by *Patricia Northlich* 83
Walden's Ridge by *Nancy Earl* 90
Understanding Chuck Cheese by *Cynthia Roberts* 93
A Fifties Girl Finds a New Thanksgiving by *Laura Kaufman* 97
Standing Room - A Memoir Chapter 1 by *Kathleen O'Hanlon Peterson* 100

Section IV: The Struggles of Living 113
The Swivel Chair by *Neil McCabe* 115
The Hawk by *Lila Naimark* 123
The List by *Kathy Nakamatsu* 129

Section V: Poetry 137
My Subatomic Awakenings by *Betty Luceigh* 139
My Vision of Beauty by *Betty Luceigh* 144
Highway 68 by *Robert Nielsen* 146
Upper East Side by *Robert Nielsen* 148
Border Crossing by *Robert Nielsen* 151

Computer Creativity by *Lynette Kent* 153
On Change by *Taly Rutenberg* 154

Section VI: The Unexpected Meets the Unexplained **155**

The Root of All Evil (Trilogy – Part 1) by *Petra LaVictoire* 157
The Root of All Evil Returns (Trilogy – Part 2) by *Petra LaVictoire* 160
The Root of All Evil – Final Eclipse (Trilogy – Part 3) by *Petra LaVictoire*.. 164
Raising More Than Cain by *Cynthia Roberts* 172
A Change of Plans by *Neil McCabe* 181

Section VII: Canine Companions and Feline Friends **191**

Do Dogs have Souls? by *Melanie Johnston* 193
Farewell, Thompson by *Lorilyn Parmer* 196
Girl with a Secret Comes Home by *Laura Kaufman*................... 200

Section VIII: Drama **205**

Taban by *Will Harrison, MD*.. 207
Fresco-1 Prolog and Chapter One by *Will Harrison, MD*........... 222
Hark the Herald Angels Sing by *Bernd Kutzscher, MD* 242
My Fish Story by *Jeanne Verville* 259
Two Toes (Part 1) by *Kinsley Earl*... 263
"Only a BB Gun" by *Fred Michaud*... 271
The Good Driver by *Jerry Thrush, MD*....................................... 279
Resigning my Commission by *James Chandler*........................... 300

Author Biographies... **303**

Notes on the Next Anthology.. **315**

Section I:
From the Pleasure of Words to the Ruminations of Romance

My words fly up, my thoughts remain below;
Words without thoughts never to heaven go.

William Shakespeare

Love is a smoke raised with the fume of sighs,
Being purged, a fire sparkling in lovers' eyes,
Being vexed, a sea nourished with lovers' tears.
What is it else? A madness most discreet,
A choking gall and a preserving sweet.

William Shakespeare

A Room of Words
Betty Luceigh

WORDS! WORDS! WORDS!
I've entered a room full of words!
They're *everywhere*...oozing out of the furniture,
clinging to my shirt, bumping me from behind.
Can you see them, too?
They're crawling up your arms,
and tickling the end of your nose.

Words! Random words, disconnected words!
I wonder where they came from?
Were they edited out of someone's life,
lost here from unfulfilled dreams,
trapped in cyberspace during a twitter?
Perhaps they snuck out of a trashcan
at a writer's conference,
longing to self-publish!

Words! Everywhere words!
I can't avoid breathing them,
this floating dictionary of gibberish,
I inhale nouns and adjectives,
exhale verbs and participles,
my lungs conjugating
in desperation for the next phrase.

Words! I see their translucent letters everywhere,
fonts of Courier and Helvetica and Times,
sticking to walls in bold capitals,
resting in italic loneliness on the empty bookshelf,
even popping out like word-dander from my dog!

"The Write Retreat" - Stanford Sierra Camp 2010

Are those *your* lofty words rising to the ceiling?
Is that a secret leaking out of your mouth?
And who left those tear-drenched words
sobbing in the shadows?

LOOK! LOOK! Do you see what they're doing now?
They're organizing themselves into groups...
sentences, paragraphs, even whole chapters!
They're suspended over each of your heads,
trying to sneak into your brains,
past your resistance to express them
in hopes of reincarnating on your paper.

So many words! They loiter everywhere,
with a few commas hovering in the corners
and periods pasted on the windows panes.
Look, a semicolon just slipped into your back pocket!

Words, some flashing with anticipation
that a poet or novelist or playwright
will string them into patterns
to express novelties of mind, fantasies of heart,
others hoping to become part of a joke,
others a deep philosophical truth.

What exhilaration to be a permutator
in this pandemonium of words,
to proclaim my sesquipedalian erudition
by creating grandiose profundity
from their otherwise paltry presence!
Ah, but first, first I must dust and mop and vacuum
the superficial words of nonsense,
to reveal my own unique expressions
from the words still struggling to be found,
squished under the cushions,
hiding behind the curtains,

and even now patiently clinging
to the very tip of my pencil!

My *own* words.
I'm ready to make room for *my* words.

Memory in a Music Box
Jerry Thrush, MD

Introduction

Tchaikovsky immortalized Russia's defense of Moscow against Napoleon's advancing army in 1812 with an extraordinary overture best known for its climactic chimes and incredible volleys of cannon blasts. In the infamous battle, Moscow safeguarded itself by setting its own buildings ablaze in a dramatic and ultimately successful attempt to thwart the invaders. The piece is entitled *The Year 1812, Festival Overture in E flat major, Op. 49* and popularly known as the *1812 Overture*. This story ties together a contemporary symphonic performance with the historical event that it commemorates.

1812

Smoke filled the air and the cacophony of cannon fire pierced the darkness. Church bells tolled and a river of tears flowed. In the chaos of a blazing city a pair of lovers made their way hand in hand through the smoking rubble. Although their voices were muted by the sound of flames licking the bones of smoldering buildings, they spoke as they walked. The woman leaned into the man and murmured into his ear.

"Our city is ruined!" she mourned.

"Only for a time. We will soon rebuild using the modern construction techniques of the 1800's. And we will do it without the French to tell us how they would have it done," he reassured, pausing to kiss her in the flickering firelight.

"But our most beautiful buildings, built over centuries, are destroyed!" lamented the girl. Her emerald eyes were moist with emotion.

"And Napoleon's soldiers will not have quarter. They will go home, and not make us their slaves. Besides – it will save more lives than if shots are fired. Tsar Alexander knew what he was doing when he allied himself with the English."

"A risky plan, this fire," countered the girl. "We might lose it all. What if the soldiers decide burning is the order of the day and set fire to our houses out of anger? What if they take the city anyway? What of our food? Will they take that too? And what will become of us next winter when they have eaten it all?"

The man suddenly stopped before a building that was just beginning to glow. Russian soldiers with torches ran past. The acrid smell of smoke bit them like a fiendish animal and their eyes smarted.

"Shhh. Do you hear it?" He held her tightly, and cupped his hand to his ear.

"Which?" she asked, "The crackling sound of everything we know going to heaven? Or the bells tolling their way?"

"There!" he said, pointing to grand hotel across the street. Flames coughed to life and smoke leaked from the upper windows.

"Another building sent to the sky! An irreplaceable monument lost!" she sighed.

"There it is again!"

"The sound of our lives turned to ashes? Of course I hear it!"

"No! There's more. Listen!" he whispered, holding her close.

Suddenly the man removed his hand from her waist and quickly wrapped his scarf around his face. He turned and dashed toward the flames.

"Where are you going? Don't go!" she screamed, tugging him back. He struggled away and pulled her hand roughly out of his.

"I must. Someone is there!" he shouted as he ran.

"No!" she screamed.

He jumped through the smoking entryway and flew up the stairs. A moment later she heard the mewling child and understood. Her man – the surgeon with the golden heart would give his all for the lives of others. As she silently worried a small face appeared in the window.

"Hurry!" she cried. "Please hurry!"

A hand appeared next to the child and the little one disappeared. Her heart skipped a beat then restarted with a flutter. He was there! He would save the child. An explosion roared and she fell to the ground as if her legs were pulled out from under her by a tether. Her ears rang and blood seeped from her nose. All was warm and dark.

The girl awoke not knowing what had happened. The world spun, and she held her head in her hands. She found that her chestnut hair was tangled and moist with sodden earth. She was disoriented for a moment and lay there in the freezing dirt, dazed and confused. Fire leapt through the roof of the grand hotel before her and lapped at the moon. She stared up at the sky, still not understanding. The roof of the building before her yawned, an orange blossom flowered and with it the gates of her memory widened. A young woman in tears appeared next to her and bounded for the building. Instinctively she tackled the mother to prevent her from entering the burning edifice.

"My baby! He's inside! Let me go!" The woman struck the green-eyed girl as hard as she could.

The ladies stopped wrestling when a figure suddenly appeared in the doorway holding a whimpering child. His clothes were smoking and his back was lit with the progeny of the monster that ate the inn. He collapsed, but protected the little one with blackened hands before he hit the ground.

As her lover struggled with the flames that were beginning to eat him alive, she ran to him and patted them out. All the memories of their brief courtship flashed before her. Among them, the image of the ornate music box that he had given her in happier times.

The mother of the child scooped him up and sat in the road smothering him with kisses and cooling him with her tears. A horse galloped by and splattered the small group with mud. The green-eyed girl stared into the eyes of her gasping lover, then glanced up to the heavens at the moon and liberated a prayer. The sound of the animal running, the chiming of church bells and the smoke drifting through the sky brought her back to an evening nearly a year before. She rocked him in her arms, hummed softly, and willed him to live. She tried to stay in the present but the mystery of his pupils staring up at her whisked her away.

She looked lovingly into his eyes. She remembered how endearing she found them when they first met. She wanted to swim in them and let them take her where they would. His eyes were one of his most striking features. The windows to his soul were dark blue, like a cobalt ocean on a sunny day. He always told her how they complimented her own emerald irises. And she thought his golden mane of long wavy hair contrasted beautifully with her rich brown locks. Notwithstanding the reflection of the raging inferno in his pupils and his toasted clothing, she let her mind pull her consciousness out of the present to the summer of 1811. She remembered it well.

On that other pivotal evening just before sunset, the full moon hung over their expectant city like a lamp. It added an extra layer of icing to the treat of the orchestra concert in the park that they had attended. After the music, the pair spoke excitedly of the symphony and the magic of the sunset as they strolled to his waiting steed. Flags waved happily in the breeze and the grass and flowers cloaked the world with the aroma of life. Clouds moved overhead like the gowns of angels, backlit by a silvery moon, and the tendrils of cooking fires snaked upward like incense in a cathedral. The scent of magic was in the air.

After the performance the couple rode his stallion through the narrow alleys and wide avenues all over town. They paused here and there in the moonlight to contemplate life and the greatness of their city. A star fell from the heavens and they wished the evening would last forever.

In the week following the concert, the handsome young man bought a music box from a man called Sergei who had a shop that smelled of cigars and silver polish. On the night he gave it to the girl with green eyes they opened it together. The flowers he placed inside released their delightful perfume of jasmine and rose, and soft music drifted out. Green eyes met blue and hope held affection. The music of the box reminded the couple of the summer concert in the park. As they looked and listened, both recalled the silvery magic of the moon, the singing violins, the drifting clouds, and a nighttime ride though a sleeping city. *A memory was born and slipped quietly into the box.*

The Present

Two centuries later, cannon blasts echoed from the hills of another great city. Smoke tarried in the sky, trumpets played, violins sang, and chimes sounded. Then all was silent and the grand finale of the 1812 Overture by Tchaikovsky was finished. This other immense metropolis – separated from the first by centuries and thousands of miles – basked in the ethereal light of the moon. In a nearby shop on Newport Avenue a memory stirred in the small gilded box where she was imprisoned. She heard the sound of a motorcycle tantivy away as a couple rode by, savoring the magic of the night and recalling the enchantment of the music they had just enjoyed. The vibrations in the air and the magic of the moonlight outside conspired, and the incarcerated memory began to wish once more...

There once was a memory who lived in a music box. The child of hope and affection, she was a creation emulsified with dreams and marinated in moonlight. The kiss of life was imparted upon her with a flurry of the bud and bloom, and a simple incantation uttered in the language of love. When released, she wafted ethereal, leaving only footprints of jasmine and rose. Her voice was the tinkling of bells. And her raiment was sewn of the fabric of purest joy. The sylph was as patient as she was beautiful, and meekly waited in the dark solitude of her home of silk and gold for the release she hoped would one day come again.

The memory knew that when the lid of her dwelling was lifted a beautiful young woman would peer in from on high and lovely pink lips would part. The sky would light up as white teeth appeared, bracketed by lovely dimples. Soft music would play, and she would leap forth, swirling and twirling, bobbling and bedazzling, climbing upwards, ever higher into the room in a mist of mirth, a geyser of glee, a cataract of creation – all reflected in emerald eyes which sparkled with delight.

When the box was opened the memory would dance. Her music, and the laughter of her girl, would blend in perfect harmony in a duet of delight. Reminiscences and bliss would fill the air like a warm sigh of springtime.

Sadly, the box in which the memory resided had been forgotten for many years. She knew her home changed hands countless times and the girl – *her girl*, was missing. The memory longed to be let out and rain happiness with dew drops of music on the beautiful one with smiling eyes and lovely patulous lips.

The memory was proud of the music box where she lived in spite of its age. Her dwelling was her tiny castle, lined with soft silk and velvet the color of moonlight. The exterior of her palace was crafted of fine gold grillwork that evoked images of one of the greatest cities on earth lost in the mists of time.

The memory sighed. The sound of the motorbike galloping by made her even lonelier. She didn't know exactly how long she had been locked in her gilded prison, but knew it was a long, long time. Passing epochs were commemorated by marks and scratches on its surface, and its interior was stained in many places. If time could be counted in dings and blots it would have spanned nearly two hundred years. But the hourglass of wear wasn't important to a memory. Memories can never be rendered obsolete, and cannot be tarnished with time as boxes and cities can. She knew she was a wonderful thing, and would spark the flame of happiness when her girl raised its top once more. If only she would.

Memories understood little of the world outside of themselves, but this one recalled the origin of her tiny home. She knew that her box was made in Switzerland and sold to a cigar smoking Russian named Sergei, who sold clocks and music boxes in his small shop in a back alley of Moscow.

The memory knew too, that the exquisite container where she lived had been purchased by a blond surgeon with kind blue eyes, and was given as a present to a beautiful girl with a lovely smile. Nothing lived in the box then except for tiny fleeting recollections of a wizened Swiss craftsman and Sergei and his little store.

She also realized that her box was sold to the surgeon one year before the world had gone mad, before Moscow lay in the crosshairs of the cannons of a small French man with a large ego. The sounds outside of blasts and chimes on this moonlit evening reminded the memory of that fateful evening nearly two centuries before. On that night the sky bled crimson as fires raged all about, and the life of a great city waned. Smoke hung in the air like an omen of doom. And it was the final time that her girl had let her out to play. The sylph in the box recalled that her girl had red, puffy eyes when she saw her last. Tears were shed and captured in the velvet lining of her gilded cottage – forever staining it. Nonetheless, the memory made the girl smile once more, albeit through the veil of her tears. She didn't know why her girl cried on that night; she only understood the language of laughter and love. Good memories are like that.

On the fateful twilight during the great conflagration, people wailed, and the city was lost by fire yet saved by its ashes. Before the coals could cool, the box containing the memory was wrapped in oilpaper and placed in a trunk by trembling hands. The next day it was moved to a horse drawn buggy that bumped down a windy lane and left the smoldering city behind.

After weeks of twisting down rocky paths, the box was removed from the trunk and taken to a cellar where it remained for many years. One day in 1850 it was found again, and brought to an old lady, who clutched it tightly to her breast. The memory recalled the touch of her girl and started with excitement. How she longed to come out and make the girl – *her girl* – smile once more. But it was not to be. The hands of the elderly woman were halted by order of death as she fumbled with the lid. So the memory was left inside, wishing in the blackness.

In spite of the desire of the being within, the cover was not raised again for many years. After the old lady with emerald eyes went to another world, the music box was placed in the back of the cellar once more. After two decades, it was opened by a young man who spoke German. The girl with the beautiful smile was not there. So the memory stayed in her box and did not come out. How could she? There was no smiling girl to delight. She did not understand that her girl had aged, or that she went to a place from which she could not return.

After a long while – again, she could not tell how much time had passed – a small girl cracked open the cover of her box. The little girl had brown eyes and a happy, inquisitive face. She liked to play princess and serve her imaginary friends tea to the music of the little gilded container. The happy child added a few memories to the box. But they were not like the remembrances of the blond young man and the green-eyed girl. The new memories stayed in their own area of the box and kept to themselves. The memory of the green-eyed girl with the lovely smile hid in the soft velvety darkness and silently wished she could make someone happy again.

Many more years passed. Eventually the box rolled and bucked over the Atlantic by steamer. As the vine of years bloomed decades, the girl who played tea with her dolls grew wrinkles, and the lines in her face lost the war with gravity. The old woman who once played princess forgot about the gilded music box as the bridge keeper of time collected his toll. She kept it safely locked away in an attic with the magical memory safely sealed within.

In 1905 the box was opened by a lawyer who said he was acting on behalf of an estate. The memory wasn't sure what an estate was. But she knew that she still longed for the green-eyed girl, with the wide smile. She knew she could conjure sunshine from that beam if only that special someone opened her home and traded dimples for recollection.

There was a sale associated with the liquidation of the estate, and her box was purchased by a collector with silver hair. The music box was kept a dozen years by the white-haired man because there was another war and many things lost value at such times. Near the end of the conflict, her box was given to a melancholy girl who cried whenever she opened it. That girl didn't put any memories inside. The memory only saw her lift the lid, cry for a while, and close it again. After her tears were spent she would shut the box and leave it on a shelf until she had recharged her ducts. The memory didn't know why the girl wept, but thought it had something to do with a thing she heard about called the "War to End All Wars."

One night the silent soliloquy of the sylph was shattered by a breaking window when a thief broke into the house of the girl who cried. The robber roughly threw the music box into a pillowcase with a candlestick, a clock, and some jewelry before he escaped into the night. The outside of the box was all the more scuffed, but the memory was safe. After all, memories cannot be stolen by thieves.

A hard man with cruel eyes opened the box the following morning. He sneered as he heard the music when the lid was up. Thankfully *that* man put few memories into the box, and those he did – could not remain. His recollections were only those of money, cruelty and something called "running rum." Loud jazz peppered with static played in the background from a phonograph and drowned out the soft music of the box. But the memory didn't care. She was not going to come out for this man. He had evil stains in the fabric of his soul much worse than those that now marred the velvet bottom of her gilded home.

The bad man threw the music box in a trash can in the alley outside. He hit his minion for putting something worthless into his bag. "Get a box with jewelry in it next time!" he scorned. "That's an empty one like your head."

In spite of this, the memory knew that her box; her home – *her* castle – wasn't empty. *She* lived there. But she wondered if she would be lost forever as she huddled in the box in the waste can. How she longed for the green-eyed girl with the lovely smile! How she wondered where she was, and if she was safe.

While the memory rested, and thought pleasant thoughts of her green-eyed girl, she felt the sensation of her home being lifted out of the rubbish. Calloused hands with tattered gloves picked her gingerly out of the trash. A toothless smile greeted the velvet lining when he opened it. The disheveled man hid the box in his shopping cart and pushed it away.

Two days later, when he began to shake for want of a drink, the homeless alcoholic traded his box to the owner of a liquor store for a bottle of brew. That night, the man from the liquor store gave it to his wife as an offering of peace in the name of love. The shop keep's wife was stout, and wide as she was high. She licked her lips with anticipation as her stubby fingers eagerly pulled the box open. She scolded her husband when she found that his gift did not contain sweets.

The memory thought that heavy people were supposed to be happy. After all, Santa was jolly, and she knew about him. She gleaned such knowledge through bits and pieces of conversations she could take in through the aging walls of her box. But the store owner's wife was not a merry soul. She was selfish, supercilious and cruel. The memory soon learned that the fat lady would tell her husband corpulent untruths about where she had been and how she had spent the family money when he was hard at work in the store. She felt she would never again make anyone happy. How she missed the girl with green eyes who would sit, and smile, and sigh, to the soft sounds of her musical voice.

Another great war came, and the box was forgotten for what seemed an eternity and a day. It remained stashed high up on a shelf behind a vase. Eventually, the big wife of the liquor store owner died in her sleep and her grandson went through her things. He found the old gilded box and placed it in a worn cardboard container and gave it to a charity. He didn't want a scuffed old box with stains inside.

The owner of the charity shop placed it behind glass in a counter in the front of the store. But business was bad during World War II and the music box wasn't bought again until 1948. One day the memory was awakened to a pleasant voice after a long sleep. A man with such a tenor and tone could be a radio announcer she thought. A kindly gentleman with a hat and a cane purchased the music box and excitedly told the cashier that it was for his granddaughter who had just been born. He was a good man. The memory could sense that as plain as sunshine. She felt warm again every time he held her home in his caring hands.

The new owner of the music box would open it and sit and listen, and stare, and smile for hours on end. He had many memories of his own but didn't put any inside. He was sad to part with the box, the memory could tell, but gave it to his little granddaughter for something to remember him by. The memory didn't know exactly how other memories could be added to her box but she knew that a person alone couldn't seem to do it.

The memory wished the nice man with the hat and lovely bass timbre would put some memories inside. She knew, like his sterling character, his memories must have been beautiful. She also thought that his recollections would have shared the little space well with her, the memory stored there by the green-eyed girl so long ago. But it was not to be. The box was given to someone else to have.

The granddaughter of the kind old man with the cane loved to play house with her stuffed animals when she was small. Although she looked at the box, and opened it now and then, it was not a prized possession. The memory was lonely, and worried about the new owner of her home. Over time however, it became clear that the granddaughter of the nice man with the cane was a wayward soul, searching for happiness that she would never find in this world.

When she became a teen, the granddaughter of the kindly old man chose a crooked pathway in life. She began to furtively hide things inside the box that she didn't want others to discover. She called her favorites "reefers," and they were joined by reds and blues, speed and Quaaludes. The sylph didn't like sharing a box with drugs. She knew that such things ate memories. So she hid under a ruffle in the velvet lining of her home and waited to see what would become of it.

In spite of her dislike for the narcotics, the memory locked in the box felt sorry for the girl. She was saddened when the owner of her music box died of an overdose of heroin at the age of twenty-four. Regretfully, it was the kind old man with the cane who found his granddaughter on the floor with a needle in her arm. After he discovered her, but before he called the coroner, he opened the box and stared inside for a long, long time. Tears rained and seeped into the workings of the music maker causing the mechanism to stall. The voice of the memory was muted, frozen by tears.

After the demise of the young lady, the music box was stored in a musty paper sack and put into a basement for another fistful of years. The memory wondered where her green-eyed girl was, and when she would return. She wished only to make her happy again.

Sixteen years later, the bag was opened by someone called an appraiser. It was then sold at an auction to a thin lady who carried a small dog in a bag. The sylph silently wondered: Will she bring me to my green-eyed girl? Will I make her smile again?

The thin lady with the dog looked at the box and grinned. She had beautiful memories of dancing with a handsome young man, but none as poignant as those of the green-eyed girl and her blue-eyed man. But as lovely as they were, she couldn't put any new memories into the box for she was alone. The memory felt sad and longed to make someone, anyone, happy again.

Two decades passed and the box was sold to an antique vendor with a rash on her cheeks and a noisy cough. She placed the box in the back of her store on Newport Avenue where it was promptly forgotten. The fruit of years fell from the branches of months and the box gathered even more dust.

The memory began to fear in earnest she would never make anyone smile again. She now worried that her green-eyed girl was gone forever, and began to lose hope. She tried to answer questions which ate at her: Are there any more green-eyed girls left in the world? Is my box too ugly for a person to love?

One day, when the memory had nearly given up, she felt her box lifted from the shelf. Gentle hands caressed it and she tingled inside. The lid was opened and knowing dark blue eyes looked right through her. The sylph was stirred – for those eyes – also framed by a wavy blond mane – were the ones from the dreams and hopes of her green-eyed girl! The man with blue eyes smiled at her box and looked in as if he could see her. He fondled the aged grillwork and touched the velvet lining. He paused, and sniffed it, and wondered what was stored inside over the years, and where the box had been throughout its life. This man had many fine memories, but he too could not store them alone. He had a golden soul. The memory could tell at once.

A price was agreed upon and the box brought home and placed on a table. There was a strange contentment that came over the memory. Classical music played in the house where she was taken. It reminded her of the piano once played long ago by the green – eyed girl. *Her* green-eyed girl.

The kind man with blue eyes took the box to a jeweler and asked how he could have it restored. He told the man that wanted to savor the music that would not play. The jeweler could not fix the mechanism, but told the new owner of the box about a skilled watch repairman who could make it sing once more.

The memory clung to the old velvet as the box was tilted and its workings revitalized. Sadly, the cost of repair was more than the man with blue eyes anticipated. The warmhearted watch repairman could see that the new owner loved the box, and agreed to do the work in trade for a bottle of wine. After a week, the box was finished and returned to the man with cobalt eyes. He picked it up one day after tending the sick in a hospital.

Although the velvet and silk lining of the music box could not be replaced without lowering its value, the outside was returned to its former glory. Now, the voice of the memory had returned, and when the box was opened, she sang once more. Her golden dwelling was placed in a position of importance in a room with a peaceful view in the home of the blue-eyed man. The sylph was excited that her little castle was loved again.

A few days later, as the memory silently contemplated her renovated palace, she heard a bell ring, and a door open downstairs. The tinkling music of laughter and memories being made filled the room like a warm breeze. The memory was eager again, for the symphony of mirth cascading around her reminded her of the girl with green eyes who put her in the box so many years ago. Would the girl who bubbled laughter be the one to let her out? She hoped that she would!

Soft hands opened the box and green eyes smiled as they peered deep inside. Lips parted and evanescent dimples appeared. The green-eyed girl stroked the blond curls of the blue-eyed man who sat smiling next to her. The memory swirled out of the box and cascaded into the room, a cataract of joy. Green eyes met blue and the new memory met the old. The memories entwined, and embraced like friends who had not seen one another for ages.

As the new memory met the old, time regressed nearly two hundred years. Fire lit the sky, cannons roared and chimes clanged. Hands touched. Hugs exchanged. A small kiss was shared by firelight. But during the blaze, the young surgeon raced into a building and sacrificed himself to save a child.

The old memory recalled how, before the conflagration in 1812, she was locked in the box from the time the green-eyed girl and blue-eyed surgeon peered into it together and remembered the magic of the symphony and the moonlit ride as one. But now, a new blue-eyed man looked into the eyes of another smiling green-eyed girl and they shared a memory of their own.

The new memory was also born of a symphony on the grass by the light of the silvery moon. Cannons and fireworks roared to the music of Pyotr Ilyich Tchaikovsky's commemoration of the War of 1812. Smiles were shared. Hands were touched. Moonlight was inhaled. The couple rode through a sleeping city on a two-wheeled stallion, and a memory stirred in a box on a shelf as they passed.

The pretty girl took the music box home and smiled whenever she lifted the lid for the rest of her life. For every time she opened it, memories danced unseen but nonetheless appreciated. The sylph in the box was content. At last, together with her friend the new memory, she could evoke a smile from her new green-eyed girl and bask, skip, pirouette and sing in its radiance.

Á la Carte
James Chandler

"Waiter, I'll have some of that endearing affection," I said, pointing toward a young couple at a nearby table. Their hands were touching, moving as they talked. They broke into blushing smiles, lost in their own world.

"Yes sir. Right away, sir," he replied in compliant fashion. Within a minute, the maitre d' escorted an even younger couple to a table within my sight. They tried to suppress a giggle, exchanging glances as they made their way. They seemed to be sharing an intimate secret, believing no one else could see what they so clearly felt.

This dinner was starting nicely. Now there were two sets of young lovers for the evening's entertainment. I heard laughter from the outdoor patio. Eight people sat around a large, circular table. I noticed several bottles of wine and a red-faced gent espousing something to the captive crowd. More laughter ensued.

"Waiter," I summoned.

"Yes, sir," he said with a magnanimous poise that was fast becoming familiar.

"I'd like one more of those," I said, pointing to the large table, "although make it a smaller portion, please."

"Of course, sir. Joviality for four then?" His right eyebrow rose almost imperceptibly.

"That would be fine," I agreed. He turned and left me to peruse the rest of the crowd, still sparse on this Thursday night at the wine bar.

I was looking at two men and a woman in the latter part of their dinner, plates askew and wine bottle empty, when the maitre d' escorted two couples to a window table. They talked excitedly, lifting menus briefly and then putting them aside in favor of the topic de jour. In response to some comment I could not hear, they each burst forth in laughter, filling the room with sound.

"Will that suffice, sir?" said the waiter, appearing suddenly at my side.

"Yes, that will do nicely."

Two women to my left had been chatting for some time, their faces remaining rather dour. They seemed to be troubled or incapable of feeling satisfied. Their conversation turned to a debate over the desert menu.

I raised my head, ready to call for the waiter when I heard a voice from my left, "Yes, sir?"

"Ah, there you are then. I'd like two older friends sharing memories and possibilities."

"Male or female, sir?"

"Doesn't matter," I replied. "Surprise me." He bowed out with his usual "Yes, sir," and vanished amidst the flow.

A line of people ran along the bar, most of them turned sideways in conversation with others. The bartender, apparently having met all her service obligations, was conversing in animated fashion with two women across the line of napkins and glasses. That struck me as nice: engaged with the clientele rather than aloof or detached.

"Are you through with that?" asked another waiter.

"No," I told him. "I'll eat the last of the Manchego cheese." As a purposely-slow eater, I was used to defending my food. He nodded and turned back toward the kitchen. I also had two olives left in my Spanish salad. They would not be wasted.

Just then I saw the maitre d' escorting two elderly women past me to a table near the window. They walked slowly yet steadily, as if they were savoring the moment, the people, or maybe the anticipation of a good meal and conversation. Their skin was pale, yet their eyes bright and observant.

They sat, looked at each other and smiled. They stole glances around the room; then picked up their menus, pouring over the offerings with apparent surprise and delight. They talked as if comparing notes.

I looked again at the first couple I had noticed. They seemed in a quiet, comfortable dimension all of their own. I enjoyed the way they touched forearms on the table so that both hands also met, fingers intertwined. She laughed, blushed and lifted her head into a kiss. Both were oblivious to my attention.

I turned back to my own table, leaving them in their delusion of privacy in such a public place. "Waiter," I said, catching the fellow as he returned with a drink order for the elder ladies. "I'd like just a bit of dessert."

"Of course, sir. What can I bring you?"

"Young, in her twenties or thirties, blue eyes, a soft smile, slight bit of mischief in her eyes."

"Blonde or brunette?" he inquired, appearing to approve of my choice.

"Doesn't matter," I said, then corrected myself. "I take that back: a brunette, mid-length to long."

"Yes, sir," he said. I wondered about the breadth of his vocabulary, and then concluded that his "Yes, sir" was infinitely better than being "86-ed" due to the unavailability of the requested fare.

I brought the last of the Chardonnay to my lips, letting the flavor linger on my tongue. Another glass? No, it was time to go; and one was enough. Often, I found greater appreciation in less of something.

As I set my glass back down on the table, I saw her settling into a seat directly across the way. He had done well: long, dark brown hair – almost black – pulled back into a ponytail. Tall, giving her a certain elegance that suited the way she moved. Her blue eyes seemed to sparkle in the low light of the restaurant. Lifting her head, she paused as she caught me looking back at her. Then she returned her gaze to the menu, the corner of her mouth rising just slightly into a quiet smile.

"Waiter," I said, assured that he would be within earshot. "I've changed my mind. I will have another glass of Chardonnay."

Section II:
The Drama of Relationships

I'll follow you and make a heaven out of hell,
and I'll die by your hand which I love so well.

William Shakespeare

Half Awake
Karen Paluska

She often wondered if nightly mummification would be her best option--as long as the linen strips didn't bunch up around her knees. And she would skip the amulets the Egyptians tucked between the layers to 'protect the body on its journey'; sure, protection would be an added bonus, but the lumps would be completely unbearable.

Perhaps she could pad herself with cotton gauze and have her husband wrap her in plaster to form a human pupa. Once it hardened she could cut it neatly in half and lay it alongside the bed to welcome her each evening. "Excuse me, darling, I'm climbing into my pupa now. I'll reemerge in the morning much more tolerant of your follies...and wingy, too." The lid would close with a soft thud.

The later the hour, the more intricate the inventions. Over the years Helen had conceptualized dozens of ways to create a smooth, snug nest that promised to hold sleep so firmly against her skin that it couldn't escape. While her husband gobbled air in heavy breaths a few inches away, she schemed of ways to lure sleep to her side of the bed. Sleep wasn't something you could bait into a trap, like the mice in the garage. If only sleep would wiggle its little pink nose and follow a trail of chocolate crumbs over to her side of the mattress, she might reconsider her rule against bringing food into bed.

It didn't help that she had married a nocturnal tornado who could roll over a few times and consume all the sheets in his path, dislodging the bedspread like a powerful wind popping the roof from a house. For six years of marriage, Helen and Carsten had shared a small, limp futon--a double, not even a queen--because their cramped apartment couldn't hold anything larger. She didn't have the luxury of hovering on the far corner of the bed.

Each night, Helen performed a routine of smoothing the wrinkles and tucking the sheets securely on all sides before slipping in gently, as if trying not to ripple a lake. Bedtime required a ritual not conducive to romance: it was difficult to fling oneself into the heat of passion when worried about collateral damage. Many nights, even the smoothness of the sheets could not release the knots within her. After a few hours, she would wander down to the kitchen to search for lost change in the junk drawer or to neaten up the edges of leftovers in the refrigerator. The width of her hips recorded the story of countless sleepless nights.

Tonight, the outside temperature had dropped and the wind had picked up. A cold stream of air spilled through the window frames and the gap below the baseboard. Helen tried to use her girth to her advantage, securing a length of bedding beneath her hips, yet she could never successfully sandbag against the storm. The tornado beside her had picked up again, stirring more than just the sheets; tonight her emotions were sucked into the twister as well.

Helen was doing her best to steer her thoughts away from the fight at the dinner table, but the wind thrashed the tree outside of her bedroom window and her mind scurried off its leash. It was impossible not to rehash the evening fiasco, the battle that had come from out of nowhere. While Helen had been tangling spaghetti around her fork, she had quite accidentally unraveled a harrowing truth; a simple question about a DMV envelope she had found in the trash exploded the conversation like a car bomb in front of her. Lying in bed after midnight, she could still feel the heat on her cheeks. She burrowed deeper. If her mind dove back into the argument now, she would never fall asleep.

Focusing on her breath, she pushed her ear into the pillow so as to dampen the choked snores behind her. Carsten sounded like a bus engine struggling to shift gears on a hill. She twitched. A wrinkle in her nightshirt pressed the wrong way against her stomach. A curl of hair slid down her cheek. She freed her hand from beneath her shoulder to make adjustments, then returned her arm as a bird would tuck in its wing. It took effort to force her eyelids down. She visualized winding rose-colored yarn around and around a skein.

Something delicate tickled the stubble on Helen's calf and she shifted to avoid it. If it was an insect, it was better not to know. She made a general habit of turning away from crawly things in the apartment and the garage. Where could she and Carsten be living now with the money he had squandered? Maybe in a neighborhood where she could take walks at night after work, get a little exercise to clear her head before bedtime.

The blanket was crooked and had inched too high, the cheap satin trim rising past her lips. It smelled of cat and closed windows. She shuffled it down and shut her eyes.

Helen couldn't fathom how much money Carsten had 'invested' in what he glorified as 'an automotive start-up'. The irony was that half of the autos probably wouldn't start up at all. Her thumb pressed her wedding band down her ring finger. The nervous habit made her wonder if the gold might be worth more than what was left in their checking account. The charm bracelet she'd circled in a catalog--not a realistic request, only a flirtatious dream--was now certainly out of the question for Christmas. No wonder he had never bought her jewelry: he was busy collecting heavier metals.

How had Carsten kept a fleet of purchases hidden from her for so long? What made him think he had the right to spend their money so recklessly--the money she had worked to earn while he supposedly marched from interview to interview? There was no way to know how many of those interviews ever truly existed. She was desperate to figure out when this ruse had all begun. There were moments in the past few years where things seemed to be not quite right, when she had dreaded Carsten was having an affair with the slender insurance agent who lived down the hall. But her suspicions had been completely misguided. Of course he met with the insurance agent so frequently--he had a lot to insure.

Helen tucked the corner of her pillow underneath itself, but no matter how perfect the nest, her mind refused to settle. She pictured her hands snapping down banks of light switches in a huge stadium, dropping the glare in chunks until there was nothing but darkness, but a voice echoed in the empty stands demanding answers. She was a fairly observant person, she thought, so how had he managed to conceal so much?

What was most disturbing was that, in *his* mind, there was never even a cover-up. He had insisted that if she had ever asked, he would have 'gladly explained everything', but until the business took off he preferred not to worry her. She was worried all right, but anger had stolen the spotlight. Honesty was something she valued above everything else. Even when she had accidentally nicked the key into his driver's door, she had been honest about it. Taking a step back now, it was his dishonesty that made her angrier than the diverted money.

Lying on her stomach, she wiggled her hips to shake her spine into alignment. Again came the tickle against her leg. Maybe the cat had snuck into the bed again for a cozy nap and had left a tuft of hair. Helen patted her hand down the fitted sheet and eventually discovered a frayed thread. Pinching the base, she tried to snap it but there just wasn't enough for her to grip. After a few tries, she tucked her arm back underneath her chest and stared at the side of her nightstand.

A metallic flash caught her eye. Resting on the nightstand a few inches from her nose, a pair of manicure scissors caught an arc of streetlight in its tiny beak. She knew she should close her eyes, (after all, sleep never came to those who watched for it), but she was transfixed by the way the glint swayed as the leaves outside filtered the light. The artificial salmon glow of the lamplight was condensed in the concave curve. The reflection pulsed like a beacon.

Carsten snored away. She resented his monopoly on sleep. Fighting didn't seem to fester in his blood the way it did hers. Perhaps the dinner confession had even lifted a weight off his chest, and now he could sleep uninterrupted for a week at a time. It was as if he had simply shrugged off his share of the anger and dropped it into a bag, and Helen was left holding it the way she would clutch a purse for a friend using the bathroom. She wanted to shake Carsten awake and shove him a handle to divide the load. He needed to carry half of the weight.

The thread from the sheets meandered along her calf like a tiny spider. How could any woman sleep with a tiny spider creeping up her leg? Carsten would call this obsessing, but she would defend herself: tiny spiders were a legitimate complaint, real or imagined. She glanced at the nightstand. The manicure blades smiled at her, promising assistance. They wanted to help with the thread, really they did. Then for a moment the leaves shifted and full lamplight hit the blades, and they seemed to promise more.

In hindsight, she should have just stayed in bed and smoothed the thread with her hand, but the wind was racing outside and her mind was keeping pace. Trying to lie still at this point was like sitting in a car with one foot on the brake while the other revved the gas pedal--it was a false stillness.

She carefully flipped back the sheets and swung her feet onto the rug. It would be a quick mission, and then she would return to bed. Running her fingers along the length of the sheet, Helen easily found the offending thread. The streetlight seemed sufficient for this minor surgery; she pulled the thread taut and with a snip the whole of it was gone.

Always thorough, she patted the area to check her work. Her fingers discovered a small hole where the thread had been. She hissed a string of curses at the thread. Clearly she shouldn't have cut to the base. With a few twists, her fingers balled up the thread and flicked it aside.

Helen stood at the side of the bed, staring down at the disheveled navy-and-white stripes on the bedspread. Ever since Carsten's mother had shipped it from Germany as a wedding present, Helen felt it was too masculine for a married couple's room. The bold pattern stared back at her through the darkness.

Carsten mumbled something incoherent about hubcaps then rolled away, yanking the sheets with him. His long, thin leg extended well past the foot of the bed and he kicked to free himself from the linens. Helen decided to do some strategic tucking before she climbed back into bed. Lifting her end of the mattress, she jammed in a handful of bedding to anchor it. Carsten didn't flinch. She lifted the futon a little higher and gave it a gratuitous pump. He kept on sleeping. Even a solid kick to the middle of the mattress elicited no reaction.

Her empty pillow stared back at her. She wasn't ready to try again. Instead, Helen shoved open the curtains and leaned her forehead against the sash that divided the window. The wood was icy cold. The outside air snuck around the single pane and ran across the backs of her hands. On the sidewalk down below lurked a few shadows, probably negotiating something illegal. If she and Carsten ever did have the children he dreamed about, this wasn't the place to raise them. She desperately wanted to move up in the world--not because she was materialistic, but because she wanted a certain level of safety and security in her life--but if Carsten's gamble didn't pay off, they would likely be downgrading soon.

How could they scrape themselves out of debt? Or more to the point how could *she*, because Carsten had no official job and she doubted his investments could be liquidated at any break-even level. Her career didn't offer any immediate upgrades. She had already hit the glass ceiling a few years ago, but she stayed out of a sense of loyalty she couldn't really justify. It was painful designing sales brochures for homes she would never be able to afford. She wished she could be as flighty as Carsten but a marriage needed balance, and she prided herself in being the ballast for their ship.

Helen fingered the smooth loop of the scissors' handle and watched the scene down below as if it were a curious play. The lurking shadows seemed to disagree over some part of the exchange. The shorter guy shoved the taller guy's chest in the spark of a fight. Helen could hear snippets through the window. He wanted money, money that was supposedly his share of a deal they had done, money the taller guy had stolen from the trunk of the car. A few bucks and a promise wasn't the same as cash. He wouldn't leave until he was repaid his half, he shouted.

It wasn't fair: half was half. As a kid, half was always split straight down the middle. The concept was mandated by adults, but eventually embraced by kids who watched without blinking to make sure that both halves had the same amount of strawberry frosting, or an equal number of orange jelly beans. Always quantifiable, "half" symbolized a certain order in the world. Now she was an adult, married, and she was well aware that half wasn't always such a clean slice. Sometimes half meant washing the dishes while the other person paid the bills, or half could mean keeping an unfulfilling job for the paychecks while your spouse struggled to get interviews. Those were simply different forms of half. But when one adult slaved to earn all the money and the other irresponsibly spent all the money, where was the half in that? And he didn't spend *half* the money, he spent *all* of it. If he'd done some convoluted calculation to determine his share of the funds and had spent up to the last cent, she could somehow digest the situation more easily. But he had blown it all, no half about it. And once again he not only ruled the whole bed, he was hoarding all of the sleep as well.

She couldn't get her money back, but it was time to get her half.

Turning from the window, Helen moved with sure steps and knelt on the rug at the end of the bed. She placed the manicure scissors on the ground beside her. With one scoop, she loaded a twisted pile of linens back onto the mattress.

Grabbing a piped hem, she slid her fingers along until she felt the lumpy corner of the bedspread. Her free hand traced back along the piping until she had a wingspan's-worth in front of her. That was likely the middle, she figured, give or take a few inches.

She gave the bedspread a few shakes until it flopped loosely across the bed, the wide stripes curving softly over Carsten's legs. How sweet, she was tucking him in. She patted the ground until the point of the manicure scissors pricked her palm. The scruff of the rug dug into her knees, but the discomfort prodded her along.

In the low light, the manicure scissors flashed like a silver fish in an inky river. With its small mouth against the piping, the fish became a hungry piranha. Her pulse sped up and she knew she would never be able to sleep until she had established a meridian.

The scissors gagged on the thickness before taking a nibble out of the edge. She heard her own breath louder than Carsten's snores now, and she tightened her grip on the fabric to force the small blades ahead. Her progress was too slow. Her fingers yearned to slice through the fabric in large pulsing waves. Helen rose and rushed down the hall.

The shears from the kitchen junk drawer lunged into the synthetic threads with a happy song of metal stroking metal. The vertical stripes now served as a perfect guideline for a straight cut. It was as simple as slicing wrapping paper off a roll. In a matter of minutes, Helen had created a matching set of two bedspreads. Confused nylon strands sprang from the freshly cut edge, but she could bind them up later. Oblivious, Carsten clutched his half while Helen tossed her share onto the bed as if throwing a hat into the ring. She felt a surge of strength she had been missing at the dinner table.

Now that she had carved out her own bedspread, it struck her that the blanket had always given her the greatest grief. She heard her mother's voice proclaim, "Success breeds success!" Helen could feel the tides turning and she was determined to ride her success forward.

She had to untangle some of the yellow blanket from Carsten's legs in order to get her bearings, to find what seemed like the middle. After all, her goal was to even things out, so it wouldn't be right if she took more than her share. Her revenge should be underscored by her restraint. The balding blanket had its own history that was rather vague but involved an ex of some sort. Perhaps Carsten would have 'gladly explained everything' if only she had asked, but now it was a relief not to know. When she pulled against the weave, Carsten slid his legs out of the way as if to help. Helen shook a last corner loose from his grasp and he moved his hands absentmindedly to his pillow.

It took only seconds to divide the blanket. The satin trim made a delicious sound as it gave way and the blanket itself disintegrated like moist cake. With no pattern from which to work, Helen feared her cut was at an angle, but she stowed her concerns. Most of her night had happened at distorted angles. The entire episode had come at her from an unexpected diagonal. She mentally saw a snapshot of Carsten, elbows splayed as he gripped the dinner table; neck jutting forward as he loudly defended the crooked vision for his business venture. Thinking about it now, she had no idea exactly how many cars he had bought, or where he planned to sell them. There were numerous angles that didn't seem to add up.

Slitting the green floral top sheet was a true joy. It was one of her mother's old guest sheets, and just seeing it made Helen feel like a child who depended on handouts from home. Clusters of geraniums were finally getting a much-needed pruning. Helen cut a wavy line around a few of the bouquets, generously giving Carsten some additional foliage. He had never been the type to bring her flowers, but maybe he could use these to woo someone else. She savored the vengeance and pushed aside the pang of sadness that came along with it.

The bed was separating into two camps, like children dividing into two teams on a field. Helen stared at the fabric and ran her fingers along the scissor blades to remove the fuzz. She couldn't see it fall, but felt it graze her bare feet. Her toes were cold, craving the warmth of a snug blanket.

In a flash of panic she realized that once she had established her own set of sheets, there would be no way to tuck in her side. Her half would have to float free. For someone who agonized over every wrinkle, the absurdity of the new situation came as a welcome relief. She would be a mummy unraveling in the wind. Her nest would be a deconstruction of itself. She was now creating…art. With rational sleep considerations out of the equation, she moved with new gusto.

The fitted sheet, of course, was a breeze. She peeled the bottom from under the mattress to get a starting point and away she went. The fabric sighed in relief as it split open. Midway, Helen had to heave herself onto the futon to complete the job. Her leg fell against Carsten's and she jumped when he reached out and patted her knee. He mumbled, "Sleep, sweetie, just close your eyes." Helen froze for a moment until his breathing deepened again, but the scissors begged to march straight up to the headboard.

Now a tingle raced around her body and she could swear she was levitating slightly over the bed. What would Carsten say if he woke up to see what she was doing? It struck her that she didn't care. Her project seemed to make more sense than anything she'd done in years-- more sense than his own ill-conceived business plan, no doubt. She was almost eager to show him her work. A giggle slipped out of her lips.

The mattress pad was quilted, and the shears hummed softly through their work. Helen found herself matching her down strokes to her exhalations. With each breath, she found a retort that had escaped her at dinner. "In many circles, withholding the truth is actually called lying." "So, your grand vision is to be a used-car salesman working out of a dark parking garage? Impressive." "Hey, if we can't pay our rent, at least we can live in a car…and lucky for me, we won't have to share one."

When one mattress pad had become two, Helen straightened up to admire her handiwork. A perfect 'his and hers' of bedding lay in piles before her in the faint light. She could now arrange her sheets in any way she wanted; it might take some significant tacking here and there, but her nest was now her own.

But something wasn't right. It made no sense for the linens to be split if the mattress remained intact. Half was half, and slicing through the icing was not equal to sharing the cupcake. She was only halfway there.

The sharpest knife in the kitchen was a carving knife, a sway-backed weapon with serrated teeth that usually scared her just to see it in the house. Now it felt powerful in her hand, the right size for her task.

As she returned to the bedroom, her eyes scanned the futon. The pile of bedding sat where she had left it, but she noticed with horror that Carsten was no longer in the bed. There was nothing but a knot of twisted sheets where he had lain only moments ago. She squinted into the darkness to see if he was watching her from the sidelines. Here she stood in a nightshirt, next to the dissected bed, with a carving knife in her fist...and now her husband was missing. If police asked around, neighbors would report they'd heard a fight through the walls earlier that night. The situation was misleading, at best. Her bare legs began to shiver.

Down the hall the toilet flushed and soon Carsten stumbled back into the room. He flopped onto the bed and jerked some sheets up to his waist. He flipped onto his side, leaving his back to her. Helen didn't exhale until she heard his rhythmic droning once again.

It would be easier to work downward, so she climbed back up onto the bed. She tried the knife at a few different angles before sinking it deep into the futon mattress. With a hearty sawing motion, she pulled the knife through the stuffing. It didn't take long before dusty particles stuck on her tongue. She spat them to the side and kept at her work. The slats on the futon frame made a perfect parallel trough, and she only had to navigate the supports at either end.

Toward the bottom of the bed, Carsten's ankle lay across the midline. For a moment Helen considered slicing right through, but this wasn't about mutilation--this was about division. Her hand cradled his warm foot as she gingerly severed beneath it. She pitied him, almost...his constant delusions about success right around the corner, with no ability to recognize the path to his own destruction. But in this case, his destruction would bring about hers as well. She let his foot fall back onto the futon and continued sawing to the end. The last few sinews of material fought her, but the serrated blade won out. She pushed her half of the mattress aside.

Helen tiptoed to the head of the bed. Carsten's nostrils twitched against the dust before his snore became a sneeze, then resumed as a snore. With a regretful smile, she whispered that if he had only awakened and asked, she would have gladly explained everything--but she preferred not to worry him.

Before she could decide what to do next, Helen noticed a glossy shoebox jammed beneath the futon frame. She kneeled down to drag it out. In the lamplight, an oversized ring held keys that sparkled like a jagged charm bracelet. She counted the keys. There were eleven toothy beasts of various sizes that all looked like they could start an ignition. Eleven. Incredible. She slid the entire ring onto her wrist.

Beneath the keys sat an envelope bursting with papers. She carried it to the window where she could make out the top page in the lamplight. It was a lease agreement, with Carsten's name signed to the bottom. He had put down a large deposit for a retail space on the main drag of the neighboring town. The document was signed only a week before. Her lungs choked in a breath and she wasn't sure how to release it.

She moved quickly. The keys clattered on her wrist as she shoved her allotment of bedding into an oversized shopping bag and slung it over her shoulder. Four years ago, it had taken two men to haul the floppy futon into the bedroom, but tonight Helen learned that one determined woman could drag half the futon down the hall without too much difficulty. Gripping the open edge of the mattress was a little tricky and often ended in a handful of stuffing, but by embracing the bulk around the middle, she was able to battle it into the elevator and down to the parking garage. Once the trailing end of the mattress passed the heavy fire door, the slam echoed throughout the garage.

Beneath the harsh glare of floodlights, Helen scanned the rows of cars and wondered which 'priceless antiques' she had unknowingly financed with her meager salary. Eleven of them, nonetheless. The dingy Beetle in the neighbor's spot was likely hers, and she assumed the title to a rusted Karmann Ghia was registered to her address. But she was headed for the Volkswagen bus that was parked across from her own tiny import. The large expanses of shiny tangerine paint had always caught her eye as she had unloaded groceries over the past few months. Hadn't she even complimented the couple in Apartment 108 on their new acquisition? How embarrassing to remember that now--no wonder they had flushed and looked away.

Thumbing through the key chain, she bristled at the hand-written labels wrapped around the car logos: "office," "recycling," and even "bike lock." And he had insisted he wasn't trying to cover anything up. For a moment she wondered if she had been too kind with the carving knife, but the buzz of the garage lights calmed her down.

The second key Helen tried easily popped the back hatch of the bus. The interior was a spotless black rubber cavern that held her half of the futon perfectly. She pulled her sheets from the shopping bag and arranged them with precision. They lay flat for the moment, but Helen dreaded climbing in. Her lungs were too tight and she needed some fresh air.

Just before dawn, forty miles from the apartment, the tangerine bus sat parked in the silence of an outcrop of trees. Helen had rolled her bedding tightly around herself to create the pupa of her dreams. With one hand left free for adjustments, she tugged the bedspread into place to fight the chill. She lay back and noticed the steam of her breath in the air in front of her.

The snoring was gone, leaving only quiet. Her mind began to wander around the layers of the cocoon in a virtual inspection. One hip seemed lower than the other; likely the stuffing was leaking from the futon. Her shoulder was raised at a strange angle, and she dug a hollow to even it out. The sheets seemed to be creeping too high on her feet, exposing her ankles, so she maneuvered the edges with her toes to seal her pupa. How in the world could the caterpillar get settled within the chrysalis so it could transform itself into a butterfly? She tried to visualize the orange and black wings of a monarch swooping above the roof of the van. Her muscles instinctively relaxed.

Looking out the large rectangular windows, Helen spotted the moon disappearing through the trees. The sky lightened too quickly. The night was gone already, and she hadn't had even a drowsy moment of sleep. She studied the simple dot pattern on the ceiling above her. As the sun stretched in, the white vinyl took on a striking coral glow that no streetlamp could ever match. Flecks of futon stuffing sparkled as they floated through the air. Helen's half was now her whole. She wondered if it was enough.

Ensenada
Kathy Nakamatsu

It hadn't even been my idea to go on the cruise. If the MSPA hadn't had that stupid silent auction last November, I never would've been there. I never would have had that picture taken either – the picture that lies buried in the bottom drawer of my desk.

****

As a member of the Menlo School Parent Association and one of the party organizers, I was obligated to attend their annual fundraiser. This year's theme was "Hawaiian Sunset" because Susie ("with an *ie* at the end!" she would exclaim at every meeting, just in case people forgot) Jacobson, the MSPA president, had spent her summer vacation at an exclusive resort in Hawaii, where celebrity sightings are common. We heard about this ad nauseam at the first meeting, in Susie's characteristic high-pitch squeal: "You should've seen Cher! She was wearing this God-awful muumuu that she must have bought at Wal-Mart! And, then we ate lunch with George Clooney. Oh, what a hottie!"

Menlo School was an elite private college-prep school in Atherton, with most of its graduates going to college. I was not your typical MSPA mom. Most of the women were stay-at-home mothers who spent their days socializing and organizing charity events. I could have stayed home--Jeff was CFO for a marketing firm in San Francisco--but I chose to work instead. I had started out as a financial planner after graduating from college twenty years ago and now ran a small investment firm. When Nathan was a freshman, I had just started my business and joined the MSPA for good PR. It had paid off financially, but I have never felt connected to the other women.

People were encouraged to dress Hawaiian style for the party, but my husband and I were in business attire. I had on a cobalt blue silk blouse with black pants and low kitten heels. Jeff was wearing a grey suit with a white shirt and blue pinstriped tie, his salt and pepper hair perfectly styled.

"Why didn't you tell me it was Hawaiian night?" he hissed in my ear. "I could've worn my shirt from college!" He was talking about the shirt I had thrown in the trash years ago with gigantic palm trees and coconuts on it.

"I forgot." I actually hadn't forgotten. I had been tempted to wear a muumuu just to see how Susie would react, but decided it wasn't worth the effort. Not that I would have had trouble finding one in the richly diverse Silicon Valley.

"How could you forget? Didn't you send out the invitations?" Jeff took a sip of his Mai Tai. We'd only been at the party for an hour, but he was already on his third cocktail. "These are good," he said for the fifth time. "I'm gonna go check out the silent auction."

Before I could say okay, he was gone. I looked around to see who was there. It was a pretty good crowd. About two hundred people paid $150 each for the dinner and silent auction. The food was typical Hawaiian with sushi, spam musubi, pineapple, and poki--all spread out in fancy geometrical patterns. Like a hummingbird, Susie hovered around the food, rearranging it as pieces were removed. In spite of her annoying habits, one had to admit she knew how to throw a great party and raise lots of money for the school. Orchid blossoms and floating candles in glass bowls adorned the tables and a floral scent permeated the ballroom.

"Hey, Ellen!" Jeff called me over to the other side of the room. He was standing near a giant basket filled with Starbucks coffee. "We should bid on something," he said.

"I don't know, Jeff. I've heard about people bidding on things they never really wanted and then winning, if you can call it that!"

"Just for fun, honey! Someone will outbid us." Jeff was combing the stations. Susie had mentioned that they raised almost $200,000 at last year's silent auction. Someone had paid five grand to get two reserved seats at the graduation ceremony. Five grand!

"Well maybe," I said. "We need to pick something that other people would want and bid low." There were dinners for two at local restaurants, tickets for "Phantom of the Opera," gift certificates for a day at the spa, among other things. Jeff was a few steps ahead of me when he suddenly stopped.

"How about this one--a three-day cruise in August to Ensenada? That'd be fun!"

"Remember dear, we're not trying to win it."

"It could be very romantic," Jeff whispered in my ear. He had his arm around my waist and nuzzled my hair with his chin. It was his signature flirtation. "We could celebrate our anniversary."

"That's not until October."

"August, October. Whatever, Ellen. It doesn't matter when we celebrate. Gosh, you're always so black and white." He pulled away pouting.

"I guess we could do that," I said, trying to smooth things over. "We haven't taken a vacation in a while. It would be nice."

Jeff perked up. "Really? You wouldn't bring any work with you, would you?"

"Not if you don't."

"Deal." He grabbed my hand. "Can you believe it's been twenty years, honey?"

"No, I can't," I said. Jeff and I had met only because he introduced himself to me. We lived down the hall from each other as freshmen at Stanford, but I didn't meet him until December, when our dorm had a holiday party. I was sitting with my roommate--another wallflower--and only there because our resident advisor cajoled and begged us into coming. A tall, lanky dark-haired guy approached us in a Frankie Goes to Hollywood t-shirt. Ministry's "Everyday is Halloween" was blaring and about twenty people were dancing in a 10' x 10' space made by moving the couches.

"Hi! I don't think we've met!" the guy yelled over the music. He bent over to shake my hand, spilling beer onto my new acid-washed jeans. "Oh my gawd, I'm so sorry!" He wiped my jeans with his napkin. When his hand grazed my thigh accidentally, I felt a surge of heat and I blushed. My roommate rolled her eyes, stood up and left. "I'm Jeff, by the way."

"Ellen."

"It's nice to meet you. Sorry about your jeans."

We were inseparable for the next four years. Soon after graduation, we married in a small ceremony in his parents' backyard. Jeff had wanted to live together first, but my Catholic parents threatened to disown me if we did. They must have thought if we didn't live together, we wouldn't be having sex. Imagine if they knew I had started taking The Pill as a freshman.

"So, how much should we bid?" Jeff asked, bringing me out of my thoughts.

"Do we want to win it or are we still just bidding for fun?"

"A little of both?" He grinned sheepishly.

"What's the minimum?" I asked.

Jeff picked up the sign. "Five hundred dollars. The package is worth eight hundred and includes roundtrip airfare to San Diego."

"Five hundred it is then. We're first on the list, so someone's bound to outbid us," I said.

"You sound so hopeful," Jeff said with a hint of sarcasm. Was I? We could use a vacation. Both Jeff and I had been so busy at work and hardly spent anytime alone anymore. When was the last time we'd been on a date? Do office parties count? God, no wonder he seemed like a stranger these days. I shouldn't shoot his hopes down.

"I'm sorry honey," I finally said. "It's just been a long day and I'm worried about missing work."

"Work will be fine without you," he said. He kissed my forehead. "I love you, Ellen. You know that right?"

"Yes. I love you, too, honey."

We ended up winning the cruise.

****

Susie had told us to contact the cruise line immediately to make our travel arrangements, but the brochure was thrown on the desk when we got home only to be covered with bills and mail as time passed. November turned into December, winter became spring, and before I knew it, it was summer. I was catching up on paperwork in my office when Jill, my secretary, poked her head in the door.

"Someone from Princess Cruises is on the line," she said.

"Unless they want to hire us, tell them I'm busy," I said without even looking up. A few minutes later, Jill was back. "She says it's about a cruise you're taking next month. She needs your information."

"The cruise, the cruise." My mind worked frantically trying to remember. "Oh my God! The cruise!"

After I got off the phone with the travel agent, I called Jeff. His company had just taken on new clients and he'd been working sixty-hour weeks lately, so I was shocked when he picked up the phone. In his usual manner, he answered, "Ellen! What's up?"

"Hi Jeff. Do you remember that cruise we won at the auction?"

"Yeah," he said. I could hear him chewing on something. Probably a muffin he picked up on his daily trip to Starbucks. "What about it?"

"It's next month."

"What?!" I pictured him sitting straight up, the muffin falling to his cluttered desk. "Are you kidding?"

"I wish!" I laughed. "It's from August 10th to August 12th."

"Honey. That's the same time as the annual fishing trip to Cabo with the guys. You know that!"

"I thought the trip was at the end of August!"

"Joe saw a weather report predicting a hurricane, so we moved the trip up."

"You didn't tell me. I didn't pick the dates…" I began.

"Can we change it?" Jeff interrupted.

I walked over to the window and closed the blinds. "I asked. We can't. Can't you skip the trip this year?"

"Are you kidding? You know how much I look forward to this trip," he said tersely. "Why don't you see if your sister can go?"

That was just like him. Choosing his friends over me. The guys had been going to Cabo for almost fifteen years - he could miss one year. But I would never tell him that.

"You were the one who insisted we bid on this trip," I said, my voice tight with anger. I knew it was a low blow, but I didn't care.

"Whatever, Ellen. I have to go," he said and hung up.

I held the phone, speechless, until I heard a recording say, "If you'd like to make a call, please hang up and dial again." What had happened to us? Were we going to end up divorced like so many other couples we knew? Nathan had been the glue that kept us together all these years, but he was leaving for college next year. What would happen to us then?

I glanced at my watch. It was ten o'clock. My first appointment was in fifteen minutes. I sat with one hand under my chin, staring blankly at the computer screen. Through the door, I could hear Jill and my partner's secretary chatting about the "Lost" finale.

****

Over the next few weeks, I tried to find someone to go on the cruise with me. It didn't help that it was in August, when most people are on family vacations. Nathan didn't want to leave his new girlfriend, Mandy. My sister's in-laws were visiting. Thumbing through my address book, it dawned on me that most of the people we socialized with were Jeff's friends and colleagues. My college friends had all moved away or were busy raising families. We communicated occasionally through email, but when was the last time I called one of them? It had been years. I couldn't call now only to admit that my husband was not joining me on a romantic 3-day cruise to Ensenada. Imagine the gossip that would cause! I hesitated when I got to my parents' number. It could be an early Christmas present, but I could just hear my mother on the other line: *Why isn't Jeff going? Is everything okay, honey? A good husband would change his plans. I told you he wasn't right for you.* It wasn't worth that headache. I walked to the refrigerator to refill my Chardonnay, my heels clicking and echoing in the empty kitchen. I sat down in the glider rocker Jeff bought me when Nathan was born. The upholstery was faded and the blue floral pattern clashed with the rest of the furniture, but this was still my favorite chair. Nathan had trouble falling asleep as a baby and I would rock him in the glider, singing softly until he closed his eyes. I gently rocked back and forth, thinking about how simple life had been back then. Jeff and I had lived in a one-bedroom apartment in Mountain View, with a galley kitchen only big enough for one. Now we lived in a six-bedroom house in Atherton with a kitchen almost as large as our old apartment. How could I have so much but feel so alone? Maybe there was a reason

I couldn't find anyone to go with me. Maybe this cruise would be an opportunity to reevaluate my life.

****

I flew out to San Diego the following Friday and boarded the cruise ship after lunch. The room was small, but cozy, with a tiny balcony that overlooked the water. There were two twin beds that I pushed together to make a double. The bathroom was so small you had to close the door in order to turn around in it. I spent the afternoon finding my way around the ship that seemed bigger than any hotel I'd ever been in. You could almost forget that you were in the middle of the ocean when you were underneath the sparkling chandelier, looking up the grand staircase that led to the ballroom. I seemed to be the only person on the cruise without a spouse or family, but somehow I felt less lonely here than at home. I stood on my balcony until ten o'clock watching the waves rise and fall until I crawled into bed exhausted from my day of travel.

When I awoke on the second day, we had arrived at Ensenada. After spending the morning walking around town and window-shopping, I returned to my room to change. I pulled out my old faded swimsuit – a one-piece of course – and put it on. I was happy that it still fit after ten years. At forty-two, I still had a decent figure thanks to running two miles a day. My few grey hairs were hidden behind highlights in my brunette, shoulder-length hair. "Not too shabby, Ellen," I said as I glanced at myself in the mirror.

I found a lounge chair near the adults-only saltwater pool and settled in with a strawberry daiquiri in one hand and the latest Nora Roberts romance novel in the other. If Jeff were here, he would've been at the bar making new friends. We used to attend business conventions together and Jeff would start working the room immediately. I, on the other hand, would find a place to read my book until my meetings began. At parties and dinners, I relied on Jeff to bring me out of my shell and into conversations. He was good for me in that way. I could never be like Jeff. I was more like Nathan--quiet, serious and hard to read. It was almost too quiet without him here.

"Ma'am? Would you like a refill?"

I looked up from my book, shielding my eyes, to see someone standing in front of me. I assumed the bar steward, but the sun was right behind him making it hard to see. He must have realized that because he moved off to the side. He was in his early 20's, dressed in white shorts and a crisp short-sleeved shirt that showed off his biceps and tan. Short, light auburn hair and a captivating smile completed the picture.

"I'd love one," I said, handing him my glass. He put it on his tray and sat down on the chair next to me.

"Are you here alone?" he asked.

"Yes, my husband is on a trip with some friends."

"That's too bad," he said. "A beautiful woman like yourself shouldn't be alone."

He'd probably told hundreds of women the same thing. I wondered if part of his job was looking for single women to hit on. Flattery brings big tips, you know.

"I'm okay, thank you."

"You're looking a little red, ma'am. Would you like me to rub some sunscreen on you?"

"No, I'm fine. I can do it myself."

"Really, ma'am. I don't mind," he said. "It's part of my job." Was he serious? I was perfectly capable of putting on my own sunscreen.

"Would you just get me another drink, please?" I opened my book and started reading, hoping he would leave. After what seemed like forever, he finally stood up.

"I'll be right back, ma'am. I'm Luke, by the way, and I'll be your server," he said as he walked away.

I was just starting to doze off when I heard the woman next to me say in a Southern twang, "I can't believe you turned Luke down."

"Excuse me?" I turned toward her. She had short, spiky red hair that matched her red lipstick and long red fingernails and was wearing a string bikini that barely covered her large breasts. It was not the kind of outfit a woman our age should be wearing, no matter how fit and toned she was.

"You must be crazy, lady!" She took a sip of her Cosmopolitan. "Look around," she said, pointing with a long skinny index finger. "Do you see how many women are in this section compared to the others?" She was right. "They all are here, ya know, because of Luke."

"What's so special about Luke?"

She sat up and turned so she was facing me, leaning close enough so I could smell the vodka on her breath. "Well, first of all, look at him. He's hot. Second, he gives the best massages evvveeer. And, third, he's hot. I'm married, too, but I left my hubby with the kids at the kiddie pool just so I could sip a Cosmo here and drool for a few minutes. He thinks I ran upstairs to get a book."

I suppressed the urge to laugh. Luke was pretty good-looking, but this was ridiculous. Picking a lounge area because of a bar steward? Really.

The woman glanced at her watch. "Damn. I have to go meet the family. I've been gone too long. Can I have your book?"

"Sure," I said, even though it would leave me with nothing to do. It was kind of fun to be part of a cover-up.

I handed her the book and she shoved it in her beach bag, along with the rest of her belongings. "It's really none of my business, honey, but what do you have to lose? It's the last day of the cruise. Live a little."

Live a little. She wasn't all that crazy. What had I done for myself on this trip? Not much except buy that cute polka-dot sundress on the Promenade. Why not be one of those cougar women I'd read about and let myself be pampered by some young cub?

"Ma'am, I have your drink," Luke said, interrupting my thoughts. He set my daiquiri on the side table and placed my drink card on his tray. "Looks like you still need that sunscreen, ma'am. Did you change your mind?"

"Actually, I did," I said, handing him the sunscreen. "You come highly recommended." I turned over so he could rub my back.

"Really? Well, that's good to know." His hands felt gentle, but strong, as he rubbed the lotion on my back. I tensed when he reached my neck and shoulders. "Are you okay?"

"It's a little tight there, that's all."

"I'll take care of that," he said. He gently kneaded the area and I felt the tension release. Crazy lady was right.

"So, tell me about yourself, Luke," I said.

"Well, I'm a senior at UCLA, majoring in Business. This is my second summer working for Princess and I love it! You get to travel around the world, housing and meals are included, and it's a lot of fun!"

"Are you from California?" He was massaging my calves now, working his way down to my feet. I was so relaxed I could fall asleep.

"Yeah, I grew up in Atherton," he said. "Do you know where that is?"

"Do I know? That's where I live!" I laughed.

"You're kidding!" He stopped massaging and picked up my drink card. "I thought you looked familiar! I think you know my mom."

"Who's your mom?"

"Susie Jacobson." Susie had mentioned she had a son at UCLA. I had met him briefly when we were planning the silent auction. I didn't remember him looking so buff and tan, but I guess that's what happens when you spend your summers on cruise ships.

"You're Susie's eldest son, right?" He nodded. "I think the last time I saw you, you were home on spring break."

"Wow, Mrs. Nicholson, you look ho…I mean, you look great." He blushed. I felt myself getting warm and not from the sun.

"Please call me Ellen. It's a little strange hearing Mrs. Nicholson."

"I can do that. So, what are you doing here, Ellen?" he asked, emphasizing my name.

I explained about winning the cruise and taking a little vacation time for myself. Luke pulled up a chair and we chatted about school and his plans for after graduation.

"I still don't understand why your husband isn't here," Luke said after some time had passed. "If I were him, I wouldn't have chosen a fishing trip over you."

"That's sweet, Luke," I said. "However, you might think differently after you've been married for twenty years."

"No, I don't think I would," he said, with a look so intense I felt myself blush. "I should probably go before my boss fires me, but..." He looked down at the ground.

"Yes?"

"Well," Luke continued. "I was hoping we could meet up later. Maybe after I'm done with my shift," he finally said. "You shouldn't spend your last night here alone."

"What did you have in mind?"

"How about a stroll at sunset? We could meet me at the tiki bar at six. I'd love to show you the rest of the ship." He turned toward me and added, "She is a beauty."

"I would love that."

****

I had a couple of hours to get ready. What was I going to wear? I had brought a black strapless cocktail dress for the traditional Captain's dinner that seemed a little overdressed for the tiki bar, so I pulled out my new sundress instead. I didn't mind that I would be missing the fancy dinner. I felt like a teenager about to go on her first date--nervous, excited, hopeful. Had I just been flirting with Susie Jacobson's son? It was only flirting, right? Or was there more going on than that? What was I doing? I was married. He was twenty years younger than me. But, he was gorgeous. I got shivers as I imagined him touching me. I tried to picture Susie Jacobson hearing that I had slept with her twenty-two year old son. What would she think? No one would believe it. No one.

I sat down on the bed and looked out the picture window at the horizon. I saw nothing but ocean for miles, so getting off the ship to avoid temptation was not an option. So far, I hadn't spent much time thinking about my marriage, which was the reason I'd come on the ship in the first place. Jeff and I hadn't been happy for years. Had we just stayed together because Catholics don't believe in divorce? Or because we didn't know any better? I didn't know anymore. I don't think either of us was to blame. We had just grown apart after twenty years. If I cheated on Jeff, I couldn't go back. I wouldn't lie to him--he deserved better than that. Why was I even thinking about this? It wasn't like Luke had invited me to his cabin. He probably just wanted to keep his mom's friend company, nothing more. "Stop reading into things," I said to my reflection in the mirror. "Just go and enjoy your last night on the cruise."

I found Luke at the tiki bar in khakis and a blue oxford that made his blue eyes pop. He was sipping a margarita and had already ordered me a strawberry daiquiri.

"I thought you couldn't drink on the ship," I said as I slid onto the stool next to him.

Luke leaned over to hug me, his lips brushing my cheek so tenderly that shivers ran down my body. "Sammy here," he said, waving at the bartender, who waved back and smiled. "Sammy promised not to tell anyone. He keeps good secrets." Still, I hoped Sammy didn't know Jeff or anyone in Atherton.

Munching on peanuts and pretzels, we chatted with Sammy for a while. Luke and Sammy had worked together on other cruises, but this was a full-time job for Sammy. I wondered how many other women Luke had introduced to him.

"Shall we take that walk, Ellen?" Luke asked, bringing me out of my thoughts. "I don't want you to miss the sunset. It's quite spectacular on the ocean."

"That sounds great."

"I'll get your usual spot set up, Luke!" Sammy shouted, giving Luke a thumbs-up signal as we walked off. We took our drinks and walked to the edge of the deck. The sun was just starting to set, a reddish-orange glow floating on top of the water. It was quiet, no children or families in sight. Nearby, a man and woman spoke in hushed voices--the kind lovers use when they don't want anyone to hear what they say. Luke and I stood next to each other, our arms touching.

"Isn't it beautiful?"

"Yes." My throat was dry and my heart was racing.

"I love coming out here," he said. "I feel so free." The waves swelled and I lost my balance and fell into Luke. He wrapped his arm around my waist and pulled me to his side. Minutes passed. I could hear the water gently lapping against the side of the ship. I could feel his hand caressing my waist. It felt nice. I wanted to kiss Luke but that would mean crossing a line and opening the doors to God knows what.

"Ellen?"

"Yes?" I turned, looking up at him.

"Look, I know you're married and this is kinda weird, but…" He paused, as if he were struggling to find the right words. "But, I just have to tell you something." He grabbed my hand and pulled me towards him. I swallowed hard, waiting to hear his next words.

"Yes?"

"You really are beautiful. I thought you were beautiful the first time I saw you. In fact, I recognized you when you first sat down in my area. I just pretended…" Before he could finish, I kissed him on the lips. I pulled away, shocked at what I'd just done.

"I'm sorry, Luke. I shouldn't have done that." Luke pulled me back and wrapped his arms around me.

"Don't be sorry, Ellen. We both wanted to. I've been thinking about it all afternoon." I wanted to tell him that I'd been, too. We stood there for what seemed like hours, neither of us saying anything, neither of us moving. I liked feeling his body against mine.

"What a gorgeous pose," a voice said behind us. "That would look *perfect* on your mantel." It was the ship's photographer with his camera poised and ready to shoot.

"We're not interested," I said, wanting to tell him that it would never go on my mantel.

"How about I take the picture anyway? You might change your mind." He went through a lengthy, but quick, explanation of where we could find the pictures and how we could pay. I wanted to say, "Really, we're not interested, thanks," but couldn't get a word in.

"Ellen, why don't we just take the picture? Like he said, we don't need to buy it."

"You don't need to buy it," the photographer repeated, as if that would convince me to change my mind.

The photographer glanced at his watch. "So? What's it gonna be? I have customers."

Before I could answer, I heard Luke say, "Let's do it." He pulled me backwards so I was in front of him, wrapped his arms around my waist and rested his chin on my head, which was easy since he was almost a foot taller than me. I leaned back, smiled and the photographer took the picture.

"They'll be for sale as you disembark. Be sure to pick one up!" He said before moving on to the next couple.

Luke and I turned around and watched the sun creep below the horizon. I shivered, prompting Luke to wrap his arms around me again. What was going to happen next? This could be our little secret, a little fling in the middle of the ocean. No one would have to know.

"I won't tell anyone," Luke said, as if reading my thoughts. He rubbed my arms and kissed the back of my head.

"I've always been faithful to my husband, Luke," I said. "This isn't easy for me."

"It's just one night. You'll never hear from me again." He kissed my neck. My resistance was melting. What was I going to do?

"Paging Ellen Nicholson. Paging Ellen Nicholson," crackled through a nearby speaker. "Ellen Nicholson, please go to a white courtesy telephone."

Luke pointed behind us to a phone on the wall. I picked it up.

"This is Ellen Nicholson." There was a lot of static on the other line. "Is anyone there?"

"Ellen! It's Jeff! Where have you been? I've been trying to reach you!"

Jeff? Why was he calling me? I thought they only did shore-to-ship calls in emergencies. Oh God, was Nathan okay?

"Jeff? Is everything okay?" I glanced over at Luke, still leaning against the railing. He smiled and raised his glass as if giving a toast. My heart was racing, thinking about what had just happened between us. I felt like a child stealing candy from the candy jar, not sure if I'd been seen or not. It was just coincidence that Jeff called at this exact moment, right?

"Yes, I just called to wish you a Happy..." His voice cut off, the static making it impossible for me to hear him.

"A what?" I shouted.

"A Happy Anniversary, honey!"

"Anniversary?" I asked, confused because our anniversary wasn't until October. Then, I remembered. This was going to be our anniversary cruise. "Oh yeah! I remember. Happy Anniversary."

"Are you having fun?"

"Yeah," I said. "But I wish you were here." I wanted to add, "Here so I won't sleep with Susie Jacobson's son," but didn't.

"I should be there, honey. The guys told me what a jerk I was for choosing the fishing trip over you. In fact, I came home early." Jeff paused, as if waiting for me to speak, but I didn't know what to say. "I'm really sorry."

"Me too. I really miss you, Jeff."

"I miss you, too."

As I hung up the phone, I realized that I really did miss him. I wasn't just saying it. Whatever troubles we had were not going to disappear with a one-night fling. When I got home, I would talk to Jeff about seeing a marriage counselor.

"Was that your husband?" Luke asked when I got back to him.

"Yes." Five minutes ago, I would have lied. "He apologized."

"Good for him."

We stood in silence, an arm's length apart. The moon was starting to rise, casting a silver glow on the darkening waters below us. The clinking of glasses and dishes echoed from the nearby kitchen.

"Luke," I finally said. "Luke, while it is very tempting, I think it's…"

"You don't have to say another word, Ellen," he interrupted. "I knew from the look on your face that you'd changed your mind." Luke stroked my cheek and I put my hand on his.

"Thank you," I said, relieved that I wouldn't have to say the words myself.

"He's a lucky man, you know." Luke paused. "I hope he knows that." He walked away, then suddenly turned around and stopped.

"What?" I asked, wondering why he was just staring at me.

"I just want to remember how beautiful you are."

I stayed on the deck for about an hour. I had no regrets. When I disembarked the next morning, I passed the photo display. Our picture was dead center. The photographer asked if I'd like a copy, but I told him no. I couldn't justify paying twenty dollars for a picture I would never be able to display.

****

Two weeks later, I received a package at the office. It had no return address and was about the size of hardback novel. I un-wrapped it carefully and found a framed photograph inside. It was the picture of Luke and me with a Post-it note on the glass. Written on the note was one word: *Beautiful*. I stared at the picture for a few minutes before re-wrapping it. I opened the bottom drawer of my desk and put the picture at the bottom, carefully burying it under a pile of folders.

The Runner
Gregg Garmisa

Through the picture window framed by sensible blue curtains, Lena strained to see the lean runner edging perilously close to her prized English garden. Alarmed he might damage the little oasis she had planted and nurtured, she headed for the screen door. Just then, the runner picked up his gait lustily as though propelled forward by a burst of wind. His sudden surge jarred her and Lena felt the weight of his steps rumble internally.

Short of breath, she sat. From the family room, she heard a TV golf commentator analyzing someone's feeble stroke and her husband's less restrained opinion. She could picture him writhing back and forth in his seat, a couch potato lap dance. Looking at the laundry pile waiting to be folded, she thought that the linens' creases formed a sympathetic frown.

The next morning at work, Lena was comforted by the natural rhythms of her responsibilities. A few hours in, however, her focus began to evaporate, as it had these past few weeks --- this damn new supervisor, his coarse micromanaging style. She lapsed into a brief daydream, recalling her sprinter, many years ago, and his stride, long and smooth. She did not notice the steady stream of shoppers being consumed and disgorged by the electronic doors to the supermarket below her office window, ants trudging to and from their hill.

Then, a runner cut perpendicularly through the mundane lines. Startled, Lena pressed her nose against the window. This runner appeared taller than the one yesterday, beefier. She preferred the thinner version. Though she couldn't recall the outfit of yesterday's intruder, this one wore candy apple red shorts and a shimmery green top. She wrinkled her nose. Men should not be adorned with plumage. Aware that she was being silly and judgmental, Lena was, still, satisfied with her visceral instinct. Because she had feared being perched on the edge of not caring about such things, she was pleased to feel that raw streak.

The week passed restlessly for Lena. The house bellowed with silence from the absence of her grown children and the presence of her husband. She poked at her food. Lena struggled with sleep. She tried warm milk. She read. She traced the fringe of her underwear and slipped her fingers beneath but found no comfort. Unfinished business, unsettling memories, kept doing laps around her mind.

The weekend returned and Lena found every excuse to garden. She had no reason to think that the runner would reappear. She did not recognize him from the neighborhood, had no clear idea what she was doing and had nothing to say to him. This is pointless, she concluded, after a few minutes of vigorously turning the soil with her bare hands, like a Cold War era Russian masseuse.

Clipping a few of the remaining unspent tulips, Lena headed into the house and nearly drowned them in a vase of water. On autopilot, she walked to the basement to switch the laundry.

Outside Lena's house, the runner slowed his pace and almost came to a stop. Then, as if gripped by fears of a recurring nightmare, he bolted around the corner and disappeared.

Early the next morning, Lena laced the dusty hand-me-down running shoes that her daughter had left behind in the mud room before moving to Boston. God, she thought, when was the last time I did this? What the hell am I doing? Her knees creaked a bit, apparently in protest of the upcoming pounding they were about to undergo.

Genetically, she had been dealt a pretty solid hand. Her good looks and all the right curves that had eased her through her twenties and thirties had given way to a near stunning mature beauty. Tiny creases cradled Lena's kaleidoscopic blue eyes. A few gray strands whispered softly around her ears and all those curves still generated appreciation.

Though still shapely, she rarely exercised. When she did, she lacked the essential accoutrement of the youthful, vigorous, set --- no iPod. Not even a Shuffle. Worse, when working out, the songs on her mental playlist looped between Kenny Rankin, Boz Skaggs and, in more carefree moods, Joan Armatrading. Not exactly the musical currency of *The Young and Beautiful*. For a few seconds, she thought of kicking off her shoes.

Instead, she picked herself up and headed outside. As she walked to the nearby running trail, she remembered the article she recently saw in the women's health magazine advising new runners to run at an extraordinary slow pace or else they'd crash. She thought that was good advice, recalling her school days when long-distance running was clocked in P.E. She'd start fast, quickly lose steam and inevitably hit a brick wall, leading to embarrassing times when they were posted on the gym's bulletin board.

Come to think of it, she realized her running strategy back then pretty much summed up her relationship approach as a young adult. She had considered herself passionate, but now had to acknowledge that, for one reason or another, the few electric relations only shone bright for a brief interlude, but then inevitably went dark. Usually triggered by an explosion. Or perhaps, she mused, an implosion. Slow and steady, she warned herself.

Out on the trail, she contemplated some of the highs and lows of her adult years. The episodes all trotted out like a mash-up of a beauty pageant, spelling bee and amateur talent night. The marriage that seemed like a sound proposition. The accidental high-profile career that flung her around the globe, sometimes with a first-class ticket and the occasional double-take from strangers. The even more accidental pregnancy and the months of medically-mandated bed rest. The years of raising the child, essentially as a single parent. The crying --- not just the baby. The screaming and yelling. The almost pointillist marriage which, from afar, appeared normal but upon closer inspection really was broken into countless unrecognizable fragments. The difficult but important process of trying to gather and reconfigure all the different pieces.

Before long, she found herself a few miles away, a distance she had never walked, let alone run. She was amazed that she wasn't tired, then checked to make sure her breathing was under control and turned around, heading toward home. Two blocks from her destination, she spied a little path that led directly down to the lake. Without so much as a second thought, she veered off the trail.

At the water's edge, she contemplated the fact that it wasn't yet close to the summer swimming season. Removing her shoes, she drew a sobering breath and sprinted into the lake. Waist deep, she dove under an oncoming wave. Lena's religiously-themed necklace bobbled near the surface for a second, sparkling, before it joined her on the short descent to the rocky bottom. She surfaced, then flung her hair about wildly and returned to the shore, shivering. Quickly putting her shoes back on, she took off like a child who hears the tinny music blaring from an ice cream truck's speaker.

Back at the trail and out of breath, but almost dry and warm again, she stopped and looked right, at the short path toward home. She turned left, swallowed hard and started walking.

In the park across from Lena's house, the runner ran a few dozen wind sprints, his movements spare and contained. Once winded, he stared at Lena's perfect Victorian house and admired her beautiful garden before easing into his car and driving away, never looking back once, unwilling to even try.

A few minutes later, Lena realized her folly and promptly headed toward home. After a quick shower and change of clothes, she picked up a few tools and trudged toward the garden.

She immediately saw the decapitated remains of a tulip clump she had sprayed with coyote urine just days ago to ward off evil deer spirits. Those damn deer. She could almost feel Bambi gloating over her. If it didn't risk her street cred as a progressive, Lena would truly give her support at the next City Council meeting if a proposal to cull the herd was raised.

Walking over to the composting bin, she held the stalks so tightly that, had the deer not already feasted on the flowers, her grip surely would have twisted any remaining life out of them. She lifted the lid and flung the limp pile inside, making her feel a smidgeon better --- ashes to ashes, and all that.

She picked up a nearby rake and began another chore. She had to. Couldn't sit still. Ever. Yet, she still couldn't figure out why? She had been this way since childhood. Director and writer of the summer theatre productions put on in basement family rooms with her friends on the block. Organizer of the effort in college to protest Apartheid in South Africa. PTA Room Mom. Sought after motivational speaker. She spoke with passion. She connected with the audience, locking eyes, making people feel as if she was talking directly to them, as if they were the only two people in a room filled with hundreds more. She was very good at helping groups and individuals tap unseen, unknown, potential. Always available to help them, to help others, grow. It had been a long time since she had asked the question, what about me?

Looking down at the rake, she saw that she had nearly removed a square foot or two of grass from the middle of her lawn. She leaned the ostensibly guilty instrument against the side of the shed, as if sending a toddler to a time-out, and, head down, walked into the house.

In the sunroom, she ran her fingers along the spine of several photo albums until she found the one she needed. There, on the last page, she found the shot of her small cadre of old college friends, arms entangled, everyone smiling. While others wandered in and out of the group over the years, these few had always been there for her, and vice versa. Through the dabbling phases. During the transitions. Picking one another up after the crises.

Lena slowly brought the photo up to her lips to offer a kiss when she spotted someone in the photo she had never noticed there before. Slightly out of focus and off to the side, she spied her runner, sprinting across the college green. He was the only one who had ever been able to keep up with her, challenge her to race faster into the unknown, and force her to slow down and look inward. The one whose touch she still tried to recall, whose lips she still tried to taste. The one she discarded. She recalled the pain she had caused him. A wave crashed over her, just like it had so many years ago. She wept.

Later, she heard her husband singing in the shower, same wretched voice as always. Lena closed her eyes, now calm, recalling how, over time, she had learned to appreciate his steady confidence, his easy comfort in his own blemished skin, even that miserable warbling. He called out, "Hon? You there? Let's run over to the hardware store. I want to show you the light gray picket fence I've picked out."

She remembered that he thought they should replace the drab, washed-out, chain-link fence that was on the verge of collapse. Without answering, she walked over to her computer and navigated to one of her favorite sites for online shopping, where she placed an order for tulip bulbs, red, yellow, orange, even purple. I can't wait until next spring to see them, she thought. I can't wait. I can't.

The First Step
Jeanne Verville

We arrive in Prague in January 1976, for my husband's long-awaited sabbatical: two parents, two young girls, four suitcases and two boxes of belongings. The weather has been raw. I have shivered in pain, the wind cutting through my skimpy green coat like a sheet of tin, my feet frozen stiff as I trod hard cobblestones in thin-soled black leather boots. The skies, grey and weeping, are darker than normal because everything is powered by soft coal. Even the off-white stucco surfaces of the newer buildings, dirty from soot and lack of maintenance, reflect nothing but drab sterility in their soviet architecture.

My heart matches the surroundings, bruised by the fact that just before we came to Czechoslovakia I discovered that Andrew, my husband of 11 years, had fallen in love with Marie's nursery school teacher. Creepily, I knew he would the moment I saw her. Rindy has big blue eyes with thick blond lashes, is freckled all over, has long strawberry blond hair (his weakness) and is covered with blond hair – her arms, her legs, even her face. At first, before I know they have fallen for each other, I thought of her as a timid, woodland animal. Now I think of her as "the witch."

And now it is May. The skies are bright. Grass is poking up through the unkempt brown bare patch outside our apartment building. Spring is always my "new year." Just as the maple sap runs with sweetness in the spring, my blood runs with energy when the earth comes alive. It is time to come out of bleak hibernation of spirit and embrace this wonderful adventure more fully.

Despite the cold, I have explored the streets and alleyways of Prague while the girls are in school and Andrew is at work and I've fallen in love with the city: the view from Strahov Monastery, the picturesque Gothic Town Square and its astronomical clock and procession of mechanical apostles, the golden Renaissance buildings on the banks of the Vltava River. I have learned this city, its history and legends. Its beauty, never destroyed by bombs, entrances me. It feels like a fairly tale come alive.

I am caught up in the newness and excitement of it all and want so much to be sharing it with my husband. I want to rebuild our relationship through happy, new experiences together. I am tired of exploring alone. I am willing to forgive his transgression. Here we are free from all the duties our respective roles entail, free to make up an adventure together in this very romantic setting and return to our normal lives, changed for the better. But every weekend I get the same response, "I don't feel like going out."

Now I want to explore the rest of Czechoslovakia and go to Poland to visit Auschwitz. And I want Andrew to come with me. "Let's do as much as we can while we're here," I've pleaded. "When will we ever have another chance like this?" My words fall on deaf ears and a stony heart. He has shown an amazing lack of interest in where we are, his interest still focused on Rindy back in Nebraska. I know he writes to her – he's told me so – and sends her emotional German expressionist poems he copies out of books. I have protested to no avail.

I decide to go on my proposed trip anyway. It feels important to do it. Andrew seems relieved at my plan to take the kids on a two-week road trip, exhaling more long sighs than usual. No doubt he can now read his German expressionist poems and write his love letters in peace.

Zdenek, Andrew's ever-thoughtful host at the science lab, questions the safety of my idea. "What will you do if you have an emergency?" he asks. He knows that my seven-year-old has hydrocephalus. "What if Carol gets sick and needs surgery?"

"I'm sure I can find an English speaker who will help me," I respond. My secret plan, completely uninformed, is to call the American Embassy and ask that a medivac unit be sent to god-knows-where in the Slovakian countryside to airlift Carol to the American base in Nuremburg. I'm not really afraid. Carol had been okay for more than five years. The chances of her shunt failing are small. I'm willing to take the chance.

The day of departure arrives. I pack our new, bright gold Volkswagen Camper and buy what food I can find at the drab market across the street from our apartment tower: a loaf of crusty and delicious sour-dough rye, cheese, a few apples, milk, and some cereal purchased the week before from the American Embassy commissary. Not much. In 1976 this is a country of scarcity and there isn't much to *be* bought.

Carol is excited. "We're going on an adventure, Daddy," she says to Andrew the night before, as she picks which stuffed animals she wants to bring along. Four-year-old Marie chimes in, "We're going on an adventure." If she gets to do what her big sister does she's good to go. "Daddy, Daddy, are you coming with us?"

"I have to stay here and work," he says flatly, a fair response, but not entirely true. There is no pressure in the Czech lab. He's told me that the people there work short hours and disappear at random times most every day. He hasn't expressed any internal pressure to do as much research as he can either. He just doesn't want to go. He doesn't want to be with us.

As I drive to the lab the next morning for last good-byes to Andrew, I feel bile rising in my throat. One minute I say, "Of course I'm going. Never pass up an opportunity for adventure." The next I shudder inside, fear of the unknown gripping my heart. As I pull up in front of the golden, stuccoed building where Andrew works, sense finally comes to me. What do I think I'm doing, going on a long trip with two small children in a country where I don't speak the language and have no confidence that anything – including emergency response – works? What if Carol's shunt does break? Without proper medical intervention she could suffer brain damage within a matter of hours. What if the car breaks down? What if...what if? And, shouldn't I stay here? As Andrew's wife, isn't my place with him, preparing his meals, doing his laundry – instead of gallivanting all over Eastern Europe? Shouldn't I be doing everything I can to win back his heart?

As Andrew climbs into the camper to hug the girls good-bye, I ask, "Andrew, should I go?" Part of me hopes he will say something like, "No, I want you with me. Don't go. We'll go together in a few weeks."

"Sure," he says. "It will be good for you." His self-satisfied grin only thinly disguises his real desire – to be left alone.

I strap on my belt and start the engine. But I can't make my foot engage the clutch to put the van in drive. I am paralyzed. Then, a voice from deep inside says, "You have to do this." I put the yellow VW baby in first gear as Andrew slams shut the sliding door.

The mapped route is clear, the roads good and soon we are in fresh green hilly countryside, singing *She'll be Comin' 'Round the Mountain*. A little wheel speed and music always cheer me up. "This is going to be fun!" I say to the girls, feeling a surge of confidence. The universe will be kind and take care of us.

We are now in Southeast Bohemia, on the old route from Prague to Vienna. Suddenly we roll into the town of Telc, an arrestingly beautiful Renaissance town whose huge cobble-stoned town square is flanked with arcaded Baroque facades. I have to stop. This is a place from a different time, seemingly untouched by modernity. "Let's go find some *zmrzlina*," I jolly to the girls, hoping to entice them to explore the arcaded tunnels of shade with me.

"*Zmrzlina, zmrzlina*," they chorus, chanting their favorite of the four Czech words they know. Ice cream is always welcome no matter how you say it, especially when you can only get it in the spring and summer.

Back in the van, the map indicates there is a *campingplatz* about an hour down the road, but I can't remember the foreign names of the cross roads while driving and feel lost. I ask some tired workers walking alongside the highway for directions but my made-up language of German-sounding words fails me. I just repeat "*campingplatz, campingplatz*" and point to the dot on the map. Finally one man understands. "I take," he says. And with that he opens the door and climbs into the passenger seat.

The young man's eyes are round with wonder at the size of the camper and its luxury. I can see now that his eagerness to help is at least partly motivated by the chance to ride in the shiny new vehicle. Guided by pointed fingers and words that make no sense, we finally arrive at a green clearing by a stream. "*Campingplatz!*" my guide announces. True. It is a fine place to pitch a tent, a beautiful spot where the air is clean and the wind whistles though the surrounding pine trees.

But it isn't what I was expecting – a campground like those in the European *cities* we have visited.

The man lingers after I park. Several people are now coming straight for us. I feel tension beading up in my chest. What do they want? The answer is soon apparent. They just want is to touch the beautiful children, want me to pop the top and want to look in the ice chest, in the little closets, and at the sink that runs real water.

The next morning as the girls and I shake sleep off a woman and her two children come to us bearing fresh-from-the-cow milk and some biscuits. "For you," the woman says, thrusting the sweet-smelling breakfast into my hands. I feel touched by this simple kindness and accept her gift with a smile – and a tour of the camper. I am beginning to realize that I will be safe on this adventure. I, a single woman traveling in a big, new vehicle, am a novelty. And having two children assures that no one will harm us. Everyone is so kind to the children.

Over the next few days we stop frequently – a castle here, a field for romping there. We meet many people who are always eager to hop into the van to show the way. The girls behave remarkably, entertaining themselves without the usual squabbling. But now I am having trouble finding food for breakfast and lunch. The milk, always an iffy proposition, is sour when bought from small, dingy stores in the rural areas. Bread is the only reliable thing to eat. We manage. Dinners of pork cutlet and potatoes are fine in the small cafes. But the campingplatz dots on the map have dried up and my budget really doesn't allow for hotels.

One night, in desperation, I drive up a steep hill in the middle of a vineyard and set up house right there. I feel lonely and after the children are asleep I break open a bottle of Hungarian *Bull's Blood*. The red wine is full and smooth on my tongue and mellows out the fears I continue to have about the wisdom of this trip. It also brings tears. I sit muffling my sobs, warm saline spilling freely as I contemplate the state of my marriage. I feel so alone. Is my marriage over? Is this little female trio the new reality of my family? The more *Bull's Blood* I drink the more self-pity fills my being. Finally I cry myself to sleep.

Ow! The next morning I awake with a banging headache. Then, as I take a squat between rows of grapevines, I hear a man's voice. I struggle to right myself and pull up my drawers.

"*Dobre den,*" the farmer says. I am sure I'm in trouble for trespassing on his land. "*Dobre den,*" I respond. I try to explain that I couldn't find a place to camp. Either he doesn't understand or doesn't care. All he wants is a tour of the camper! With that accomplished he sends me off with good cheer.

We roll into Poland, visit the castle in Krakow and stroll in the old plaza where I buy some colorful paper-cut art. But I'm restless. The real reason I came to Poland is to see Auschwitz, to gain a better understanding of what the Holocaust was all about.

Auschwitz, the German concentration camp built on annexed Polish lands, is only about 30 miles from Krakow. I drive up to the gate where the commonly used and insulting slogan "ARBEIT MACHT FREI" (work will set you free) welcomed more than a million Poles, Russians, and Gypsies who were sent here to do forced labor – and die in the gas chambers.

In these Eastern Bloc countries many of the old women wear printed dresses, heavy stockings, black shoes, a sweater and, invariable, a babushka, a word whose etymology means old woman or grandmother. Such women are affectionately called "babushkas." At the ticket counter at Auschwitz, rounded babushkas tell me in broken German that I cannot take the children on the tour of the camp. "*Nein, Kinder! Nein, Kinder,*" they scold me in broken German, shaking their fingers at me. "*Nein, Kinder.*" They want me to leave the children with them. I see that Carol and Marie fear these well-meaning women and I would no more leave my children with strangers than with the devil. Plus I want Carol to see this death camp, hoping she will remember something of it and become tolerant of differences. I want her childhood to be different from mine, where everything was presented in sanitized interpretation. I want her to become strong through experience, strong enough to resist falling into the usual passive role women are expected to assume. I ignore the babushkas and start the tour.

I hold both girls on my lap as we watch an introductory film. They are quiet and don't squirm. What are they thinking when the emaciated figures welcome the soldiers of liberation? Are the babushkas right that this is not child's fare? I go forward. Europe at the time is just coming out of years of denial about what happened in these camps. This is important. This experience will not be denied to me or to my children. I want to face the horror straight on and I want my children with me, watching me be brave.

I carry Marie and hold tight Carol's hand. All the way through the tour I receive scowls and finger shakings from fellow travelers. I resist feeling like an unfit mother.

"Mommy, why are all those glasses there?" Carol asks.

I try to explain. "Some very bad people took those glasses and everything else from some people they didn't like. They didn't like them because they were different. Then the bad people killed them, even the little children. It was a terrible time. We have to see it and pay attention, to make sure it doesn't happen again."

Carol looks seriously at the exhibits and grips my hand. When we come to the bunkhouses I explain that four people had to sleep in each straw bunk and crowd together for warmth because they only had thin blankets. She looks solemn.

We pass cells where certain people were imprisoned. "This is where they put people who tried to disobey the rules," I say to the girls.

I hold it together pretty well until we come to the crematoria. The smell of death permeates the buildings. I feel woozy. I can't take any more. Lucky for me the children are getting restless and hungry, and provide an excuse for not enduring the entire horror show. I turn and we leave.

Despite the downward spiral of my marriage I know I am lucky indeed. I have my beautiful children. In this place of ghosts who braved the very worst that could possibly be offered I have found courage.

Back in the camper, I ask the girls what they learned from our visit to Auschwitz.

"It's not nice to be mean to people because they are different," Carol says. I beam with pride that my seven-year-old has gotten this message. "Carol, you are such a smart girl."

"Mom, did any of the prisoners live?"

"Yes, honey. Many did live. They had a huge will to survive and many of them lived much longer than anyone would have guessed, given how little they had to eat and how hard they had to work. The will to survive is a very strong thing. Many were still alive when the Americans and their friends rescued them at the end of the war."

"Well, that's good," Carol states with relief.

"You know, Carol, you're a survivor too. You could have died as a baby with your hydrocephalus. But you didn't. You are strong. You are a survivor."

"Yes I am. Nobody's going to hurt me."

I wistfully hope that will be true.

The trip through the death camp stifles any remaining wanderlust. I want to go "home" to Prague, to my real life, to my husband. I feel refreshed, inspired and proud of myself for having taken the trip.

Although I won't realize it until years later, the moment I engaged the clutch back there on the shaded street by Andrew's lab, I said "yes" to my innate will to survive. And the determination to take my children through the camp stood as inspiring proof that I could push through obstacles and no longer be led docilely by those who think they know what I should do. Although it will take another six years to find enough courage — or be given further excuse — to leave my marriage, I have taken the first step toward proving to myself that I can survive.

The Photo Gallery
Tori Ritchie

    In the hallway outside of our bedroom, one wall is lined with framed pictures. My wife's photo gallery I call it, for this is her project. She chooses what goes on the wall, she buys the frame, she puts the photo or clipping into it, and she does the hanging. There is no real chronology. If a picture of our golden retriever fits the spot between our son's grammar school class photo and the aerial shot of our garden, she'll put it right there.
    I don't notice the photos very often. Mostly I've passed them in the dark, not wanting to disturb my wife by turning on the hall light when I leave for work in the morning, and usually feeling too tired at night to stop. But I'm thankful that she's done it and I should tell her that someday.
    Near our bedroom door, there is a black and white portrait of our children taken alongside an expansive oak tree on their grandmother's property. My wife hired a professional to shoot it and each child is crisply dressed, hair combed and shoes tied. I wasn't there when it was taken and I'm not sure what ages the children are. They're little. The youngest is still in diapers, the edges peeking out from beneath her dress. Her neat little saddle shoes are turned in slightly and her fingers are curled into the cuff of her brother's gray flannel shorts.
    In years past when I did look at this picture, I was more taken by the quality of the frame, a piece of craftsmanship not easy to find today, than I was by the photo itself. I just didn't like to linger over that part of the past. But lately, I stop often to look at our little girl. Truth be told (and I would never tell her mother this), she is my favorite. This morning she called from the city, asking if she could come down to talk to us. Her mother answered the phone. She doesn't like it when the children want to come by without advance warning, especially on Saturdays, which she prefers to devote to her rose garden. But Annie insisted. Her mother signaled me to pick up the extension in the den.
    "I need to come down to talk to you and Dad today," Annie said.

"Today? Why today? I wish you'd given us a little notice," her mother answered.

"Well, Mother, you know how hard I work during the week and I just didn't plan this ahead."

"Is Warren coming?" I asked.

"Warren?" Annie hesitated. "Um, well, he's working today. You know how it is. He's always working weekends. Pricing some deal that's going public Monday."

"That's a shame. We've seen so little of Warren lately," her mother said.

"Actually that's kind of what I'd like to talk to you and Dad about."

Silence, and then a buzzing noise as her mother switched the portable phone to her other hand.

"Are you two having problems?" I asked.

"Look, let's talk when I get there," Annie answered. "It's better to discuss this face to face. It has to be today. It really can't wait until it's convenient for you."

"Well," her mother replied, "we'll have to see if your father can make the time."

Actually, I don't have much to do on weekends anymore since I transferred the business to our son. It's just that my wife doesn't like unpleasant scenes and when the children have problems in their personal lives, it usually falls to me to hear the details. I am not particularly comfortable in this role and I don't think the children like it either. But that's the way it's always been done in our family.

We don't see much of Annie these days. When she moved back from the East after college, we saw her much more. She and her friends would come down during summer, escaping the fog. She had such attractive friends, lively and energetic. There was a new man every so often and we'd meet him. I didn't like some of them, but Warren was the exception. Handsome and athletic and from a fine Eastern family. Newly minted MBA from Stanford. The first time we met, he came straight to me and shook my hand firmly, looking me right in the eye. And he always asked how my business was doing. Before they were engaged, he took me to lunch to ask for Annie's hand.

Sometime around two in the afternoon, I heard the crunch of Annie's tires as she drove down our gravel driveway. I was standing in the hallway upstairs, looking at the photo gallery on the wall. I walked to the deck off our bedroom to watch her get out of her car. My wife was standing at a rose bush near the pool, trowel in hand, face shaded by a straw hat. She walked over to Annie.

"Your father's upstairs. You know he usually takes his nap around now, but I asked him to stay awake so he could talk to you."

Closing the car door, Annie said, "You mean you're not joining us?"

"I don't think that's necessary. Your father can speak for both of us."

"This is more about listening than speaking, actually."

Her mother waved the trowel in the air. "I'm not good with emotions, Annie, you know that. If you need to speak to us about your personal life, your father is in charge. Please don't make it unpleasant for me."

Annie looked up at the house and saw me. I gave her a smile and motioned to her to meet me in the entry hall. I walked downstairs. She was in a skirt, flip-flops, a t-shirt she called 'yoga top'."

"Hi Dad."

"I'm so glad you're here, Annie. We haven't seen you in weeks," I said. "We really miss you." I squeezed her hand.

"I'm sorry. I've been really busy."

"Do you want something to drink? To eat?"

"No, I just want to sit down," she said, sounding tired. "Where shall we go?"

I gestured towards the den. As I followed her down the hall, I couldn't help noticing her feet. She wears a small shoe size, an anomaly in our family. When Annie was a little girl, I taught her to dance by having her stand on my wing tips. I would dance her around carefully, exaggerating the steps so she could feel them under her feet. We'd dance this way to Ernie Hecksher and Glenn Miller. She loved Gershwin, too. Her favorite was *Love is Here to Stay*. She arranged to have the band play that for the second dance at her wedding reception, when she and I were paired up, while Warren danced with her mother.

"How's work?" I asked as we sat down.

"It's okay. I'm doing an interesting project on Xeriscaping. You know, landscaping for less water use." She was avoiding my eyes. "There's a wonderful guy in Berkeley who's written a book on Xeriscaping for city gardens. I'm doing a lot of work with him."

Annie is a writer for the home section of the local paper. It's a respectable job, but we don't like it that she has to be in a union. And her pay is a source of aggravation to me; I don't approve of working for so little money. Fortunately, Warren makes more than enough to support them both nicely.

"You ought to tell your mother about that Xeriscaping," I said. "She'd be interested to know the latest in gardens. Maybe she'd like to meet this fellow."

Annie shifted in her chair. "It's not for her. It's the opposite of her gardening credo. Besides he's only interested in city gardens."

When Annie was little, she loved to play at gardening. My wife had a miniature set of tools made for her – a rake, a hoe, a shovel and a tiny trowel. Each one had a different bug painted on the handle, with Annie's initials on their backs. But the pictures of the bugs scared Annie and she didn't use the tools much. They still languish in our gardening shed. Once I suggested to her that she should take them to work, sort of a talisman as inspiration for her articles. She said she'd rather her colleagues didn't know too much about her childhood.

"I meant to call Warren this week and see that he gets you to transfer your IRA to a growth fund," I said. "I just hate to bother him at work. He's so busy, poor guy. What a tough business he's in. I'm so thankful we didn't have to travel like that in my day. But I suppose it's nice to get all those free airplane miles."

"Dad, why are you always so worried about how hard Warren's working? Don't you ever think about me?" she said.

I was taken aback. "I do Annie," I said. "It's just that I want to see you both happy."

Shifting subjects, I added, "Your mother and I are thinking about taking a trip to Virginia for Garden Week. Why don't you and Warren come along and relax a bit?"

She looked at me. "Warren and I aren't going anywhere with you and Mother."

"What does that mean?"

"I'm leaving him. We're separating. I'm moving out. I already have an apartment lined up. It's just a studio, but I'll be comfortable. The rent is manageable and I can bring the spare bed from the guest room and a few other pieces of furniture. I may need to take some things from here. You know, that old love seat from my room. I could slipcover it and it would work fine as a couch."

Again, I noticed her feet. They were turned in slightly, the exact same position as in the photo in the hall upstairs.

"What's the problem, Annie? Warren is a super husband. What could be making you unhappy?"

She pushed her palms into the seat cushion, lifting herself up slightly from the upholstered chair. "All he ever does is work or work out," she said, then dropped back down into her seat. "And when he's not doing one of those two things, he's sleeping. Recharging his batteries for the next deal."

"But Annie, that's what it takes. You know that. What do you think I did all those years you kids were growing up? It's not easy supporting a family. Your mother never complained when I worked hard."

"We don't have a family yet."

"Yes, but Warren's laying the groundwork. Doing what's necessary so you and any kids will be very comfortable. You'll never have to work. You can still write books or articles if you want to, but you won't have to slave away for those cheapskates. You're pretty lucky, Annie, if you ask me."

"Lucky? Lucky to have a husband who's so tired he can't laugh, can't talk, can't enjoy life? Do you know we've never had a conversation in bed in four years of marriage? He's asleep the minute he hits the pillow. And he's up and out before I'm awake!"

"Well, Annie, maybe it's time you had kids. That will bring you together. And it will give you something to do so you won't need so much from Warren. You can't expect a man to give you everything. A secure home and a nice life – that's more than most women get."

Kids would also make her so tired she wouldn't care much what happened in bed, I thought, but I didn't say this.

"Kids?!" Annie's voice tensed. "Kids would just make Warren redouble his efforts. He'd never be there for them. He'd be traveling constantly. He's a workaholic, Dad. Can't you see?"

"Listen, there are worse addictions than work. How do you think we get ahead in life? Not by designing gardens that use less water like that guy you mentioned in Berkeley. How would you like to have a husband who did that for a living?"

Now Annie looked at her feet. And she blushed to the skull. My heart pounded; I could hear it inside my head. I had to choose my words carefully. "Annie, whatever you do, don't end up regretting this for the rest of your life."

She told me it didn't matter what I said, she'd made up her mind to leave Warren. After that, there wasn't much more to discuss. I went into the garden to get her mother. Annie calmly told her that she and Warren were separating. Her mother took it well. She didn't ask any questions about Warren, she just wanted to know where Annie planned to move, did she need any money, had they told Warren's parents. Once Annie was gone, I told my wife I would take that nap I'd put off. She headed back to the garden. Don't overdo it out there, I said. I never do, she replied.

I had no intention of napping. I wanted to be in the hallway, to look at the photos. To remember what my children looked like growing up, to remind me of their smiles, and of the smiles their mother and I wore on our wedding day. To look at the picture of my parents on their 50th anniversary and all the other accumulated mementos of a marriage. To try and believe that this wall tells the whole story.

But in my head I see another picture, one I took of a woman around the same time that the children were being photographed under that oak tree. She's on a boat off the coast in Mexico. She's wearing my white button-down shirt and swabbing her neck under her dark, curly hair with my bandanna. I can almost smell the sweat and sea salt on that bandana, feel the heat of her back under that shirt. She loved the sea, wanted to be out in it all the time. She never liked to be landlocked. She didn't own a home and she didn't want a family. She hated to garden. I tore up the picture a few years later.

"The Write Retreat" - Stanford Sierra Camp 2010

    A photo on the wall catches my eye and brings me back. It's from Annie's wedding, just as she and I entered the church, the same church where her mother and I were married. My hand is holding tight to hers. Right before the photo was taken she had turned to me and said, "I love you, Dad." It was the first time she'd said it since she was a little girl. I didn't have time to say it back because the camera went off at that very moment and we had to walk up the aisle.

1492#
Kathleen O'Hanlon Peterson

The guard waved and opened the gate for her. Christina smiled and raised one hand in recognition as she swung around the delivery truck waiting to be signed in. She knew it was a violation of the rules. Every visitor was to be given a guest pass and the address to be visited duly noted in some log to be studied later if necessary. But the guard must have remembered her from all those afternoons she came to the Humphries to pick up Ethan after school. She felt a little chagrined, sneaking into one of the leafy, old money developments in Newport Beach, a little worried that the guard might get in trouble if his lapse was discovered. But she pushed the thought away. None of that would happen. They had nothing to fear from her; just another toned, chipper woman in her forties, tooling around in an oversized vehicle wearing jeans designed to be worn by a 14-year-old. Like it or not. When she was younger, when they had first moved here, she never thought she would end up being one of those women.

She waited for the gate to complete its creaking progress to open. She looked down at her hands in her lap and congratulated herself on not biting her cuticles for several days. She moved the car slowly along the main road, bracing herself for the speed bumps. She counted the streets she passed, still unable to remember or distinguish any of the individual street names even after years of visits. The names seemed to be plucked randomly from a French dictionary, with no connection to the actual physical location they labeled -- Beaulieu, Bordeaux, Sancerre. After five streets she made a right into the circular street. She pulled to the curb, one house down and across the street from her target. She cracked the window against the October heat and turned the ignition off.

The house was quiet in the late afternoon. Halloween decorations were already up. Cutouts of skinny, stylized black cats skittered across the windows. Amused ghosts peered out from behind the bushes. The black front door looked freshly painted, nestled into the front alcove, against the mossy green of the rest of the house. It all was so fresh, so new, warm and welcoming. She remembered flipping through the book of allowed paint combinations with Shelley last spring, paying detailed attention to almost imperceptible variations of green and taupe. It looked like Shelley had finally gone with her initial selection and had ignored Christina's input. Not a surprise. Just more fallout from a friendship gone inexplicably awry.

Before even the first tear rose over the edge of her eye, she had the car in gear, making a sweeping U-turn, on her way home before Shelley or anyone else saw her on their way home from late afternoon sports practices.

On Saturday morning, after a long, thoughtful period awake in her bed and then in a verbena bath, she drove into Shady Canyon. She still had a transponder that opened the heavy wooden gates. In the confusion of the property settlement no one had thought to demand that she return it. But she stopped at the keypad and punched in "1A," perhaps the most predictable two-character combination that could be imagined. It was strange that the people in this innermost sanctum of privilege and privacy relied on this mundane code to provide protection from the rest of the world. Most of the other developments around here had more inventive codes, which were supposed to be jealousy guarded but always ended up being distributed indiscriminately on party invitations. The jaunty "1776" and the risqué "6969" in writing for all to use.

She drove to the street where they had all lived together. Even though it had only been three months since she'd been here the street was almost unrecognizable. More of the houses had completed landscaping and dozens of spindly trees competed for space along the side of the road.

Two little boys in purple soccer uniforms raced out into the street from a driveway and swarmed back up onto the lawn of the house next door. The house, her house as she still thought of it, had a for sale sign in front. There were a few others down the long block. It was an abysmal time to sell. The sign was enough of an announcement of failure to eliminate any need for discussion with neighbors. Only the financially or marital fallen needed to face the market right now. She wondered if anyone was really looking after the house, making sure that the blinds were closed at the right angle to keep the chestnut colored floors from fading, making sure the pittosporum in the rear garden looked properly lacy and inviting. It really still was her business to know the status of the house. She would call Carl and ask him about it.

She knew she should want the house to sell. Until it was disposed of, she was tied to Carl, and tied only financially, the least of the ways she could fathom remaining linked to him. But she felt an inexplicable lift every week the house remained uncommitted. Until then, she would stay in her rental, getting quieter every week as the summer crowds at the beach continued to diminish. And that morning, as she felt the first grey wisps of winter fog trail across her in bed through the open windows she thought it wouldn't be too distasteful to be in the apartment all winter, to be able to experience all those Pacific storms firsthand, one of the diehard people on the beach waiting for the gusts to reach land.

The garage at the house next door started to open and Christina quickly drove to the end of the street and hovered in the cul-de-sac until the neighbor's car was out of sight. She followed the car down the street and to the other end of the development, where the view lots and eight figure price tags clustered together.

This was where the houses had been built first, now with mature fruit trees and full driveways. She made a left and climbed up higher, where the houses were under construction or just stakes outlined on the ground. She passed a taco truck with a dozen workers clustered around it. A red hawk wheeled to her left, dancing on a current right at the edge of the canyon.

Carl's new house was near the top, almost the only house built up here. She pulled up higher on the hill and turned around so she could get a full view of the property. She felt an odd calm of appreciation as she studied the cool grey-blue stone that she had suggested, the elongated curve of the windows, and the beginnings of the grove of olive and lemon trees that she had envisioned. She opened the window and heard the tink, tink, tink of a worker chipping apart pieces of slate, fitting them into the walkway from the house to the grove. The hawk glided over the man's head. She wondered if she could go walk through the house, see what Carl had decided to keep of her ideas and which had been erased. Was the Jerusalem stone still a prominent feature? What about the stenciled Venetian etchings on the dining room ceiling? She hesitated; forming the conversation she would have with the workman with the chisel, and then let the idea float away. It was too much, too invasive. She didn't want to think of herself that way.

That night she thought about Matthew, who had been her son Ethan's friend since pre-school. His parents had divorced in kindergarten and all the time Ethan and Matthew had been friends he had lived with his mother and two little sisters in a narrow house not far from the school. She remembered wondering how they all fit in the house, even though she knew there were three bedrooms, and she had speculated about how Matthew's father had ended up with the big spread of a house in south county while the mother and the children compromised here. At first she hadn't been excited about Ethan's friendship with Matthew and had looked for signs of instability or poor parenting in Matthew. But he was a sunny, bright boy with an even temperament and a bubbly sense of humor. He always bounded happily out of the car when she dropped him home and when she saw his mother at school events she too had an aura of calm about her that both invited and dispelled comment.

She wondered where Matthew was now. In the haze of last spring she had paid little attention to the diaspora of graduating eighth graders. Her frozen horror at finally agreeing, after months of Carl's insistence, that Ethan could, indeed should, go away to school this year had robbed her of any ability to find any joy or sadness in the achievements of the other kids.

On Tuesday, she went to the grocery store near Ethan's old school to get the Italian truffle cheese that she loved. She would put a tablespoon in an omelet for dinner and would feel on top of the world when the richness filled her mouth. While waiting in line to pay, she flipped through a magazine. Her attention was snagged by a large bold quote from Lindsay Lohan, now in the middle of one more fresh start. The young actress explained that her new clothing company was called "6126," which was Marilyn Monroe's birth date. Pathetic. She slapped the magazine closed and stepped forward to pay.

As she left the parking lot, she made a right, away from her apartment, and drove to Matthew's neighborhood. She remembered the gate code here. "1492#." She smiled as she pulled up to the keypad and tried to guess who the Christopher Columbus fan was who had been in a position to select the code.

She pulled through the gates and made the series of turns to Matthew's house. A leering six-foot transparent pumpkin was on the lawn and two toddler girls tumbled on the grass in front. They weren't Matthew's little sisters. A new Land Rover sat in the driveway. She couldn't picture Matthew's precise, self-contained mother driving that. They must have moved. She should ask Ethan when she next spoke to him.

Her phone rang. It was the cleaning service for her apartment needing to arrange a different day. When the call ended she sat with her Blackberry heavy in her hand. In a rush, she thought of all the little boys Ethan had been friends with in his nine years at the school. She saw a parade of blond, freckled boys in navy sweatshirts with the sailboat logo over their embroidered names. Now, only four months after they left the school, they were spread to the winds, her own son and Matthew among them. She scrolled through her address book, looking for one after another of Ethan's friends, as if the listing of a mother's name or a phone number would lend them permanence or even intimacy. In each entry she had included some information to help her keep everyone straight. Siblings' names, father's occupation, address of stepparents for weekend play dates. But in most entries that consistent entry: the gate code.

As she studied them, she started to laugh. Each neighborhood was linked in her mind with some fact of history triggered by the gate code. "1066" – the code for St. Michel, peopled in her mind by tall, Norman-featured men; "1865" – always expecting to find a Civil War battle reenactment underway; "1963" – imaging the narrow, booted figures of the Beatles getting ready to appear on the Ed Sullivan show; "1620" – the smell of turkey almost palpable in the air. She put down the phone and pushed her head back hard against the seat. Her laughter was almost a forgotten practice and she experienced the physical release as if for the first time.

Was there one lucky person at some central management company in an office near the Irvine Spectrum whose job it was to select these numbers; something he had turned into a special perk as he created one more layer of artifice for all of the unsuspecting residents? She wanted to meet the person and congratulate him on his work. And to get his advice.

If she ever got her money from the house, she wanted to live in a place with a gate code to her liking. Maybe she would even be able to talk him into letting her choose it. Her mind flitted through possible dates, considering and rejecting the birth years of the women all her friends admired – Coco Chanel, Audrey Hepburn, even Madonna. No, those wouldn't do. She needed something removed from herself, in no way self-reflective, and also somewhat dark, so that each time she gave it to a visitor she would have a little private joke. What was the year the plague struck Europe? The battle of Waterloo? The great Chicago fire? The invention of gunpowder? She relished the bitterness of making a choice and then living with it.

Now she would go home, make her omelet and maybe have a glass of good Chablis from that case Carl had left with her. After her dinner she would think some more about her code.

Section III:
Family Reminiscences

The voice of parents is the voice of gods,
for to their children
they are heaven's lieutenants.

William Shakespeare

A Fine Way to Treat a Steinway
Patricia Northlich

"I know a fine way to treat a Steinway
I love to run my fingers o'er the keys, the ivories..."

> ...line from tune, "I Love a Piano" composed for Broadway Revue,"Stop, Look, & Listen" 1915, by Irving Berlin

"It is a mystery. The same workers at the Steinway & Sons factory bend and shape the wood the same way. The sounding boards are designed to the same specifications. Strings and pins, hammers and keys – there should not be noticeable variations. Yet every Steinway has a unique sound. Some are modest, some monumental. And no one is quite sure why." (From a nine part article in the New York Times, 2003, 2004, by James Barron)

It was my first break from the Concierge desk since 7 a.m. In the early afternoon, I stood up, stretched, and turned over my three telephones and two guest chairs (empty at the moment) to the bellmen. Then I escaped with my water bottle-- out the lobby side door to the veranda of the huge, historic hotel, leaving the uproar of the computer convention, Junior League luncheon, and Mackintosh Clan 25th Reunion behind. The temperature outside matched the number of the hotel occupancy percentage – both had climbed to 89. I sank into an Adirondack chair with a thick green striped cushion, finally having a pause to think about arrangements for an unusual request concerning a Steinway piano. The Steinway belonged to a celebrity musician, who I was expecting from New York City at any moment now. I closed my eyes, and my mind drifted...

It was a long way from my parents' one-bedroom flat in Queens to their modest two-story house with the maple tree pushing up through the front porch. In 1948 they climbed into their new black Chevrolet and moved our family to Dobbs Ferry on the Hudson River in Westchester County. There were separate bedrooms for my sister and me, a stage with red velvet curtain in the basement, and a bright, spacious dining room. Most important, my mother's old Knabe spinet piano (a precious gift from my young accountant father, which he bought on time over two years) fit nicely against the inner wall of the small living room.

Stardust and scales quickly surrounded us as they had in New York City. My pianist mother had accompanied dance classes in lofts for 35 cents to $1.00 an hour. I loved to listen to her lilting music before falling asleep at night -- lying backward in bed, walking my feet up and down the wallpaper from rose to rose in time to the notes.

Music was in the air. My mother's piano refrains were heard in the evenings, and also in the mornings, beginning at dawn. Every Tuesday at 3:00 p.m., Mr. Woods, kindly, tall and dressed in his brown wool suit, white shirt, vest and green tie, came to conduct my sister and my piano lessons on the Knabe. He corrected our hands with his long fingers, sporting two huge gold rings, nails clean and trimmed. Under his tutelage I was transposing simple tunes in elementary school. Meanwhile, our basement stage inspired the creation of a continual stream of plays, mimicking those we attended with our mother in New York City; and featuring our own original stories, sets, costumes, make-up, ticket sales, audiences, and all starring my sister and me.

There was music in our neighborhood as well. My sister and I noisily rode our bicycles round and round the hills, shouting back and forth with the many children who lived in nearby houses.

On autumn weekends we laughed as we jumped in piles of leaves raked up by fathers dressed in plaid jackets. In the winter we skipped to a nearby pond to ice skate, dodging small ice chunks, breaking and falling with tinkling sounds, from the tree branches above us, or packed snow into forts and snow men. Burl Ives, and Betty White and Allen Luden were neighbors.

One summer on a sultry morning the doorbell chimed. My mother received a telegram. In a Norman Rockwell-like domestic scene of the late 40's, she stood at the screen door in her blue flowered house dress with white apron tied around the waist, calico cat and two young daughters at her feet peering up at her as she opened the telegram. Breaths were held. A fly buzzed. My mother's initial frown and expression of alarmed curiosity was soon replaced with a calm smile as she read the brief message over and over again. Finally she plopped down on the entry bench and explained.

After high school she had attended Oberlin Conservatory of Music to study piano. This was only possible because she had been awarded the prestigious Edward Drummond Libby Scholarship from Libby Glass Company in her hometown of Toledo, Ohio. She attributed her achievement largely to her music teacher, Sue Love. The telegram said that Sue Love had died, and when her will was read, my mother was named to inherit Sue's Steinway Grand Piano. The piano in its original cover would arrive the following week. Suddenly, my mother scurried into our living room where the Knabe piano took up most of the inner wall. She walked around, looked up and down, and finally declared: "The Steinway will go in the dining room."

The day the Steinway arrived in a moving van, it was hoisted up on the porch, knocking a branch off the maple tree, and then angled through the front door. Dining table and buffet were shuttled off to the sunroom, and the dining room was exactly where the Steinway went. My mother invited the three expert piano delivery men to sit down and have a glass of lemonade. Everyone sagged into a dining room chair, and one of the men asked if he could play a tune. My mother was quite willing, and the house heard its first Steinway strains – a jazz tune which the man performed in clubs in the evenings.

Overnight, life changed. Now there were rules galore concerning the Steinway. No playing the Steinway unless mommy is home. Always close the keyboard cover when you are finished with your daily practicing for your lessons with Mr. Woods. No "Chopsticks." Never put a glass or anything else down on top of the piano. Never touch the tools of the piano tuner. Without supervision, you were only allowed to play the Knabe piano, which still resided modestly in the living room;

unless you were favored like older cousin Dave, who was allowed to play Claire de Lune for hours on the Steinway when he came to visit.

A steady stream of troubadours descended. There was the boisterous local glee club that gathered around the Steinway for rehearsals (my sister and I would sit at the top of the stairs in our pajamas eavesdropping and enjoying the sounds of the Steinway accompanying their loud, lively voices). There were three bustling ladies sporting hats with feathers, who came to practice intricate classical two-piano pieces on the Steinway and Knabe pianos. And any old day could turn into a special day, when neighbors of all ages came at my mother's invitation for sing-along parties. Then, in great anticipation, we would set up white folding chairs, place a song sheet on each seat, and prepare trays of our famous pink punch or holiday eggnog in paper cups. One year my boisterous dance group arrived for a chaotic final dress rehearsal for our June recital, with featured guest star, Eddie Fisher. Eight-year-old dancers with sequins flying assembled in our hot living room. My mother valiantly accompanied us on the Steinway for this rehearsal, before she accompanied us on the theatre Steinway for the performance itself.

Our Steinway, with its warm, magnificent tone, became the heartbeat of our family, celebrating music, and shaping each of us in some way. My mother practiced with her uniquely soft but sure touch, alternating works of her classical training with popular and show tunes. She seemed to embody a comment by Austrian-American pianist, Artur Schnabel: "The notes I handle no better than many pianists. But the pauses between the notes – ah, that is where the art resides." She went out to perform often, and I remember drama and glamour before she departed – the rustle of black taffeta, her sparkling rhinestone pin, shiny red nail polish, and the scent of Joy perfume wafting behind her.

My father's muse arrived. He composed score and lyrics for a masterwork, dedicated to my mother and titled "Jane," my mother's name. I remember many evenings up to the time of my father's death in his 70's, when my mother and father would sit side by side on the piano bench, my mother playing, and the two of them singing this tune in harmony.

My grandmother undertook a two-year task of needle pointing a canvas painted with musical instruments against an aqua colored background to cover the piano bench lid. After the canvas became a cushion, the seat was soft and much nicer. My mother purchased a little aqua Chinese oriental carpet to go under the bench, and the colorful effects of the piano bench lid and carpet were handsome against the dark finish of the Steinway.

Most significant for me, the piano awakened and gave strength to an inner rhythm that led to my passionate, lifelong study of ballet and tap dance. My favorite pastime was dancing to my mother's playing, a ballerina in flight, executing grand jetés off the round yellow leather hassock with the fringe around the sides, which sat next to the Steinway. I have often thought of my career as a Concierge in a large, historic hotel as a similar dance, where each day "on stage" at my lobby desk, I gave my best creative efforts to organize requests and events with graceful timing and choreography for successful results.

When my mother was in her 80's, she recorded a tape cassette and C.D. of piano standards in a sound studio in Phoenix, Arizona, near her home in Scottsdale. She sold these recordings and netted several thousand dollars, which she donated to a foundation in Arizona. She would often play one of her CDs on her little player that sat on the music cabinet and accompany herself for "stereo sound." She played regularly for a convalescent home, the children's program at her church, fall festivals, and charity fashion shows. She daydreamed about playing a few sets on her local Nordstrom Department Store Steinway. During her regular evening gig playing the piano in the dining room residence where she lived, she was a popular entertainer, taking requests from Bach fugues to University fight songs. Hawaiian prints replaced the black taffeta; her small fingers were curved with arthritis, but her nails were still beautifully painted with "Love that Red" nail polish.

My mother's musical gifts have been inherited by my two children. My 34-year-old musician son shares her relative pitch. He composed eleven piano etudes in his grandmother's honor, which were aired at his recital in support of his Masters Degree in Music Composition from New York University, and played beautifully by a young female pianist on a Steinway Concert Grand in NYU's Black Box Theatre. One summer evening, I overheard my mother and son swinging on our front porch glider in a lively discussion of the key in which they thought our resident mocking bird was performing his repertoire from the top of the live oak tree. My 32-year-old daughter shares my mother's vibrant personality and sense of rhythm and timing, which she has utilized in her artistic career. She has been a dancer since she was a toddler, leading to a scholarship to study dance and dramatic arts in a competitive University program. My daughter also clearly shares my mother's passion for New York City, where she too has lived and performed for many years.

The Steinway resided with my mother in the dining room of her apartment in Scottsdale until her death at age 95. In later years she played by ear because macular degeneration prevented her from using the large collection of sheet music and piano books bulging from her walnut music cabinet handcrafted by her father. Fortunately, she learned to play by ear as a child, when her six-member family gathered on Sunday afternoons for sing-alongs. Each member of her family played an instrument; and my mother told me that at that time she took piano lessons from Sue Love and played her mother's Boardman and Gray piano.

I have inherited my mother's Steinway, and consider it to be a great honor and responsibility. I have paperwork on the 5'7" long Steinway M, which includes its serial number and "birth date" of December 10, 1924, in the Astoria, New York factory, making it a highly prized Steinway Vintage piano. I have carried out some research about the Steinway and its one hundred and fifty year history: the inventive, colorful Steinway family; the company intrigues; the New York and Hamburg factories producing two different Steinway sounds; the numerous patents; and the fascinating explanation of the complicated design and meticulous handcrafting required to create each unique Steinway piano by a cadre of trusted and dedicated artisans. At www.Steinway.com one can find a listing of artists, composers and symphony orchestras that use the Steinway exclusively; as well as available books such as "The Steinway Saga by D.W. Fostle, and DVDs about the Steinway, such as "Miracle In A Box, a piano reborn" and "Note By Note, The Making of Steinway L1037..."

A bellman was tapping me on the shoulder. I started, jumped up, and raced back to the Concierge desk. My long-awaited V.I.P. guest and Cabaret star, who would be performing in San Francisco, was at the front desk checking in with his entourage. He bustled over to tell me that his Steinway piano would be arriving shortly. Nervously he asked if I would please see that it got placed safely in his suite. I acknowledged his concerns, and replied with confidence, "Don't worry, sir. I understand. Arrangements for the delivery of your piano are in place." And with a broad smile I added, "You see, I also have a Steinway in my family."

Walden's Ridge
Nancy Earl

It was a lovely place to have grown up: Walden's Ridge, on the back half of Signal Mountain. The woods that surrounded my grandfather's old house on Key Hulse Road were full of loblolly pine, dogwood, sweet gum and swamp maple. In the summer, Queen Anne's lace, day lilies and black-eyed Susan ran riot along the roads and fences; afternoons lasted forever and were fragrant with the smell of honeysuckle and cut grass.

My grandfather had a small manufacturing plant at the foot of the mountain and when I was five, he put up two tall swings under an old oak tree on a grassy rise above the driveway. From those swings, I commanded a view of daily events: the wash drying on the line, Mr. Quakenboss walking his swaybacked beagles, the yard man, snoring under a walnut tree, an RC Cola by his side and remnants of a cheese sandwich rising and falling on his broad chest. I could hear before I could see the postman everyday about noon shifting gears before he started the long grind up Key Hulse Road.

What I didn't like to see was my grandmother, dressed for town, come out the front door and head for the garage. I knew what was coming. I'd hear her car door open and close and the motor start up. Then she'd back slowly out of the garage in her 1957 cream colored Chrysler with her ancient cat who usually slept on the hood usually still on it. "Mary Helen," she'd call, rolling down the window, "come and get this cat!" The cat was mean and he didn't want anything to do with anybody except my grandmother. My eyes would narrow. I'd go peel his claws out of the windshield wiper, carry him struggling and howling to the basement, open the screen door and try to throw him in before he could take a chunk out of me. "Dumbhead!" I'd say under my breath, watching him in the dim light stalk indignantly toward my grandfather's workbench. I knew he would sleep away the summer afternoon curled up on a burlap sack among an array of brushes and dusty paint cans. Then I'd head back to the swings, picking my way barefoot over the chalky gravel in the driveway and through coarse grass rife with sweat bees and big black ants. And there I'd sit and swing and dream to drone of the bees and the sound of my grandmother's two hundred pound cook, Fairy, banging pots and singing Beulah Land.

Fairy (long on the *Fai*, short on the *ry*) sang other songs when she thought no one was listening. "Fairy?" I said one day, "Fairy, what was that fella doin' to Dinah with his ol'banjo?" Fairy allowed as how she had work to do and I could just get my smarty pants self out of her kitchen and out of her hair. "You don't have hair, Fairy," I said. "You're bald." But I was already in full retreat down the long ell of house. "You're baaaaaaallllldd!" I shouted running for the front door.

Fairy wasn't bald but she didn't have much hair. What she did have she wore skinned back in a knot no bigger than a wad of bubble gum, fastened with a red rubber band. She didn't have many teeth either. They sat in her pink gums like tombstones. A few were gold and glinted when she talked. All of them pointed in different directions.

What Fairy did have was a voice that my grandmother said came from some place deep in her soul. Her words came out slow and easy like honey from a glass jar. And listening to Fairy sing was like being wrapped in a fur coat on a cold day.

But the words that floated after me that day down the long ell of the house had an edge to them and suggested that had someone thought to smother me in my crib, it would have saved everybody a cartload of trouble. "Not funny, Fairy!" I shouted from the other side of the screen door. "Not funny. Not funny. Not funny."

Called in for dinner late that afternoon, I came up from the basement, moving quickly and sucking a scratch on my finger. I was just about out of the kitchen when Fairy wanted to know exactly what it was that I have been doing down in the basement. "Well…Fairy," I said, "Well…I been praying for you, Fairy. Praying for your sins." I hummed a few bars so she'd know what sins I was talking about and I flounced out of the kitchen. "Not funny," said Fairy to my departing back.

That night at the dinner table when my grandmother was wondering aloud for the third time how the cat had managed to get green paint all over himself, I looked up to see Fairy standing in the kitchen door. Her arms were folded across her ample bosom and she was looking at me from under arched eyebrows. I folded my arms across my non-existent bosom and stared right back. An unspoken deal was struck.

I kept quiet about Fairy's songs. And she in turn kept quiet about the paint, the shoe polish, the trick with the cheese and what she knew about why the mailman always looked twice before putting his hand in our mail box.

Fairy died not too many years later. As far I know she kept her bargain to the end. And I kept mine long after I'd forgotten the words, the songs themselves and long after it could have mattered to anybody what Fairy sang in my grandmother's kitchen.

Understanding Chuck Cheese
Cynthia Roberts

"I do not understand zis Chuck Cheese," Antoine huffed.

He looked distressed, so I tried not to laugh. Antoine was a recent arrival from France, who looked uncomfortable sitting in the bright orange plastic booth. He was eying the pizza set in front of him distrustfully. Behind us at the other side of the room, six-foot mechanical animals were starting their musical routine for the fourth time.

"Where's your son?" I asked, making an effort at keeping a straight face.

"I do not know. He went into a tube. I do not know."

Turning my head to hide the grin, I pretended to watch the mechanical puppets act out *Born to Be Alive*. My sister, Chris, was sitting next to Antoine across from me in the booth. She was hiding her mouth with a napkin. Mercifully, he seemed not to notice.

I had come directly from the doctor to my niece Lonnie's fifth birthday party, making it just in time. The last hour had been spent losing to Lonnie at gopher smacking and bee scooping and crawling around in the human habi-trail. Tired and bedraggled, I had turned down an offer to dance on the floor lights and escaped to sit with the other adults in the booths instead.

I looked at my sister, slightly in awe. How did she handle the mom thing? How does any woman do it? When you have kids, the choices as I see them are to either manage a job and motherhood, abandoning any pretense of having a life, or to stay at home and put yourself completely in your husband's hands. I'm very happily married, but I don't trust anyone that much, probably because my family is full of examples of women who made that choice with disastrous results. In fact, I'm pretty sure that having a second child causes divorce. Of my grandparents, parents, aunts and uncles, and recently my first cousins, there is only one marriage that has survived past potty training the second child. The women were then either left to be struggling, single moms, or to make unhappy second marriages.

The doctor's appointment I'd had earlier was going to fix that, by fixing me. I was going to have myself spayed like a stray puppy. No children. The paperwork was in the car to present to my husband when I got home.

Something bumped my leg. Bending down, I saw a toddler-sized face with big brown eyes peering up from under the table. I looked a question at Chris.

"That's Rahim," she said. "He's one of Erin's sons."

Erin had been one of Chris' friends since college. She was asleep in one of the other booths. Quite a few of the parents were having a nap right then. I nodded and slid under the table to meet Rahim, smiling at the dark, cherubic face. He peered warily back at me. I reached out and tickled his stomach. He smiled shyly at me, just as I noticed that his shoes were off. I slowly moved my tickle finger toward his unprotected, sock-clad foot. Rahim giggled and jerked his foot back out of the way, striking the table leg with his shin as he did so. Suddenly, the giggle turned to a shriek and Rahim started wailing for his mother. Erin appeared and scooped him up and out of my line of sight. Crawling out from under the table, I sat back down in the booth feeling sheepish. Chris flashed me an encouraging smile. Erin was in another booth rocking Rahim on her lap and holding a conversation with one of the other moms. There were no rebuking looks from that corner, so I assumed all was well. Then it hit me that no one would ever cry for me like that when they were hurt or afraid, and I realized I was envious of Erin.

A cake had appeared and the kids were migrating from the games toward our table. Chris began lighting birthday candles as Lonnie enthusiastically plunked her behind on her mother's lap. We all sang to Lonnie as she grinned and nodded. Cake is always my favorite part of a birthday party, so I was surprised some of the kids bypassed dessert and ran right back to the games after the singing.

My little cousin Monica stayed behind, but she didn't have any cake either. Monica was nicknamed Lady Em, for though only three years old, she had a commanding presence and regal bearing. She was staring intently toward the stage at the front of the room. I followed her gaze and saw that Chuck E. Cheese had come out to wave at everyone and pose for pictures. Lady Em looked horrified. Though fearless with other humans, especially grown-ups, Em tended to shrink from loud noises or large animals. I guess Chuck E. counted as a large animal.

Em's grandfather, my uncle, was sitting in the booth with her. This uncle had been stern and strict with all of us when we were growing up. He had seemed autocratic and unreasonable at times, and I don't remember him smiling much. So, I was amused that his granddaughter, Em, could get him to do just about anything for her. They were inseparable at family events, and Uncle now smiles constantly.

"Grandpa," Em commanded, "go and touch the mouse."

I grinned. She was obviously afraid of Chuck E. Cheese and wanted her grandfather to show her that the six-foot rat was not a threat. Uncle understood too. He smiled and started out of the booth.

"Em," I asked. "Want some cake?"

"No," she answered, still staring toward the stage. "Grandpa is touching the mouse."

I thought with amusement about how different my uncle and my parents were now that they were grandparents. The mood turned wistful as I realized that I would never be a grandparent myself.

"Chris, remember when Dad fed Lonnie that whole box of cookies?" I asked.

Chris frowned. "And he said it was because she wanted it? Yes, I remember."

"What happened to the man that raised us?" I laughed.

My sister laughed in response, but held her reply as our cousin Danielle came walking up, looking excited.

"Sorry I'm late," Danielle said, "I've just come from the doctor."

"Me too," I said at the same time Danielle followed up with "I'm pregnant."

I sat there in stunned silence while everyone else began congratulating Danielle and asking questions.

"So, is Mark excited?" Erin asked.

I tried not to cringe. Mark had been Danielle's on-again off-again, boyfriend for years. He usually had a primary girlfriend and relegated Danielle to "other woman" status. I hoped she didn't think he was going to suddenly put her first and marry her now that she was pregnant. Here's another one, I thought, another struggling, single mom in progress.

"Mark and I are broken up," she replied. That didn't surprise me. He seemed like someone who would duck out on this situation. What surprised me was Danielle. She was glowing and happy, actually bouncing up and down slightly while she stood there. She had been chasing after that man since I could remember, weeping inconsolably whenever he dumped her, making excuses for his bad behavior. Now she was dismissing him as a non-issue while carrying his child. She was that excited about becoming a mother.

"I've got a crib you can have," Chris offered. "Lonnie's crib is still in the garage. I knew someone would need it."

"I've got clothes," Erin chimed in. "All yellow and green, since we didn't know what Rahim was going to be."

The offers poured in. Several of the cousins were willing to babysit. Some of Chris' other friends had clothes and appliances to donate. Everyone took turns standing up and hugging Danielle, who seemed too wired to sit down. Finally she sat, and an animated conversation started about planning a baby shower. Even Antoine was beaming and throwing in suggestions.

Erin turned to me.

"So, what about you?" she asked. "When are you having children?"

I hesitated.

"I'm thinking about it," I finally replied.

A Fifties Girl Finds a New Thanksgiving
Laura Kaufman

Ever since I hit my fifties (quite recently thank you) everything has changed. Well, ok, not that much has really changed, but I am touchier about it. My car looks older, as a beige Camry truly can. My house looks like a middle-aged person lives there; things from my past are sold as "collectibles" in antique stores. My pets have slowed down. But at least I am getting slightly more focused on comfort and being myself.

Some things have not changed. Fall is the same, even though the rituals accompanying it are different. Though the season might make one bittersweet about the passage of time, it still makes me feel full of promise. Fall is absolutely my favorite time of year – gorgeous, no matter where I have lived. It's full of the scent of wood-smoke and wonderful tastes – crisp apples, pumpkin pie, fluffy, fattening dinner rolls. Fall also has a color palette to die for.

For me, giant meals with groups of friends have recently taken the place of holidays at home in Seattle. In the past two years, my beloved elders have quietly faded from my grasp into my ever-present thoughts. And now that my teenage son would rather share a Thanksgiving bag of tortilla chips with his girlfriend than sit at a table full of fun adults, tradition is taking on a new twist. Turkey Day this year will be a group activity, with my foodie friends who are insanely good cooks, who make and bring their own wine, and other such delights. I find that I fit here, and that my surrogate family of friends is becoming more important to me, almost forming a new tribe.

At any rate, this time of year also reminds me of some funny episodes we have shared on our block. My neighbor delights in the story of a new boyfriend who appeared one week in the neighborhood, with an impeccably gleaming car. He would polish it and strut around it a bit, menacing anyone and their dog that got within a few yards.

That week, our hill was visited by a flock of wild turkeys. My neighbor watched with fascination as one male turkey began to move back and forth in front of the boyfriend's car, sizing it up. Or rather, sizing up his reflection in it.

Pow! The tail feathers came out in full battle dress, and he began to dart at the shiny car surface, pecking mightily at his nemesis. It was a rather giant turkey (probably could serve 12-14.) And so the car alarm went off. Milliseconds later, the boyfriend dashed out of the house, and there was a rather large, er, flap. The turkey retreated, but the car was already tattooed. Poor boyfriend, he didn't last long in the wilds of the suburbs.

Something else is going on this year that is also an accidental gem of silliness. I got a random email from someone I have never met, and it is just so delightful that I must share it, with apologies to the sender.

Thanksgiving is coming soon – I am excited – but unfortunately Iris and Bernie are not coming (going to LA) and Flossie and David are not coming as well.

Here is the menu so far:

Linda and Buddy – sauerkraut, and shrimp appetizer

Amy and Les – fried turkey with extra legs and wings (Note: that must be a hybrid.)

Flossie – making her famous ladyfinger cake and chopped liver! (Hopefully this is two separate dishes.)

Suzy and Rob – I forgot!!

This is such an intriguing cast of characters. Understandably, they also need some vegetarian dishes, as someone named Octavia is vegetarian. Good thing they have the sauerkraut covered. And an update: Suzy just replied that she'd still contribute her platter of roasted vegetables and a salad even though Cathy is bringing one.

OK, I am beginning to think that I should reply, and offer to bring something too, but the fact of the matter is that these people live somewhere in *Maryland*. Yet there is something so sweet about the planning that I didn't have the heart to send a message back yet. That might forever put me out of the family.

But wait, while I was looking through my own Thanksgiving recipes, more emails came through:

Amy wrote, *"I love our family and am so happy we'll be together!"* And Cathy added, *"I am so excited to be with everyone again!! Love u all."*

I found myself shopping at CVS for one of those "Across the Miles" cards to send to this family, with warmth and affection. Truthfully, despite the fact that I don't know these folks, this lovely email trail is certainly providing a window into the feeling of this season, the warm anticipation of being together with loved ones and friends (even if Iris and Bernie are going to LA.)

I wish you wonderful holidays with your favorite old, and perhaps some new, traditions.

Standing Room - A Memoir
Chapter 1
Kathleen O'Hanlon Peterson

Maria raced up the stairs and made a sharp right. I rushed to catch up and nearly collided with her, my dance bag bouncing off my shoulder. We stood in a long enclosed catwalk that ran the length of a hallway, above all of the dance studios. On each side large windows gave a view down into each studio. Maria stood rigid, looking down into Studio 2.

Below us a photographer was running crab-like across the floor, shooting pictures. I couldn't see the target, who must have been in the part of the studio directly under where we were standing. A few seconds later a large black poodle loped out into the open area of the room. Maria took a deep breath and then was completely still.

"It's Mischa," she finally hissed. I didn't understand and she must have sensed that. "That's his dog."

I looked down again and as if on cue, the floppy, golden hair of Mikhail Baryshnikov appeared below me, mid-leap. He was unmistakable even at this angle. He wore beige rehearsal clothes and misshapen black shoes. It didn't seem real. I squeezed my toes within my shoes and held my breath. I felt like I'd opened a door by accident and was seeing something I shouldn't.

He came to a stop in the middle of the studio and I remained still, studying what was before me as if he would disappear at any moment. His dark blond hair was the same color as his skin and the same color as his loose T-shirt. He looked tired, even insignificant. In his caramel-colored woolen tights his legs looked too short, his quadriceps too big, his feet knotty. I couldn't process these images.

Then he started to move again. He circled the studio in a series of leaps that I would come to learn were a well-known portion of the Albrecht role in *Giselle*, with the dog bounding after him, almost catching his trailing leg each time. Now the entire room looked completely different. It was like I was looking through a camera with a special lens, that drew out and then in again, focusing just on Baryshnikov. His powerful, compact frame was all there was to look at. All of the energy in the room, perhaps in the building, was drawn into him and was now scaled to him.

The photographer was like a machine gunner in the middle of the room, turning, turning, turning to keep up with the fleet movement. Then Baryshnikov came to the center of the room and performed an astonishing series of open *a la seconde* turns, spinning rapidly, with abandon. His mouth was open in a smile and the dog also circled madly, barking now. Baryshnikov spun to a halt and reached down to grab the dog's head in both hands, laughing. There was only brightness now, no fatigue. When he came to a stop I breathed in and heard my heartbeat pulsing through me. I wasn't sure the last time I had taken a breath. Baryshnikov straightened up and stood talking to the photographer, his arms crossed in front of him, one powerful leg casually to the side, but at the same time just a little bit off fourth position.

Maria and I stood silently for just another minute, finally feeling silly about watching two men talking to each other.

She turned to look at me. "Welcome to ABT," she said, smiling. She started walking further down the catwalk.

"Tell me this doesn't happen all the time," I said, catching up to her. I wanted to sound suitably casual but I couldn't completely mask my excitement. In the two years or so since Baryshnikov defected from the Soviet Union and come to New York, the entire population, not just the dance world, had been fascinated by him. The newspapers constantly covered his late nights at clubs, his dates, his favorite foods, as well as giving glowing reviews of his performances, with descriptions that seemed impossible for anyone to live up to.

"I don't see him all the time. But a lot." Maria paused. "You see all of them, especially now that the season is starting. Makarova, Gelsey, Cynthia Gregory, Eric Bruhn, Bujones, they're all here. And people like Jerome Robbins and Oliver Smith. It's wild." Her big brown eyes shone.

"Come on," she continued. "Let's get ready for class."

"The Write Retreat" - Stanford Sierra Camp 2010

For the tenth time that day, I wondered what I was doing here. But I knew there was no way I was going to leave voluntarily.

I had met Maria at the corner of Broadway and 60th Street about an hour before. I had already taken class that morning at my old ballet school so I was warmed up. I filled the two hours before I met her by walking most of the way across town and eating just half a slice of pizza to try to quell my nervousness. This had the added benefit of saving a subway fare. Maria had taken a jazz class across the street at Luigi's and she was relaxed and sunny as we walked the block to 61st Street, her wiry black hair springing out from her coat collar. I had met her only about a month before and I still couldn't believe she had suggested that I come to take class with her. I tried to tell myself it wasn't a big deal. How different could it be from ballet class anywhere else?

The dirty white stone building stood in the middle of the block with a narrow glass door at the corner nearest Central Park. There was no sign outside to indicate it housed one of the leading ballet companies in the world. The lobby had fake wood paneling and beige linoleum. Maria pushed the button to call the elevator and it churned into action. Even though I was seventeen and she just a year younger, I felt like I did the first day of kindergarten following my mother onto the playground. In a moment the chipped green doors opened to a metal grate with a smiling older black man behind it. A group of girls bustled behind him and spilled out into the lobby as soon as he opened the grate. They chattered out into the sunshine of the mild March afternoon, tight hair buns announcing all too clearly where they had been. The man nodded to us and when we entered he sat on the stool in the corner and placed a hand on the brass handle to start the elevator. We rose, watching the doors of each floor pass by in a steady parade. When we stopped my stomach dipped, from nerves rather than motion.

Unlike the rest of the building, the seventh floor lobby looked sleek and modern, if somewhat beat up. Matte white walls rose up two stories from low pile grey carpet but there were dark scuff marks a foot above the floor in several places. The man at the reception desk was the only person in the lobby. We approached the desk and I hoped Maria would show me what to do. I didn't know her very well. She was a friend of a friend and we had been introduced because of our mutual interest in ballet. She had been taking class at American Ballet Theatre for a few months and had encouraged me to come along with her to try a class.

Maria smiled at the receptionist. "Hello, John." He was around thirty and had thick dark hair and pursed lips that looked ready to say something surprising. Maria picked up a form from the desk.

"I need a new card today. Let's make it for forty classes." I tried not to stare as she pulled out a fat spray of twenty dollar bills from her bag and handed them to John. "And this is my friend, Kathleen. This is her first time here so she just needs a single."

John nodded at me with a serious but comic air. "Welcome. That will be eight dollars." I pulled the five and three singles that I had cajoled from my mother that morning from my jeans pocket.

As I handed John my money, he cocked an eyebrow at Maria. "You might want to take a peek in Studio 2 as you go upstairs." His voice was low and casual.

"Oh?" Maria said. She looked at me but I didn't understand what John was trying to tell her. John nodded and handed her a new card for forty classes, with the first one punched out.

Maria jerked her head sideways to show me I should follow her to the open staircase that led up from the doorway to Studio 2. As she passed she peeked in through the window and then shot up the stairs, leaving me no choice but to follow her and get my first unexpected glimpse of Baryshnikov.

After we peeled ourselves away from the window of Studio 2, we went down the stairway at the furthest end of the walkway and Maria pushed open an orange door. Inside it looked like any other locker room and we found empty lockers side by side and started to strip off our outer clothes. I was glad I had left my tights and leotard on under my jeans and sweater. I didn't like having people see me without clothes, especially at ballet school and even more so at this ballet school. My waist was a little too thick, my hips a little too wide. But somehow the thin nylon of the leotard and tights was enough of a disguise. We slipped on our soft pink ballet shoes and went back into the hallway.

    The door to Studio 7, where our class would be held, was closed. Through the window in the door I could see that a class was just finishing but it was unlike any ballet class I had ever seen. All the students were male, ranging in age from mid-teens to thirties. They took turns across the floor doing pale imitations of the turns that Baryshnikov had just finished down the hall. A few boys came to the Manhattan School of Ballet, where I had been taking class for the last year, but they were all younger brothers of girl students or boys looking for some basic training so they could pass musical theater auditions. Here was a hardcore group reaching for the ceiling, or at least the light fixtures, as they did *grand jetes* across the floor. I felt another little surge of excitement.

    Out in the hallway, Maria and I spread out on the floor to stretch along with the other people waiting for class. The students were mostly teenage girls but there were some women in their twenties and a handful of men and boys. Even though the setting was more serious and sophisticated, with the possibility of famous Russian émigrés wandering down the hall at any time, the sidelong looks and showy stretches of the girls in the hall were just like any dance class I'd been to. We rocked from side to side in splits, we placed nose to knee, we bent backwards from the waist in a broad *port de bras* to study the person behind us in a disturbing, unblinking way. Even though I didn't have anywhere near the desired shape of a ballet dancer, I was fairly flexible and felt I could hold my own in some things. But when the door of the studio opened I felt pangs of fear. I'd been so taken by seeing Baryshnikov and watching the dancers around me that I'd forgotten that I would need to dance myself and see how I would measure up. I knew I wasn't in the league of the people strewn on the floor around me. All of a sudden it didn't seem like a good idea to have come after all. I felt foolish rather than brave. My lunch turned over in my stomach and I thought about going to use the bathroom. The idea of just staying in the locker room while class started, hidden away, was appealing. But what would I say to Maria?

The boys filed out from the class and everyone pulled themselves to their feet. I let the idea of escape float away. We passed into the studio and I waited to see where Maria would go, to see what the pecking order of the class was. Maria headed to the far side near the big windows. Three of the walls had double barres, serious looking affairs with heavy brackets. The front wall was covered in mirrors and in the corner where Maria headed was a small piano. A tired looking woman with an untidy bun stood there and stacked and restacked piles of music. It looked like she would be staying for our class. I'd never been to a class with a live accompanist before.

It was late winter and the tall windows were opened about a foot at the bottom. I could see the back of a brick apartment building across the way with tangles of cables and air conditioning units hanging out of windows, like cigarettes on the lip. The windows of the studio looked like the unblinking ones in the abandoned industrial buildings that lined the shore of Staten Island.

I stood next to Maria, watching her twist her back, trying to think of yet another stretch to do to keep myself occupied. Maria was a few inches shorter than I and while she didn't have a traditional dancer's body either, her shoulders perfectly framed her neck and her legs were nicely proportioned and well-muscled. There were about twenty people in the room by now, evenly placed along the barres on three walls.

The array of leotard colors surprised me. Elfrieda Merman, the teacher I had been studying with since I was eight, had very strict rules about clothing. Students wore a long sleeved black leotard, pink tights, and pink slippers with satin hand sewn ribbons. Nothing else was permitted, although we did add a little sheer pink skirt for our once a year "open class." Now, the room swam with hot pink sleeveless leotards, torn T-shirts over black camisoles, purple unitards, a garish array of color and cut that made the studio look like the opening scene of *A Chorus Line*, which was in its first glorious run about fifteen blocks down Broadway.

At the stroke of two, the door flew open and an older woman with blond hair and perfect posture strode into the center of the room. She looked a little older than my mother and she wore a robin's egg blue leotard and a filmy ballet skirt in a bright floral pattern of blues and pinks that came to just below her knee. She was tanned and wore a glittery gold necklace that caught the light as she walked. She clapped her hands twice and with a broad smile said, "Good afternoon, everyone. Let's get started." Her accent was like Boris and Natasha in the Bullwinkle cartoons. This must be Madame Merinowa. Maria caught my eye and raised her eyebrows as if to say, "See what I mean?"

Madame Merinowa turned and almost skipped over to the pianist in the corner. She said something in a low voice to the dark-suited woman, who smiled and sat to adjust the piano bench. Even though I could hear each heartbeat pounding in my chest, I had the feeling that this would be fun. As Madame Merinowa returned to the center of the room and stood still, every molecule in the room came to attention and waited to begin.

Without another word we all stood and placed our left hands gently on the barre. I straightened my spine and placed first one foot and then the other in as good of a first position as I could achieve. Turnout was not one of my strengths but I was in the ballpark. I felt the thrill I did every time my heels touched properly and I pulled up the front of my thighs to stand as tall and as perfectly placed as I could. I didn't look around. I didn't want to know how good the turnout of the others was.

The pianist played the two introductory chords that begin any barre exercise. First, a lingering seventh chord, meant to feel unfinished, as we all raised our right hands from our hip to the front, and then the longed-for major chord, at which we swept our hand to the side, to indicate we were prepared for the exercise. No one had said a word and yet we all knew exactly what to do – what dancers have done for at least two hundred years to begin their daily routine – two *demi plies* in first position. So far, so good.

After the first two bends, Madame Merinowa chimed in to provide a welcome if unnecessary direction. "*Grand plie*." Her full, warm voice pushed her words into the air, where they hung as we dropped down toward the floor. I hoped my knees wouldn't crack as I got to the bottom of my sweep. I found my balance fairly easily when we went into *releve* after the first side of *plies*, rising up on the balls of our feet to balance for a few seconds, and I began to relax a little. I could do this. Madame Merinowa walked slowly around the room, about ten feet from the barre, watching each of us and stopping from time to time to push a hand a few inches higher or move a shoulder a bit further back.

Tendus were next, in which we slowly and precisely stretched one foot in each of the three directions that make up ballet exercises – front, side and back. Madame Merinowa came to my side of the room. She stood and watched my rear *tendus*, a move I found challenging because I couldn't see what my foot looked like when it was stretched out behind me. A surge of energy came off her, unfamiliar yet welcome. She gently touched the end of my hand, and curved my index and middle fingers a bit more towards my palm and raised her chin, showing me I should look up a little higher. I did so and she smiled a broad, shining smile that brought out an array of small lines at the corners of her sapphire blue eyes. "Yes," she said. "Beautiful." My face got hot. She wasn't looking at my feet, so what did she think was so beautiful? My face? Unlikely. And if she was thinking about my face, was that the only thing she could make a positive comment about? This was not good. I wanted her to let go of my hand and move on.

"I am Mrs. Merinowa," she said, in an odd sing-song fashion, pronouncing her name "Merry-KNOW-a" instead of the much more exciting "Mair-IN-ova" that I had heard everyone else use. I nodded. I didn't know what to do. Under no circumstances should you ever speak in class, especially during an exercise. She remained next to me, still holding my fingertips. She lifted her chin to the right, creating a perfect curve down the side of her head, through her shoulder and down to the hand that was holding mine. "And you are?" she said.

"I'm Kathleen," I said in a low voice. By now the exercise had ended for that side and everyone stood, waiting for the next exercise and listening to our exchange.

"Kathleen," she repeated, in the clenched, delicious Russian pronunciation that sounded like "KETT-lin," which would become so familiar to me. "Welcome to my class," she exclaimed, nudging my arm over my head before turning to walk to the middle of the room. "Other side." We all turned and started our *tendus* in the other direction.

We went through the rest of the barre exercises. I worked hard and I felt a glow from doing good work. I didn't look around me to see what anyone else was doing, other than watching the girl in front of me to check that I was following the directions properly. During the *frappes*, Madame Merinowa had us turn and face the barre. When I looked out the window I saw a woman across the way wearing a robe as she pulled down a shade in her bathroom. I didn't know why that small moment of voyeurism did it but I felt a shiver of excitement. Here I was in class at the American Ballet Theatre school and beyond not being asked to leave, the teacher had welcomed me. This was wonderful.

When we returned to the barre for the final exercise, the *grand battements*, the quick, controlled leg lifts that the rest of the world would call chorus line kicks, Madame Merinowa called out, "Valya, find something fun for us for *grand battement*." The woman at the piano rummaged through her stacks. She found whatever she needed and raised her hawk-like profile to Madame Merinowa to show she was ready. Madame Merinowa nodded and Valya leaned down on a huge uncomfortable chord. It took me a few notes and then I recognized it – the scene from Prokofiev's *Romeo and Juliet* where the Capulets display their warlike attitude at a family gathering. It was one of the fiercest pieces of music I'd ever heard and it put shivers down my spine. Usually I was tired by the time I got to *grand battements* and needed to steel myself to get my leg up past my nose, my own personal measuring point of whether I was having a good day or not. But today, with this stirring music, I was ready to perform the *grand battements* for an audience. What fun. At the end of the exercise, everyone burst into discussion and laughter at the joy of getting to move to such wonderful music.

We arranged ourselves in the middle of the room for floor exercises. I lingered toward the back to see how this was going to shake out. The best dancers should be in the front row, usually with the strongest one in the middle, in an unspoken arrangement that just seemed to work out correctly every time. The front row of dancers went into position, leaving an appropriate gap between each person. This was not just to make sure no one would be hit by a flailing arm during a turn but also to give those in the second row, who, depending on the class, could also be extraordinarily good dancers, an adequate view of themselves in the mirror. I followed Maria's lead and took my place in the third row.

I wondered whether she would have gone to that position if she were here by herself. I'd been too busy worrying about myself during the barre to pay much attention to the level of the other dancers in the class, but I knew that my skill level would be near the bottom and that the center exercises would prove it. Here, in the middle of the floor, there was no barre to lean on to correct an incomplete balance, and everyone in the class could clearly see what everyone else was doing in the mirror. My enthusiasm had always outpaced my accomplishments as a dancer and there was no reason it would be any different here. Well, I would just have to do the best I could.

We started in with the same ritualistic order of exercises, but for the floor portion of class Madame Merinowa had more freedom to innovate and she gave us different steps for each variation. She described what she wanted and at first I found it a little hard to understand her Russian-accented French as she described the variation – *"Glissade, assemble, pas de chat, pas de chat, prepare and turn, entrechat, entrechat!"* As she talked she demonstrated the steps, using each arm as a substitute for a leg, as she marked the steps she was describing in the air. Everyone nodded and followed along in a watered down way, cementing the arrangement of steps in our minds before we began.

When she stepped to one side of the room for the group to perform the exercise she had marked out, I could finally see how everyone else danced. The students in the front row were incredibly steady and used the floor in a forthright way, brushing and digging their feet in as if it were a tool for their use. Their turnout was almost 180 degrees and their landings from jumps were soft and clean. I knew my cheeks were red, not from fatigue but from chagrin over my poor turnout and mediocre extension. I was glad I was in the back of the class where no one could study my wobbly arabesques and single turns. I began to wonder how exactly they went about telling you not to come back. I hoped Maria didn't regret inviting me now that she was actually seeing me dance. I studied Maria out of the corner of my eye and while I couldn't conclude much, she seemed closer in skill to the direct, assured people of the front row than to me. I continued, trying not to grit my teeth, trying to breathe, urging myself to be invisible. But through the *adagio* exercise no one paid any attention to me. I unclenched my stomach muscles.

When it was time for small jumps Madame Merinowa stopped a moment and stood studying the floor. Then she clapped once and turned to face us. "I'm so sorry boys, but I am going to make you all be Giselle today." The boys, a handful of males ranging from my age to some who looked like they might be on a break from a Broadway show, groaned and laughed. "We do Giselle's opening variation."

She clapped again once and Valya started to play music familiar to any ballet student. Madame Merinowa turned to face the mirror and started to mark and explain as she had done before. Then halfway through, Valya picked up the speed a little and Madame Merinowa began to fully dance, her strong, tight leg peeking out from her frothy skirt as she finished one small, controlled jump after another, showing us how to hold back and extend at the same time, making the viewer wait to see the full extension of the pointed foot. I studied her reflection in the mirror and her face, already friendly and approachable, looked even more inviting and joyful, and I couldn't believe I was there having her show me how to do this. I'd never even seen *Giselle* performed before and now I was learning how to dance it. She finished and turned to us and briskly said, "OK, you now."

We took our places. Valya gave us the preparatory chords and then we began. As I took one tentative jump and extended my leg in front of me and then did the same in reverse, I forgot all about my uneven balances in the earlier floor exercises and felt my body responding to what she had shown us. I allowed myself to fill up the straightforward steps with the feeling of being in character. As I went on to the next set of eight measures and finished with the small *jetes* forward, I felt my heart soar. I could do this. I was doing real repertory and I could do it, maybe not very well, but I could do it and feel it fully. All I needed was a dirndl skirt and a crown of harvest flowers in my hair to make it complete. It didn't matter that I would never be on stage. I was being given the secrets of something I barely understood my desire for and it was something I could hold inside me long after we stopped. I wanted to know more, to find out how to feel like this all the time.

Class ended, as all classes did, with *reverence*, a series of choreographed bows, perhaps designed to accustom dancers to the overly orchestrated tradition of taking curtain calls. As I sank into as deep of a *plie* as I could in the middle of the floor, Madame Merinowa strolled over to me.

"KETT-lin," she said. "Where did you study before." It was not said as a question but as a declarative sentence.

"The Manhattan School of Ballet," I said, finding it a little hard to get it out in one breath. "With Elfrieda Merman."

She looked as if she was thinking and then she nodded. "Ballet Russe?" This time it was a question.

"I think so." Mrs. Merman was a more reserved but equally elegant version of Madame Merinowa. It wasn't like she and I went out for ice cream after class and discussed her dance genealogy but I did know that she had danced with the Ballet Russe de Monte Carlo before coming to New York.

"Good." Madame Merinowa said it as if that was all she needed to know and she went back to the front of the room. Either Mrs. Merman or I had passed muster. I imagined it was Mrs. Merman. I took a deep breath and we finished our *reverence*. As we applauded, Madame Merinowa ducked her head in thanks and swept out of the room leaving the impression of the flowery gauze of her skirt lingering in my vision.

I couldn't believe it was over. I stood, not sure what to do next, even as the other students bent to pick up their dance bags. Maria came next to me and said, "Let's go." We joined the crowd making their way through the door and I was still in a fog as we went to the locker room and I pulled on my jeans.

We climbed back up onto the catwalk to make our way to the front and as we passed Studio 2, Baryshnikov sat on the floor, his legs stretched wide on each side, the poodle on the floor in front of him. He was chatting and looked relaxed. A woman was at the barre at the window turned away from me. She was wearing an elaborately tied patterned scarf over her hair and as she raised her hands over her head I could tell who it was. I recognized the shape of her back from photos.

"Is that Makarova?" I was tired from two classes and all the adrenalin pumping through me. There was just too much to take in.

Maria looked down into the studio. "Yeah. I think they are doing *Other Dances* tonight for some special performance. But we should go so we can get the 4:30 boat." She nudged me along, all business now.

Then Baryshnikov stood up and walked toward the door. Maria was off like a bullet, as she had been when we first arrived, pounding down the stairs to try to be in the lobby when Baryshnikov emerged from the studio. It took me a second to propel myself into action and I was afraid of falling down the long flight of stairs. Maria was alone in the lobby but as I hit the bottom step, the door of the studio flew open and Baryshnikov emerged. I pulled myself up short, barely able to keep from plowing into him. I sucked in my breath as I succeeded in finding my balance. He turned to me. On the stair, I was a half head taller than him. He smiled and a little wrinkle appeared at the edge of each eye. He knew exactly what had been going on. I felt too hot, too breathless to do anything. He raised an eyebrow and backtracked into the studio, closing the door behind him.

I turned to look at Maria, frozen twenty feet away. Neither of us said anything. She pressed the button to call the elevator and I joined her, silent, trying to process what had just happened. We entered the elevator, nodding to the operator, who looked like an old friend now. Maria asked, "So, will you be back next week?"

Section IV:
The Struggles of Living

Sick now? droop now?
This sickness doth infect
the very lifeblood of our enterprise.

William Shakespeare

The Swivel Chair
Neil McCabe

The caster was loose and hung out at an angle as if it were signaling for a stop. It fell out of the foot when Sam turned the chair over to take a look. Something seemed to be missing. The wood was gouged-out where the caster should go. Why hadn't he looked sooner instead of just sticking the wobbly wheel back in? Now the swivel chair was ruined.

Sam stood looking at the chair, his once athletic body slumping. Alice had helped him find the chair at a used furniture store forty years ago when they were furnishing his accounting office. The chair was solid oak with a yellowish stain. Its smoothly dished seat was comfortable without having any upholstery that would wear out. He kept the chair even after he could afford to buy a modern one, and he brought it home when he retired.

He and Alice had new, matching honey-colored chairs, side-by-side at their computer desks in the family room, and neither of them used the old chair anymore. Randolph, their Maine Coon cat, had claimed it as his.

Sam set the broken chair upright near the window, where Randolph could sleep in the sun's slanting rays. Sam selected *Western Civilizations*, an old college textbook the right thickness, and placed it under the wheel-less foot.

Alice glided into the room and stood watching, hands on hips, as Sam lifted Randolph's fluffy basketball body onto the seat. "We should get a new chair for Randolph," she said.

"But he likes this one."

"We can't let the grandkids twirl around in that broken-down wreck."

Sam flung out his arms, palms up. "It's OK as long as you don't try to roll it."

"Let's buy another new chair. One that matches ours," Alice said, reaching for a Pottery Barn catalogue.

She scoured the catalogue and website and then talked with customer service on the phone. But to no avail. It had been seven years since they bought their new chairs, and although the same style was still available, the honey color was not.

"I have an idea," Sam said.

"Quick, write it down," Alice said, with a mischievous smile.

Sam glared down at her. "Do you want to hear my idea, or not?"

"Of course I do," Alice said, tousling his silver hair. "What's your idea?"

"Let's get the old chair fixed," he said, looking proud.

"It still won't match, even if it could be fixed."

"Randolph likes it, and it would be nice to be able to roll it again. I'll call Tony."

Alice frowned. "Tony?"

"My barber. He makes furniture in his spare time. He might be able to fix it."

Alice grabbed Sam's ear and gave it a playful tug.

"Hey, what are you doing?"

"Hold still. I'm trying to see if any sawdust is falling out," Alice said. "Whoever heard of a barber making furniture?"

"Well, you've heard of it now. He's a craftsman. Sometimes he'll have one of his pieces for sale in the corner of his barber shop."

Sam said Tony was the best barber he had ever had. Tony had encouraged him to change how he parted his hair and had cut it just right to lie naturally. But Sam's opinion wasn't based on haircuts alone. Tony was amusing. He was a dozen years Sam's junior but called Sam "Young Man." He complained about his own baldness while complimenting Sam's thick hair. He was a gifted conversationalist, almost always agreeing with Sam on gardening, energy conservation, the war, and the other wide-ranging subjects they had discussed every five weeks for the last six years. They had joked about one of them running for Congress; each saying it should be the other, to set things straight in Washington.

Sam called Tony and described the problem with the chair.

"Bring it over to my house. Let me take a look at it," Tony said. "And bring those heirloom tomato seedlings you promised, if they're ready."

On Monday, Tony's day off, Sam struggled to load the chair into the back of the station wagon. He settled into the familiar seat, congratulating himself for the hundredth time for his wisdom in buying the wagon fifteen years ago. Why would anyone buy a sedan, he asked himself, when a wagon was just as comfortable and so much more useful?

He drove across town to Tony's, down the driveway alongside the carefully groomed lawn, past the tidy rows of lettuce, peppers and corn to the workshop in back. Tony hurried out and helped carry the chair inside, past his planes, chisels, saws, clamps, drills and sanders, which were as neatly arrayed as his scissors, combs, and shavers were at his barbershop.

"It's a great chair, except for *this*," Sam said, handing the caster to Tony. "It won't stay in."

"The caster," Tony said. He stroked his neatly trimmed mustache and turned the chair over to look at its damaged foot. "Oh, that's not too bad. See the metal in there, where the wood is gouged out? That's what's left of the sleeve that held the caster. If you go down to Collier Hardware, I'll bet you can find a new sleeve, and it'll cost you next to nothing."

"I don't have to buy four new casters, so they'll match?"

"No, you can use your old caster. See if you can get the sleeve, and then come back."

Sam drove downtown and parked on 1st Street, next to the side entrance of Collier's. He walked across the worn wooden floor, past the bins and cubbies of screws, washers, nuts, and bolts, of all sizes. A clerk wearing an apron with big pockets was standing near the register. Sam showed him the caster.

"Do you have the whatchamacallit that holds this doodad in place?" Sam asked.

"A sleeve? Sure," the clerk said. "Let me show you."

They walked together past an aisle of electrical switches and turned down the next, where there was an assortment of rubber tips for various table and barbeque legs, wheels of all sizes, a myriad of casters, and caster sleeves. The clerk eyeballed Sam's caster and selected from among the sleeves hanging on the rack.

"There you go," the clerk said. "This should fit perfectly."

A smile crept onto Sam's face and broadened as he paid. Fifty-one cents, including tax! He was amazed. He hadn't really believed Tony. He thought it would be impossible to find the right sleeve.

Varnish vapors were drifting out the open door when Sam arrived back at Tony's workshop. Tony was brushing the finish on a new bookcase.

"That's nice," Sam said. "I like that honey color. That's the color of our new chairs. We would have bought another new one like that if it was available."

"Good color. Why do they change the colors on furniture every year? They'd like you to buy three new ones that match, in the color-of-the-year, that's why. But you don't need to buy a new chair. Got the sleeve?"

Sam handed it to him.

"Good. We're going to beat the system and fix the old chair," Tony said, re-examining the gouged foot. "I can drill out a little more of the wood, put in an oak dowel, drill a hole in it the right size for the sleeve, and presto! Good as new! Nothing to it."

"What will it cost?"

"Oh, it's nothing," Tony said with a dismissive wave.

"But your time is valuable, and you'll have expenses for materials."

"I'll get it done, and we'll talk about it. I'll give you a call when it's ready," Tony said. "Say, did you bring those seedlings?"

"Seedlings? Oh, the heirloom tomatoes? I'm sorry, Tony, I forgot all about them."

"OK. No problem. You can bring them when you pick up the chair."

Sam polished off his oatmeal, and, on his way to the family room, he put the empty bowl in the sink where Alice was washing dishes. He turned on his computer to check his email and almost sat on Randolph. He shuffled back to the kitchen.

"Alice, where's Randolph's chair?"

"It went to get a haircut," she said, with a twinkle in her eye.

"What are you talking about?"

Alice's twinkle faded, and she gave him a long look. "You took the chair to your barber," she said.

"Oh, yeah," Sam said, turning to go back to his computer.

He gently lifted Randolph out of his chair. "Sorry, Rand. I've got to throw out the spam before it clogs up my system."

The next morning Randolph was in Sam's chair again. Sam eased it and Randolph out of the way and rolled Alice's chair over to his computer.

"Where am I supposed to sit?" Alice asked when she came into the room.

"Ask Randolph," Sam answered.

Alice sighed. "Let me know when you're through with my chair. I'll find something to do in the meantime."

Two days later when Sam went to his computer, Randolph was in his chair again and Alice was in hers. Sam jerked his chair away from his computer, almost dumping Randolph out, and stomped out to get a dining room chair.

"What's gotten into you lately?" Alice said when he returned. "Poor Randolph. His chair is gone, and there you are jerking him around, waking him up. It's not *his* fault."

"Well, whose fault is it?"

"Your barber's?"

My barber, Sam thought. Tony. Right. Tony has Randolph's chair. Maybe Tony has had a problem fixing it and made it worse rather than better. Or what if he had fixed it and sold it? Sam didn't even have a receipt proving he had delivered the chair to Tony. He didn't have an estimate. Nothing.

But all Sam said to Alice was, "I wonder when the chair will be ready."

"Why don't you call – what's his name? Tommy? – and ask what the hold-up is?" Alice said.

"It's Tony. And what do you mean, 'hold up?'"

"Delay. What's the delay. And what are you so grouchy about?"

"I'm not grouchy," Sam said, a little louder than he intended. "I can't call and complain. He probably isn't even going to charge me! It would sound like I was ungrateful, or like I was accusing him of something."

"Oh, for goodness sake! You wouldn't be accusing him of anything! You would just be asking about the chair."

"It wouldn't seem right. I can't do it," Sam said. Then he added, wondering if it were really true, "Tony's my friend."

Alice looked closely at Sam. "What are you thinking? That he sold your precious chair to finance a vacation to Tahiti? That old chair wouldn't sell for enough to get to Los Molinos! He couldn't even get across the county line," she said, laughing.

"Don't be ridiculous," Sam said. "Tony wouldn't sell my chair. And if he did, he could make it a lot farther than Los Molinos. He could make it to Red Bluff at least, maybe even Redding."

The day before Sam's haircut appointment, Tony called.

"Hello, Young Man," Tony said. "I've been meaning to call you. The chair's done. Do you want to come to the house this evening and get it, or shall I put it in the back of my pickup and take it to the barbershop tomorrow? You could pick it up when you come in for your haircut."

Sam hesitated. He didn't want to waste the gasoline for an extra trip out. He could wait another day, especially since he'd forgotten about the chair.

"What would be most convenient for you, Tony?"

"Either way would be fine."

"OK. I'll pick it up at the barbershop."

"Good. And, say, could you bring the seedlings this time?"

As Sam was leaving for his haircut, Alice asked if he would mind dropping by Long's Drugs on his way home, to pick up some pictures of their grandkids.

"Stick this note to the dash," she said, "so you won't forget."

When he walked into the barbershop, Tony greeted him with a handshake and a cheery how-are-you. Then, with a smile, he pointed to the swivel chair sitting in the corner. "Take a look at that."

"Very nice. Where did you get that? I like that color," Sam said.

"A customer, a nice young man, asked me to fix it for him. It needed some repairs, and it was an ugly yellowish color. So, I'm surprising him with a nice new honey-colored finish," he said, still smiling and looking at Sam.

"What's a chair like that worth?" Sam said.

"About two hundred and fifty. But it's not for sale. I'm giving it back to my customer."

"I bet he'll be very happy with that," Sam said, walking to the barber chair. "Shall I climb in?"

Tony nodded. His face was still smiling, but not his eyes.

"Look at that head of hair! What I would give to have hair like yours," Tony said, fastening a smock around Sam's shoulders. "Let's see if we can lower those ears a bit."

Sam eased back in the barber chair and felt himself getting drowsy.

Tony chatted amiably as he snipped with his sharp scissors.

"How's your garden doing?" he asked. "My peppers are looking terrific this year. Say, you didn't bring me any of those tomato seedlings, did you?"

"Seedlings? Was I going to bring you some seedlings?"

"No problem. You can bring them another time."

After the haircut, Sam and Tony exchanged pleasantries like always, walking together to the door. But this time Tony stayed at the door. When Sam got to his station wagon, he glanced back and was surprised to see Tony, still standing there, looking towards him. They waved, and Sam drove off.

When he got to Long's, Sam sat in the station wagon for a few minutes. Then he picked up his cell phone.

"Alice, I'm at Long's. Was I supposed to pick up something here?"

"Pictures of the grandkids. Didn't you look at the note?"

"Well, I saw something on there about Long's," he said.

There was a long pause.

"How about the chair? Did you pick it up?" Alice said.
"Chair? What chair?"

The Hawk
Lila Naimark

From the dim corner of the dim old family farmhouse living room, she watched me. With her dim eyes, she watched me like a hawk. Watched me come and go, in and out, always on the move. I knew what she wanted. She wanted me to say, "Hey Mama! Let's go for a ride. Maybe over to Amish country? Get some of that good clover blossom honey. Then find a Red Lobster? If they've got one between here and Bowling Green?"

She wanted escape from the dim corner, from the brown Naugahyde recliner, with the pocket for magazines and eyeglasses velcroed to the side.

She wanted my energy, my attention, life forces she had lost; life forces that started ebbing away just after Daddy's sudden death many years earlier. She wanted to go out to eat.

In and out, back and forth on the route from the kitchen through the living room out into the leafy-bright Tennessee sunshine I buzzed. I'd traveled 2,000 miles to see her, but I can't seem to focus on that. Gotta go for a run…must go to the post office…have to go to Bowling Green for a decent cup of coffee. Go go go.

She and Daddy used to go go go. Then Daddy shocked us all by dying suddenly, dropping off a Saturday night ride home from an evening at Hardee's Hamburgers to hop onto an express train to Heaven. That's when she started slowing down. Her feet, her mind, her eyes. After thirteen years, they've all pretty much come to a stop and she's had to move from her own house to the family farmhouse so that Sue can care for her and Aunt Gladys. So they don't have to go to the nursing home.

On my way out to go to the grocery, Aunt Gladys stops me. "I wonder if you wouldn't mind dropping me off at home on your way," she said, taking her pale blue acrylic sweater from the coat rack, draping it over her thin shoulders. Mama shakes her head, mildly amused, as she always is when Aunt Gladys steps into her Alzheimer's time machine, the time machine that takes her back almost 70 years to when Aunt Gladys' home was Miss Daisy's farmhouse, just over the border in Kentucky. Mama turns her eyes to me, smiles, sharing the moment. One brief smile back, then I turn to smile apologetically at Aunt Gladys and to tell her I'm sorry, not going that way today, and I'm out the door. Firmly, quickly leaving the Naugahyde nester and the time traveler behind, I almost trip over the old stone planter in the front yard with the cherubs--their wings worn down by time--perched atop its four corners. Once upon a time, the planter stood proudly as a brilliant testament to Aunt Gladys' green thumb, overflowing with petunias, begonias, and coleus. Today, long-dead unidentifiable plant stalks and leaves rustle when I bump into it.

Two hours later, I return, my grocery bags full of chicken satay stir fry ingredients. The dim eyes look up hopefully as I come in the door, "Hi Mama. How's it going?" "Fine, I reckon," she replies, turning her head a bit to follow me as I zip into the kitchen. She pulls a tissue from her deep blue housedress, from the white pocket that looks like a smiling apple with rosy-red cheeks sewn onto it, and blows her nose. I start dinner – or 'supper' as they call it here in rural Tennessee–eager to impress Mama and Aunt Gladys' caretaker, Sue, with my adventurous cooking, my California style. No Southern fried chicken and white skillet gravy cooked here tonight!

Sue and I set the table using Aunt Gladys' ancient white Melamine plates with the gold wheat trim, then we help "the girls" to the table. I guide Mama into her seat, carefully, and push her chair in. She's so light these days, it's easy. We're all seated and Sue says the blessing. We all say "amen" and start eating. Sue and I prattle on about recipes, about nothing. Mama eats silently, the black eyes with dim vision, still the unspoken hope, occasionally looking at me, smiling, nodding, willing herself to speak.

Aunt Gladys isn't eating, but staring at her plate, her body tense. "What's wrong, Miss Gladys?" asks Sue. "I'm afraid I don't even begin to know how to sew this," she said, looking imploringly from person to person around the table. "It's all right, hon," Sue tells her. "You're supposed to use your fork–right there–that's right…pick up your fork…and then you can eat it. It don't need sewing." Aunt Gladys' face brightened, her shoulders relaxed.

"Well, I swannee. I thought I'd lost my mind for a minute."

"You're fine, Aunt Gladys," I assure her.

Mama smiles over at me and winks. I take courage from the wink, the shared conspiracy, the supper table camaraderie. Tomorrow, I think. Tomorrow...sure I can do it. She loves lakes and oceans so much. Maybe I'll take her to that little lake that's off the dirt road we pass on the way into town. The one where she had stepped into quicksand 40 years earlier, back when she was plump, sharp-eyed and had freckles instead of massive age spots. She'd sunk waist-deep in a second, and I'd unthinkingly rushed in to try to pull her out. After the lake we can go over to Cracker Barrel, or Applebee's. Any restaurant, really.

Restaurant. The word starts that awful movie in my head again: me on my knees, at that Cajun restaurant last year in Nashville, mopping, mopping, mopping...cleaning up the stall floor, its walls, the soiled Depends, the toilet seat...then the trail on the ladies' room floor...me crawling along that trail, crawling and mopping, following it out of the ladies' room, gulping breaths of less-smelly air when I'd stand up to walk back into the restroom, dripping, soaked paper towels in hand, returning to the paper towel dispenser, apologizing to horrified restaurant customers, trying to erase the trail that led almost all the way back to our table. Life force on the floor, Mama slowly shuffled, stone-faced, zombie-like, as my brother led her outside to the car.

It wasn't the first time for that. But it was the worst. And it was not the last, I knew. I can't. I just can't.

Two more days I'm at the farm, buzzing in and out. Gotta find a nail salon around here...gotta go drive around the square in Bowling Green one more time before I head back home...gotta go where there's cell phone reception. The dim eyes in the dim corner, watching me come and go, always wishing, still hoping.

When the time finally comes to go back to California, I go to the Naugahyde corner and tell her I'm going back home now. Sadness – a great sadness – burns from her eyes, as great as the sadness that was there when I married a man who wasn't Pentecostal, as great as the sadness the first time she saw that I'd violated the faith I'd been raised in since birth by cutting my hair. The sadness that had lurked there ever since. That ever-present sadness of picturing her child in eternal hellfire that had made me avoid her eyes for decades. The wedge between us. Today, her sadness is so great that she breaks her usual silence, "Why do you have to leave?"

"Mama, you know I live in California," I say. I could've just taken her for a brief ride into town, couldn't I? It didn't have to include a restaurant. A half-hour ride through the countryside. Perhaps a drive past the now-burned-down house where she'd been born. What sort of person am I, anyway?

Hoping to make it up, just a little bit, I finally look straight into her eyes, willing a bit of my life force into her. "I love you, Mama," I say. "I love you," she replies. Firmly, slowly, I walk away, tears welling up, as I go out the door into the leafy-bright Tennessee summer day, back to California.

Summer goes, winter comes and the day before her 85th birthday, fluid surrounds her heart and then attacks it. Sue calls to tell me of the middle-of-the night ambulance ride to Highland Hospital, red light twirling silently through the dark countryside; a few days later, the crisis over, a mid-day ambulance ride to a shared room in the 'convalescent home'. The nursing home I'd avoided so long. "It's real nice there," reports Sue. "Nice and bright."

Some awful wheel seems to have been set in motion and things fall apart quickly. Two weeks later, Aunt Gladys goes to the hospital and within the week is gone forever. Back in Tennessee for the funeral, I find Mama at lunch in the fluorescent-bright nursing home lunchroom, around a table with eight strangers, all lost in their own worlds. She sees me…eyes light up. I feel I must tell her that Aunt Gladys is gone. "Oh, no!" Two big teardrops roll down her cheeks. Her eyes go blank as she retreats into herself.

I push her wheelchair back to her room. The attendant helps her back into bed and she goes to sleep immediately, as if I weren't even there.

The awful wheel keeps turning. My second day back in California, Sue calls to tell me that on her daily visits to the nursing home, she's noticed that Mama keeps her eyes closed all the time now. Shutting out the world. Shutting out the dim.

A week passes. Sue reports that at yesterday's visit, she'd entered the room saying, "Guess who?" Hopefully, with a lilt in her voice, Mama had guessed that I was the visitor. My heart breaks. I arrange with my manager to work from Tennessee for an indefinite period of time starting next week.

But the call came the very next day.

Although adrenalin cancels out the effects of the red eye flight back to Tennessee, still I sit numbly in the undertaker's office, making choices I never thought of making before: what color metal for the casket? What price point? The lining color, style and fabric? What newspapers do you want the announcement sent to? When do you want the visitation to start? What day do you want the service to be held? Traditional or graveside? Here or at her church? Who'll be conducting the service? All this and I've not even seen her yet. I picture her lying naked, cold, life forces fully drained, on a slab in the back room and want to hold her, warm her, refill her.

Instead, I leave for the florist's to order the bouquet that will cover the casket that I've chosen…it's one she would like, I know.

I return to the funeral home from my awful errand. The black felt sign in the entry foyer with the white plastic letters arranged in slots announces: "Mrs. Lena Perdue, Visitation Mon and Tues, 11AM – 9PM, Peace Like A River Salon. Services Wednesday 11AM in The Chapel."

I walk slowly, with dread, toward 'Peace Like A River'. There she is. Her white hair beautifully done, that plum-colored dress that always got compliments; she nestled into cream-colored satin. Eyes forever closed.

The funeral singers – old family friends who have driven up from Alabama – arrive a scant ten minutes before the funeral services are to start. They'd brought sheet music for a selection of contemporary Christian songs, but I insist on Mama's favorite. The singers seem a little disappointed in my old-fashioned taste, but they agree, voices unaccompanied by musical instruments, in perfect harmony, sweet as clover blossom honey:

Some bright morning when this life is o'er
I'll fly away
To that home on God's celestial shore
I'll fly away
I'll fly away oh glory!
I'll fly away (in the morning)
When I die hallelujah by and by
I'll fly away

When the shadows of this life have gone
I'll fly away

Like a bird from these prison walls has flown
I'll fly away

    I close my eyes. I see the four-year-old me sitting on her lap in church, both of us clapping our hands in time with the up-tempo beat and singing, "I'll Fly Away." The joy of the Lord is on her face, a look of love for me is in her eyes, and the warmth of her fills my body.

    My first morning back in California, a hawk swoops playfully in front of my car, looking right at me with those bright hawk eyes. Joined by a second hawk, she hesitates for a moment, hovering, then dips her wings toward me. Then she and the other hawk swoop away, happily, spiraling up up up, soaring a thousand feet into the bright blue sky.

The List
Kathy Nakamatsu

On September 18, 2002, my husband of just two years, Jayson, died from sepsis. He had been diagnosed in February 2000, a month after we were engaged, with a rare form of cancer called multiple myeloma. The following is an excerpt from a memoir about my experience as his primary caregiver and as a thirty-four year old widow. Some names have been changed for reasons of privacy.

If I could give one piece of advice to someone who is a caregiver for a cancer patient, it would be to ask for help. I could not have survived Jayson's illness and death without the help of family, friends, support groups and my therapist.

I am often asked why I stayed with Jayson after his diagnosis. We had only been dating for a year and engaged for only one month. Breaking off the engagement didn't seem like an option for me. His parents, in their eighties, were in frail health themselves. His sisters lived too far away and his brother had his own family responsibilities. I was the obvious choice for a caregiver. So when Jayson asked me to stay, I said I would. I left my job and my apartment in Cameron Park, California and moved about a hundred miles southwest to live with Jayson in Clayton, a little town at the base of Mount Diablo. In many ways, being Jayson's caregiver was one of the best things that ever happened to me. Yes, one of the best things. As the youngest child in my family, I was always dependent on others. At 32, I was *still* asking my parents for help, even though they lived in San Jose. When I became Jayson's caregiver, I was responsible for someone else for the first time in my life. It forced me to grow up.

After Jayson's diagnosis, his oncologist referred us to support groups at the Wellness Community in Walnut Creek. Jayson tried a group for cancer patients, but didn't find it helpful and went only a couple times. I attended a group for caregivers and hardly missed a meeting for almost three years. There, I could share my feelings without fear that I was boring people and found comfort in shared experiences. I found that the type of cancer didn't matter – the feelings and emotions were always the same.

In March of 2002, about six months before Jayson died, I began seeing a therapist. Up until then, the support group had been sufficient. It was around this time that Jayson and I learned he now had acute myeloid leukemia (AML), an unfortunate side effect of the stem cell transplant he'd had in 2001. We were told that ten percent of stem cell patients develop AML post-treatment. Ten percent. Why couldn't Jayson have been part of the ninety percent who go on to live healthy lives? In contrast to chronic leukemia and multiple myeloma, AML cells spread quickly and patients usually die within a year or two of diagnosis. The myeloma and the transplant had already weakened Jayson's body and his oncologist only gave him six months to a year. Our hopes were crushed.

Everything changed for me that day. Even the meaningless somehow became significant. I looked at our redwood deck in the backyard, cracking from years of sun exposure. When Jayson was well, I had asked him to repair it, but two years later it still wasn't fixed. Now that Jayson was sick again, it would be *my* responsibility. I saw the overgrown lemon tree, desperately in need of pruning. That would be *my* job too. Like a tidal wave, grief engulfed me and I had to sit down, tears pouring down my face. I stayed there for a while wondering whether I should share my pain with Jayson. Would it make him feel guilty? Would it make him get better? No, I had to be happy and strong for my husband. But after years of hiding my pain, cracks were starting to show. The deck was eroding.

At the next support group meeting, I asked the group leader for recommendations for private therapists. She gave me a couple names, one of which was Dr. Sommer, who worked specifically with cancer patients and caregivers. She also provided support and guidance for children of cancer patients. Her office was in a stark white building with no magazines and no receptionist in the waiting room. How did she know when patients arrived? Yet somehow the office itself was warm and inviting, with stuffed animals and toys for her younger visitors. A brown leather couch was in one corner opposite her desk. I usually sat on the couch with Dr. Sommer across from me in a white sofa chair drinking a cup of Peet's coffee. At first, I wasn't sure if Dr. Sommer was the right therapist for me – she was young and her approach was abrupt and straightforward. Instead of giving advice, she asked questions, making *me* figure out the answers. I didn't have any answers.

"So, how was your week?"

Having just returned to work six weeks after Jayson's death, I said, "It was okay. I'm getting tired of people asking me how I'm doing."

"Why is that?"

"I don't know. It's just, well, sometimes I wonder if they really care."

"What do you mean?" she asked, looking up from her paper.

"You know," I said, hoping she would answer her own question.

"No I don't. Explain it to me."

"They'll say, 'How are you doing?' and then start walking away before I even answer," I fumbled.

Dr. Sommer waited a few seconds before responding. "How does that make you feel?"

"Mad! Sometimes I want to tell them the truth just to see their reaction."

"What would you tell them?"

"That I go home every night and cry. That it takes all my strength just to get through the day." My tears were no longer restrained.

"What do you think would happen if you told them that?"

"I don't know." I waited, hoping she would chime in and help me formulate my thoughts. That rarely happened. "They don't want to hear it. Someone told me to just say 'I'm fine.' Do you know what 'fine' stands for?"

Dr. Sommer shook her head.

"F**d up, Insecure, Neurotic, and Exhausted," I said. "Isn't that great?"

"So is that what you say now?"

"I think I will from now on."

This exchange was fairly typical. She asked difficult questions and I struggled to find answers. Initially I saw Dr. Sommer twice a month, but after Jayson died, I saw her weekly. I cried at every session and I continued to see her for the next two years.

At the beginning of 2004, with Dr. Sommer's help, I decided to make a to-do list for closure. Being a highly organized person, I have lists for almost everything. But this list didn't include things like "donate the last of Jayson's clothes" or "visit the cemetery every month." Instead I listed activities that Jayson and I had enjoyed together but I was nervous about doing alone. If I could complete all the tasks, I could find closure and begin a new life. Seven years later, I can only remember three items but these three were the hardest to accomplish and the most significant.

Task No. 1: See a movie. I tackled this first thinking a lot of people see movies by themselves. Still a lot of thought went into what movie I would see. A romance? No, too many couples. Disney was out too: Jayson was a huge Disney fan and he died before we could have children. No comedies. How could laughing be appropriate?

I finally settled on "Super Size Me," where Morgan Spurlock ate only McDonald's food for thirty days. It wasn't too funny, sad or romantic. Although I was acutely aware that I was the only single person in the theater, this was definitely the easiest task to complete. I was done in less than two hours, I could eat popcorn, and I could be incognito in the darkness. I proudly checked off the movie and moved on...

Task No. 2: Dinner. Having just seen "Super Size Me," I decided against the easy choice – fast food. I chose the Buttercup Grill and Bar, a non-threatening neighborhood coffee shop. Located next to a hotel, I thought it could be the refuge for the hungry solo businessman. No families or first dates there. Even before Jayson died, I had never eaten at a restaurant alone (unless it was from a drive thru) and this was much more daunting. I drove past the restaurant two to three times before parking. I sat in the car and watched people go into the restaurant before working up the courage to enter myself.

The young hostess greeted me in a friendly voice, "Welcome to the Buttercup Grill and Bar! How many people tonight?"

"Just one," I said sheepishly.

"Would you like to sit at the counter?" she asked, gesturing toward the counter in front of the kitchen, where it seemed all the single people were sitting. While tempting, I didn't want to jeopardize the point of the task.

"Actually, I'd prefer a table." She walked me towards a booth large enough to sit five and handed me a menu. After ordering, I pulled out a book – something I shouldn't have done if I had been graded on this task. After finding it too difficult to read a book and eat simultaneously, I people-watched while I ate; an activity Jayson and I had both loved. A few booths to my right, a flirty couple couldn't keep their hands off each other; at the table to my left, a couple didn't talk the entire meal. Finally, the check arrived and I paid my bill, breathing a huge sigh of relief.

Task No. 3: Take a trip. BY YOURSELF. This was going to be the hardest one. This would be my first trip, in every sense, truly alone. Dr. Sommer and I spent a couple of sessions discussing this task. If I could accomplish it, I could give myself permission to move on. It had been a little over two years since Jayson died. I no longer cried at every therapy session and Dr. Sommer and I had even discussed the prospect of dating again.

On Dr. Sommer's recommendation, I decided to spend only one night in a hotel at a location less than two hours away – close enough to race home if the experience was too difficult. The location had to be meaningful, but also a place of peace and solitude – a place where my soul could be rejuvenated. While Disneyland was meaningful (we had gone there several times), it did not provide peace or solitude. Jamestown, where Jayson proposed to me, met the solitude and meaningful requirements, but was a far cry from peaceful. Besides, those hotels are haunted, and no one should sleep there alone. I finally decided on one of my favorite places in California – Pacific Grove, the location of our brief honeymoon and first date.

Spring is the best time to visit Pacific Grove. The ice plants are in full bloom and the beach is bursting with bright pink and purple flowers. As a child, my parents let my sisters and me choose a family activity on our birthdays. With a birthday in April, I always chose a trip to Pacific Grove. As we walked along Ocean View Boulevard, I would always stop in front of the Seven Gables Inn to take in its bright yellow paint and Victorian architecture. "Someday I want to stay there," I would tell my family.

My dreams came true when my parents gave us two nights at the Seven Gables Inn for our honeymoon. Jayson was using a cane at the time, so we had to stay in a ground-floor room, but it was one of the best times of my life. We strolled along the pathway that parallels Ocean View Boulevard, ate fresh crab at Bubba Gump's, and spent a day at the Monterey Bay Aquarium.

This time I did not stay at the Seven Gables, a place advertised on its website as "a romantic getaway." My trip was as far away from that as one could get and I had no interest in earning extra credit on this task. I found a simple hotel down the road and booked a room for the day after Thanksgiving.

I arrived at the hotel around noon. After checking in, I went for my usual walk along Ocean View Boulevard. I thought about going into the Seven Gables. It had been three years since I'd been there. What would I do? Ask to see the room where Jayson and I had stayed? Then what? What good would come of that? Maybe some sympathy, but it all seemed too manipulative. I sat down on a bench near the inn instead and wrote in my journal. I wrote to Jayson.

Dear Jayson. It has been over two years since you passed away. I'm in Pacific Grove right now, my first time back since we were here for our honeymoon. It's a little colder now though. I wish you were here right now. We'd be walking hand-in-hand, listening to the ocean, and watching the elephant seals. We'd probably be sharing teaching stories and laughing about the goofy students we have. I miss you. It's just not the same without you...

I sat and watched the ocean until it got too cold, then headed to Cannery Row to do some window-shopping. It was a brisk November day, but there were still lots of tourists wandering through the stores. Everyone was in a group of family or friends or part of a couple. I felt very alone. I had no one with me to share my experiences. Today you can communicate instantly through a blog or email, but that's not standing next to someone experiencing a shared present, a shared moment.

That night, I decided to see a movie. Pacific Grove had only one small theater that was showing only two movies: *Love, Actually* and *Mystic River*. I'd heard *Mystic River* was good, but it was about death and murder. Unappealing. *Love, Actually* was about couples meeting and falling in love, which could only made me feel more alone. I chose that. In retrospect, I probably should have skipped both movies. My only solace was eating popcorn and not having to be alone in my hotel the entire night. As soon as I woke up the next morning, I left Pacific Grove and headed home. Forget breakfast.

"Well, how was the trip to Pacific Grove?" Dr. Sommer asked at our next session.

"Terrible. I hated it."

"Terrible. That's a strong word. Tell me about it."

I hesitated as I tried to find the right words. "Well, I felt lonelier than I've felt in the last two years. I was bored. All I wanted to do was go home."

"Are you glad you did it?"

"I guess so. I don't know what I was thinking putting it on the list."

"You've completed your list," she smiled. "How does that make you feel?"

I waited a while before answering, "Happy. Proud of myself. A little scared too."

"Why are you scared?"

"Because this means I'm supposed to be free now. I've accomplished everything." I looked at her certificates on the office wall. "What do I do now? What's next? I've always known what was next for me. There is this great unknown now. That scares me."

"You should be proud of yourself, Kathy," Dr. Sommer said, making me cry. "What you did wasn't easy. You've accomplished so much in the past two years. I don't think you need me anymore."

And in that moment, with my completed list a vague, distant thought, I realized that this could be the most difficult separation of all.

Section V:
Poetry

Poetry is the breath and finer spirit of all knowledge.

William Wordsworth

My Subatomic Awakenings
Betty Luceigh

Science met puberty met poetry for me at age 16 in my high school chemistry class. The topic was the substructure of the atom. I was so amazed to learn about the nature of protons, neutrons, and electrons and their relationships to each other. So amazed, I believe my emerging teenage hormones first expressed the "love molecule" (oxytocin) upon sight of the Periodic Table of the Elements. So amazed, I was inspired to create one of my first poems, "The Atomic Theory of Love." It began like this:

"All love is but the image of an atom,
An infinitesimal universe impervious to sight;
Yet the complete aggregate of all existence
Lies within the boundaries of its might."

It was 1960 and, at that time, my primary heartthrob was the physicist Niels Bohr, not Elvis-the-pelvis. The photo of young Dr. Bohr in my chemistry textbook made him look so intellectually sexy. Sometimes as I pulled up my bobby socks on the way to chemistry class, I would imagine romantic discussions with him about electronic configurations. I didn't know much then about the many other physicists of the early 1900's like Einstein and Heisenberg. I was too young to appreciate a sense of history beyond a decade, so I didn't realize I had been born into the era of a revolution in physics that far surpassed the understandings of the classical, not-so-handsome Newton himself. All I realized for sure was that there was something mysteriously appealing about the well-defined social order of those fundamental particles. My high school poem, in retrospect, was a written record of the *first* of what I now call my "Subatomic Awakenings."

*"That nucleus clutched by the binding energy of God,
That inmost core intermarriaging [sic] the indifferent
    and the sure,
Is the centrum around which the electrons of emotions
Whirl in an eternal shell, without demur."*

I should mention I was also in secret, hormonal awe of my high school English teacher, Mr. Bates. I learned from him the joy of writing book reports, the search for double meanings in passages of *The Scarlet Letter*, and the spelling of "sesquipedalian" he wrote in red on one of my essays. As I was convinced the way to his heart was by extending my vocabulary, Roget's thesaurus became my "manual of love."

In the decade that followed, miniskirts replaced crinoline and I replaced that first love manual with some hands-on, serious dating/marriage. I continued to believe in the popular romance tales of the times. I also continued to write poems, but kept them private lest my rational thinking be called into question. My vocabulary expanded with personal experiences that taught me to distinguish between true lust and true love, loyalty and betrayal, and even bigger words like autonomy and subjugation. In short, I learned there was no Santa Claus of the heart! To counter that jolt to my emotional reality, I kept faith in the chemistry education I continued to pursue. At least molecules and their behavior, I remained convinced, were undisputed facts of existence--predictable, dependable, and, above all, *certain*. Imagine my surprise when even *that* presumption burst! I went, dare I say, nuclear.

*"The quantity of matter, the magnitude of the mass,
Determines the degree of altruistic activity;
The stableness of the diverse isotopes
Results in either amorous fluctuation or constancy."*

It was in graduate school that I learned just how incomplete my understanding of the chemistry of matter had been. The shocking truth came in the form of two words: *quantum mechanics*. Quantum theory took decades, starting in the early 1900's, to develop. Quantum mechanics is the modern description of the behavior of subatomic particles. That behavior turns out not to be so certain, after all. In fact, it can be very weird! Chemistry texts that had once read like the poetry of logic to me were replaced with the equivalent of advanced sci-fi novels written in complex math. The worst part was discovering that Niels Bohr had been in on it all along! I felt so betrayed I wanted to tear up my Periodic Table and light it with a Bunsen burner! Since that seemed unlikely to secure my future employment, I chose a more effective option: study, study, then study some more.

I passed the courses in quantum mechanics, in part, by remembering Mr. Bates and my love of words. At first, I focused on the esoteric, and frequently sesquipedalian, vocabulary of quantum theory. I even hummed the words as if top hits by James Taylor: Wave-particle Duality, Quantum States, Electron Clouds of Probability, Superpositions, and the ever-melodic Uncertainty Principle. When that didn't bring instant quantum enlightenment, I took a more poetic approach and tried elaborate visual images, metaphors, and analogies to describe the abstract concepts. Although doing so truly improved my basic understanding, I remained always secretly afraid someone would find out that I was clueless what quantum mechanics *actually* meant and thus invalidate my academic degrees.

Fortunately, I ultimately made the major intellectual leap I now call my *second* Subatomic Awakening. Introductory chemistry became advanced chemistry and poems that once rhymed became free-form. As for those love molecules...well, they just got more confused. Back in high school, I had asked important teenage questions. Would my spirit soar by an actual exploratory sloppy kiss with a skinny geek or by a poetic attempt at a naive metaphor imagining it? Quantum mechanics changed the nature of my later young-adult questions by introducing deeper uncertainty into my view of life. That change was reflected in my "iffy" questions. *If* I write a poem about a truth today, is it possible I won't believe it's true tomorrow? *If* I try to live without creativity, will I go insane? It seemed the more I accepted ambiguity, the more probing all my questions became. Fascinating.

"Any spontaneous or forced emissions of love,
Any radiation from the source which is nuclear,
Has the penetrating power, the enormous energy,
To ionize the impermeable elements of hatred and fear."

In the four decades (1970's-2000's) that passed since my second Subatomic Awakening, the story of my life has continued its personal and professional maturation process. My reflections expressed in more detail here, however, are of those early, formative experiences of science, love, and words, because of their profound subsequent impact. My first Subatomic Awakening revealed my life's multiple interests. Within each area of interest, my second Subatomic Awakening expanded my reality from limited certainty to boundless ambiguity. Somehow uncertainty in establishing scientific facts then seemed important to drive science forward. Somehow uncertainty in relationships then seemed important to draw forth more loving attention to them. Somehow uncertainty in the phrasing of a poetic expression then seemed important to enhance the creative process. Bohr and Bates, I thank you.

I have grown to believe that all forms of inquiry, scientific or not, are moving toward an ultimate integrative answer to our common longing to know the meaning of being human, especially the experience of loving. Throughout the years I have held an innate sense of a mystifying link between the structural features of matter and the human experience of lovingness. Rather than science diminishing the meaning of love, I find that detailed knowledge of the highly complex molecules and conditions required for the awareness and expressions of love are intensely beautiful. Factual knowledge of atomic reality has also become a personal entryway for me to a co-existing realm of love/spiritual awe. We need only to engage lovingly to know love, to write/speak poetically to know the beauty in life, and to explore matter and energy to know their mystery. No sloppy kiss, Periodic Table, or thesaurus is required anymore!

At my first chemistry teacher's request, I reluctantly read my poem "The Atomic Theory of Love" to the class. Fortunately, no one laughed. That was 50 years ago. Here, I have shared it again and can be amused by the memory. I like to think Niels Bohr and Mr. Bates would as well. What I have changed since 1960 is the rest of my life. What I have not changed since then is a single word of that high school poem. It ended this way:

"For love is but the image of an atom,
An infinitesimal universe impervious to sight;
And all creation, all felicity, all knowledge
Is concealed within the boundaries of its might."

My Vision of Beauty
Betty Luceigh

I saw Beauty in the night
as radiance without form,
the light of a thousand suns bright.
She offered her vision to my unprepared mind,
 on its own too small to contain her brilliance.

As she pulsed her invitation to surrender,
I accepted her wordless mergence so complete
there could be no ecstasy greater to surpass the gift
of being nothing into nothing, all into all,
 self into the Source of Self.

Even so, as my structure dissolved
to enter Beauty's realm,
I knew somehow it was not yet the time
to stay forever disembodied
or erratically spark my temporal lobe,
but rather to return to the constraints of my form,
return behind the veil of material forces
that must shade Beauty's radiance
lest her intensity evermore disable
 my earthly comprehension.

Why, Beauty, why
why touch me so, only to leave me untouchable,
why reveal yourself so, only to leave me a greater mystery.
Where are you now, radiance of Beauty,
that I cannot reach into the bliss of your fullness,
only seek fragments through your reflections everywhere--
flower and stream and child,
simplicity and innocence and compassion,
 knowledge and understanding and acceptance.

How can I live, Beauty, so filled with your offering
and not pass on the overabundance of it,
tender assurances to other hearts
lest they despair in their illusions
of your absence or temporariness in their lives.
How do I explain what defies the limitation of language
as I learn to transcend the limitations
of my own resistance to serve you.
How do I explain that you imbue forms
to lure us beyond our human weakness,
draw us away from violence and fear,
that all may one day be embraced
 in the shared wellspring of your glow.

I have learned to return to you, Beauty,
when I choose to behave Beautifully,
when I choose to see the Beautiful in living and nonliving,
when I choose to allow the Beautiful to flow through me,
as when I strive to create an expression of your reality
and release it freely for all of us,
not as my own but from you,
in hope others will be likewise transformed
as together we evolve
 into ultimate reunion with you.

Highway 68
Robert Nielsen

She drove up beside me.
Our windows were down.
"Tight fittin' jeans,"
the song on her radio.
FM.
K-TOM Country.

The light changed.
She shot ahead and out in front.

"Insurance by Smith & Wesson,"
said the sign on her rear window
below the gun rack
which carried a long red umbrella.

"California Rodeo,"
said her bumper sticker.
So, too, did her Stetson
and the color of the shirt she wore.

Rodeo Week.
Big Week in Salinas.

And in the side mirror
of her black Chevy truck
I still could see
her gum-chewing smile

Smooth soft skin,
big brown eyes,
auburn hair in a thousand curls,

And love for someone.

She winked at me in her mirror
And accelerated down the road to town.

Upper East Side
Robert Nielsen

    Back in New York,
    tea one spring afternoon
    with the mother of an old girlfriend
    from college; open-faced sandwiches,
    fresh pastry, first-flush Darjeeling;
    one of those perpetual places
    on the Upper East Side
    where this family lived

We'd just planned everything

    The woman said of her daughter

Wanted to make sure she had the best
education; private school;
winning soccer teams;
seven-sister college;
you know the path

    She went on

Good friends, freedom to travel
community service at Lennox Hill
parties at home with her friends,
none of the hassles we got for pot

    The woman paused,
    looked down
    folded unfolded her napkin
    nestled it on the table
    by the saucer,

> Limoges,
> lifted the cup
> wrist correct
> sipped

Now she's quit

> She resumed

Left publishing
abandoned her editor track
moved to Huntington Beach
with some surfer kid from New Jersey

They drove out West last week

He's clean, my investigator says
Nothing on his phone taps either

But still
And he didn't go to college

> The woman took a small bite of madeleine
> sipped again
> tea room clatter continued
> I felt her foot press against my shoe
> she looked at me over the rim of her cup
> sighed, paused appropriately
> waited,
> said slowly

What
is a mother to do?

> Nothing, I thought.

"The Write Retreat" - Stanford Sierra Camp 2010

Let it be.
Good God, lady,
your daughter's free.

But what could I say?

I smiled empathically,
looked away.

And the waiter,
watching us,
hearing all of this in bits and pieces,
stepped forward
asked if there was anything
more the woman needed,

And before she could answer,
nodded his head
told me the taxi I ordered
which I hadn't
was here

And I thanked him
stood up
shook hands
with my ex girl friend's mother
sitting there
slipping her foot
back into her shoe

Her face smiling pro forma
as I turned, headed for the door

And slipped the waiter
sixty bucks.

Border Crossing
Robert Nielsen

These people,
he lectured from the podium,
are taking American jobs.
Work for substandard wages
paid by opportunists,
farmers perverting
our free enterprise system,
undermining the American way of life.

    He shook his finger in the air
    The crowd in the ballroom nodded
    Waiters poured coffee
    Cleared dessert plates away.

These people don't assimilate.
Make us print ballots in fifty languages.

Bankrupt hospitals near the border
giving birth to their babies for free.

Populate gangs that pollute our cities.
Make crime the wave of the future,
here now, my friends, here now.

    I wondered how much lebensraum
    this guy wanted
    as I poured a blue-haired bobbing-head lady
    more coffee,
    then handed her the cream and sugar.

    I looked over and smiled at my friend,
    Jose Luis, working

"The Write Retreat" - Stanford Sierra Camp 2010

the other side of the table
and, like me, anxious to blow this gig.

Start our date
studying together
for the Bar exam
which starts tomorrow.

Computer Creativity
Lynette Kent

Turn on the computer, pull up a chair,
My hand on the mouse, screen mirrors my stare.
I click the mouse once, and click it again,
Click, drag, click. Does this thing have a brain?
Why does it seem to control what I do?
Inanimate object, why write with you?

I open a page, put fingers on keys,
"Index fingers, press TH, third finger, press E."
Three letters appear, I click, drag, delete.
"Fingers, press more keys!" I click, drag, repeat.
My eyes close then open, again I try.
"He laughed...she cried," I type, click, drag, sigh.

A moment ago, or so it seems,
Ideas for a story flooded my dreams.
Now ready to write, thoughts sputter not flow,
One word maybe two, no paragraphs though.
My mind is a void, my visions are gone,
Inspiration is missing. Has the mouse now won?

Storytellers and poets remember this phrase:
'True art can appear in mysterious ways!
A work is not measured by marks on the page,
Nor creativity judged by a computerized gauge.
So artists and writers must never confuse
The mouse in the hand and the touch of a muse.'

On Change
Taly Rutenberg

Some days are arid,
an endless afternoon
on a stagnant sea:
windless and graceless,
flaccid sails,
no land in sight.

On other days
I ride the water's back
full tilt:
the big city skyline
bright and blinking,
calls me
to shore.

Section VI:
The Unexpected Meets the Unexplained

Man can believe the impossible,
but man can never believe the improbable.

Oscar Wilde

The Root of All Evil
(Trilogy – Part 1)
Petra LaVictoire

<u>**Setting:**</u> *Envision a stunning old mansion. It is beautifully constructed in Neo-Romanesque architectural style with impressive arches, soaring steeples topped with delicate spires and perfectionist details that would make any great artist feel inferior. The inside has the allure of a fairy tale castle, decorated with the most delicate of fabrics and carefully selected natural wood and stone. When entering the grand living room, the centerpiece is a striking stone fireplace with a large hand carved mahogany mantel, and majestic picture windows with views of the beautiful Victorian rose gardens outside.*

This manor truly exceeds every visitor's expectations – with the exception of one very ugly thing …
something of an eye sore …

On the antique fireplace mantel stood proud an old and very ugly tree root. Norma, the live-in housekeeper, had been instructed over the years to never touch it, and to never throw it out. Mrs. Dudley, the 90-year-old owner of Briarwood Mansion, said that it had been given to her by her deceased husband back in 1861.

Every afternoon, when Mrs. Dudley relaxed next to the fireplace, she would say, "Norma, in those days my husband was a cowboy in Montana. When he asked me to be his wife, he said, 'Agatha, my love, take this tree root as a symbol of my never ending love for you. Always keep it close to you, and we will be together through the ages.'"

All Norma could think was…"Blah blah blah…How can an unsightly twisted thing like *that* have anything to do with eternal love…That's rubbish!" But Mrs. Dudley insisted that within it lies a secret. A secret so dark, she didn't dare speak it from her red painted wrinkled lips.

That summer, sweet old Mrs. Dudley died. Norma had found her lifeless body draped like a forbidden blanket across the rocking chair. Beside her lay a note. Written on it was the name of an attorney. After a brief phone conversation, Norma found out that she had inherited the mansion…but under *one* condition…she was to keep the tree root – **FOREVER!**

Norma picked it up, looked at it with disgust, and uttered, "I'll burn it! No way that I will keep *this* around the house! Besides, no one will ever notice that it is gone." Having said that, and with a heavy heart, Norma threw the root into the burning fireplace.

…Blackout…

…Complete Blackout…

Norma shook her pounding head and seemed confused. "What happened?" she thought out loud. Everything around her had changed. It was most unusual, the furniture, paintings, even the clothes she was wearing were different – and dated. The only object which remained familiar was the old tree root which had magically resurrected itself from the ashes, and was now sitting proudly once more on the hand carved mahogany mantel.

Looking through the large window, Norma could see a strangely dressed man standing in her rose garden. Not recognizing the gentleman, she stepped near the pane and shouted, "Hey! Get off my property!"

He turned his handsome face towards her, then lovingly replied, "Well, I see you are finally awake, my Dear. How was your slumber?"

"Such audacity, *who* does he think he is?" she mumbled loudly.

"Excuse me? Who are you?" she furiously asked.

"I am Walter. Walter Dudley, **your** husband," he replied with a devoted smile.

If it hadn't been near the end of June, this bizarre happening could have been a great April Fools Day joke – but *this* was summer!

Norma's throbbing head simply couldn't make sense of the situation, so she ran down the hall into the powder room to splash cold water from the washbasin into her face. That's when a mysterious voice eerily chimed through the room:

"Normaaaaaaa ... NORmaaaaaaaaaaaa ..."

Spooked, she quickly turned around only to find that no one was there. While grabbing the towel to dry her face, Norma glanced up and piercingly screamed in horror as it was ***NOT*** her own reflection that stared back at her in the mirror. NO – it was Mrs. Dudley!

Terrified, she pulled on her face and the skin on her arms…but there was no mistake…Norma was no longer Norma. She was now trapped inside of the youthful body of Mrs. Agatha Dudley!

At that very moment of ghastly discovery, the nearby window flew open and the voice in the wind echoed:

"She who gets rid of the old tree root becomes Mrs. Dudley back in 1861 for all ages to come!"

*****To find out what happened next, please read the second part of this trilogy when
'The Root of All Evil Returns'*****

The Root of All Evil Returns
(Trilogy – Part 2)
Petra LaVictoire

Pennington had always been a quiet little town. It was picturesque, sprinkled with Victorian style houses and a few plantations. A local newspaper article once pointed out that it was a fantastic place for walking dogs, raising children, or simply enjoying a quieter way of living.

Some of the older generation planted themselves in rocking chairs on porches and store fronts; happily returning a friendly wave and smile to anyone who passed by. The people here took pride in keeping up their homes, with the exception of one property. It was just at the edge of town, right at the corner of Fernvalley Road and Magnolia Avenue.

Only if you looked really close, you could recognize the almost vanished outline of Briarwood Mansion. Just a few short years ago it used to be the most stunning structure in the entire county.

Sadly, after the last owner Mrs. Dudley had been taken to a mental facility, it stood empty and no one came to care for the grounds. Many had heard her wild stories of a tree root that turned evil, and that she was Norma, the missing live-in housekeeper, who was trapped inside of Mrs. Agatha Dudley's body.

Not more than five years after being admitted there, she died outside on the balcony of her room, sitting on a chair, smiling. Her stiff hand still held her long white embroidered cotton skirt. On it, she had written her last living wish.

It revealed that after twenty years of having to remain uninhabited, Briarwood Mansion was to be given to Pennington's Historical Society, and whatever money was left in the bank account was to go toward its preservation.

Prof. James Buckner, the director of the Historical Society, decided to hire well renowned horticulturist Leo Archer, and his niece Phoebe McDowell who specialized in arboriculture.

"Uncle Leo, a courier just dropped off a very important envelope for you."

"Yes, I know. I received a phone call regarding it earlier this morning. Phoebe, we have been asked to do the landscape preservation for the Dudley Estate."

"You mean Briarwood Mansion, Uncle Leo?"

"Yes, that's right. The funny thing is that some of the old folk still believe that the manor remains haunted by its terrible past. Apparently every live-in housekeeper that ever worked there vanished, and their bodies were never found. But if you ask me, that's just one of those ridiculous small town legends!"

It was late Thursday morning when Mr. Archer, his niece and crew arrived at Briarwood Mansion. Phoebe stepped out of the truck and said, "This is going to take a few months before it will be as beautiful as it once was." Everyone agreed.

The gardeners began clearing leaves and lifeless branches, placing them into a large pile to be burned. An exceptionally small tree caught Phoebe's eye. She decided to relocate it to a less shady location. While attempting to dig it out, her garden spade hit a rather firm object. At first she contemplated that it might be a bigger stone, and was pleasantly surprised that it was something far more intriguing when she took a closer look.

She happily exclaimed, "Uncle Leo! Come here! Quickly! You've got to see this. I believe I stumbled upon a treasure box!" She carefully lifted it out of the hole, and gently brushed the dirt off the hand-stitched fabric.

Leo stood next to her and jokingly asked, "What is it? What have you unearthed? Perhaps a *mummy?*"

"No! Not quite. It's a large ornate puzzle box. Whoever made this, spent a lot of time creating it – such masterful detail and perfection in the wood-inlay. But the unfortunate thing is that I have no clue how to open it."

Uncle Leo eagerly replied, "How about *I* give it a try? I'll be careful not to break it. I always enjoy a good challenge. Besides, my cousin used to have a much smaller one, and even though I didn't know the combination, I was pretty good at figuring it out."

After countless attempts of subtle squeezes and complicated maneuvers of sliding the individual wood pieces around like a pendulum clock mechanism, it became clear that something was preventing it from opening completely. Finally, Leo succeeded and pulled a somewhat shriveled old piece of wood out of it.

"Ah, a little wiggling did the trick. Someone had jammed this ugly tree root into it. It's amazing how tightly it fit in that compartment. But why would anyone want to save this unsightly thing?"

He handed Phoebe the puzzle box and threw the root on top of the burning leaf mound.

...Blackout...

...Complete Blackout...

Uncle Leo woke up on the lawn with a pounding headache. "What happened? Where is everyone?"

As he looked around, he could clearly see that all of the landscaping had been flawlessly completed. Everything was perfectly manicured, but not how it was proposed on his approved plans. Even Briarwood Mansion no longer appeared weathered and old. It was stunning – just as it was in those old photographs that were displayed at Pennington's Historical Society.

Leo was greeted by a man dressed in dated garments. The gentleman reached out his hand to help him up, and then leaned in for a *romantic* kiss.

Leo promptly jumped back and cautioned, "Sir, I must *warn* you! I am NOT afraid to hit you if you try *that* again!!"

The man lovingly responded, "Why are you so shy, my Sweetheart?"

Leo turned around, but there wasn't a female to be seen.

He firmly told the stranger, "I'm Mr. Archer, and I have been hired to do the landscape preservation on this property. Who are you, and why are you referring to me as a ***she***?"

The man charmingly smiled and answered, "Do you not feel well, my Sweet? Perhaps you have been out in the hot sun for far too long. Let us go inside, my Dear, and I will fetch you a glass of water."

Uncle Leo responded sternly, "You're crazy! Who are you talking to?"

"Oh – my dearest Darling, I have been speaking to *you*, **my** beloved wife Agatha! I simply adore it when you play those silly games with me, claiming you do not know that I am your husband – Walter Dudley. Hmm, I must say ... you are simply breathtaking today!"

Uncle Leo's headache seemed to get worse as he kept on mumbling to himself, "Could it be true? The legend ... could *IT* be really true?"

Walter graciously assured, "If you don't believe me how absolutely stunning you look, why don't you look into the mirror and see for yourself?"

Leo ran into the manor and gazed upon his reflection. It was true. Not only was he wearing a Victorian Civil War era purple and white plaid checkered dress with black wool straight sole high top boots...Uncle Leo was no longer Uncle Leo.

NO – he was now trapped inside of the youthful body of Mrs. Agatha Dudley.

At this very moment of horror and disbelief, an eerie voice creepily whispered through the air:

"He who gets rid of the old tree root becomes Mrs. Dudley back in 1861 for all ages to come!"

Stunned and frozen with shock, Uncle Leo heard Mr. Dudley softly beckoning from the grand stairway, "Ready Darling? It's getting late. Let's go to bed my Dear!"

***To see what happened next, and for the final conclusion of this trilogy, please make sure you read
'The Root of All Evil – Final Eclipse'***

The Root of All Evil – Final Eclipse (Trilogy – Part 3)
Petra LaVictoire

Kokia cookei, also known as Molokaʻi kokiʻo, is a small, deciduous tree, which is considered to be one of the rarest and most endangered plant species in the world. Even when it was first found in the 1860s, only three trees could be located. It was presumed extinct in the 1950s when the last surviving seedling perished. However, in 1970, a single plant was discovered on the same Kauluwai estate where the "last" individual grew, presumably a surviving relict of one of the plants previously cultivated there. Although this tree was destroyed in a fire in 1978, a branch that was removed earlier was grafted onto the related, and also endangered, Kokia kauaiensis. Currently about 23 grafted plants exist.
(Source: Wikipedia)

It was still mid-afternoon when Phoebe McDowell woke up on the dried grassy unkempt lawn behind Briarwood Mansion. One of the gardeners came running toward her, yelling, "Miss McDowell, are you alright?"

She propped herself up slowly; her eyes squinting, desperately trying to adjust to the brightness of the sun. Her head was pounding worse than any migraine she had ever felt before.

"Yes, I think so," she whispered in agony.

"Are you sure? I was up on the ladder over by the fig tree, trimming some of the branches, when I saw this sudden bright flash. Next thing I know you were flat on the ground. If it hadn't been for the cloudless summer sky, I could have sworn that you were struck by lightning!"

Phoebe's fiancé ran to her aid, too, and helped her stand up on her feet. "What happened? Are you okay?" He worriedly asked.

"Oliver, the last thing I can recall is that I was standing right here, next to this big pile of burning leaves. I was asking Uncle Leo if he could figure out how to open the wooden box. Then I must have blacked out somehow. Where is my uncle?"

"I don't know," replied the gardener, "it's the strangest thing...after the flash...he was gone. Perhaps he went to get some water for you."

After almost an hour passed by, Oliver sent the crew looking for her uncle. He was nowhere to be found. Oliver wondered, "Sweetie, what wooden container were you referring to?"

"Oh, I was in the process of replanting a small tree when my garden spade hit a rather hard object. It turns out it was a large wood-inlay puzzle box which was carefully wrapped inside of a hand stitched cloth. I tried opening it, but to no avail. Uncle Leo was only a few feet from me, so I had asked him if he could help. That's when I must have passed out."

Phoebe's head was still throbbing when she went on to say, "Wait, I think there was something else. I'm not certain if this is of any importance, but my uncle did mention something about a local legend. A root that turned evil. Missing housekeepers – right here at Briarwood. After many attempts to open the box, Uncle Leo eventually succeeded and pulled out a chunk of dead wood – a twisted looking tree root. But could that have anything to do with his disappearance?"

Oliver pondered for a few minutes, and then his face turned serious. He looked at his fiancé and said, "Phoebe, the only reason why the police ended their investigation in the cases of the missing housekeepers was because they couldn't prove that there was foul play involved. Plus, dear old Mrs. Dudley had some sort of multiple personality disorder, which is why she was eventually placed in the local mental ward. We need to find your uncle, and I'm hoping we'll find him fast! Let's start with where you first saw the puzzle box."

She pointed to the location and walked over to it. To her astonishment, the hole was no longer visible, and in its place stood once more the little tree.

"I can't explain it! This is incredible! I know I replanted it. I'm sure of it!" Phoebe was shocked. Her face turned pale, and her heart suddenly began beating faster. She was nervous, and now extremely worried about the well-being of her uncle.

"Whatever the meaning of this is...let's not waste any more time! I don't have a good feeling about his mysterious vanishing. Hand me a shovel!" Oliver began to dig. He swiftly removed the little tree, and then suddenly shouted, "Look! Let me pull it out. Is this the infamous puzzle box you mentioned?"

Phoebe was speechless. She couldn't explain how it got neatly wrapped again and re-buried there. Her fiancé noticed another peculiar item the dirt. It was a leather bound journal. Hoping to shed more light on the situation, they believed it would be best to drive to Pennington's Historical Society and show their find to Prof. Buckner.

It turned out that it was the personal diary of Sebastian H. Dudley, first owner of Briarwood. Phoebe eagerly flipped through the worn pages in hopes that there was anything of importance.

"Hmm. From what I can make of his handwriting, it reveals that Sebastian H. Dudley left his native England to pursue his dream of becoming a bullfighter in France. During his first year there, he befriended a German tourist who was a sugar farmer on one of the Hawaiian Islands. After accepting an invitation to visit his new friend, he tells about his voyage across the ocean and first impressions of arriving on the island Molokai. Babe, I really don't see any connection to my uncle's disappearance. Let's just call the police and file a missing person's report."

Oliver calmingly replied, "He hasn't been gone for twenty four hours yet. Keep reading. If he's not back by the morning, I'll call the police myself."

"OK," Phoebe answered hesitantly, "Sebastian goes on to say that he met some of the royal Hawaiian family at their vacation ranch, and had given them valuable tips on how to herd their cattle better. In deep gratitude, and to thank him properly for his help, the chief granted him one wish. Not wanting crafts or riches, Sebastian asked for a chance at everlasting love."

She took a quick sip of water, and then continued to summarize out loud, "He tells of a sweet young maiden who he met near the sugar fields, and that he intended to marry her. I still don't see how this journal is going to help, but I'll keep going. So, to be granted his wish, he followed the chief into the lowlands and sat down with him next to an 'enchanted' tree. Mr. Dudley further states that the chief told him that it was no ordinary tree, and since ancient times it had been passed down through generations that only three of this rare deciduous Moloka'i koki'o exist – this particular one apparently had magical powers. Then ancient words were spoken by the chief, and a good size piece of the twisted root was broken off and given to Mr. Dudley."

Oliver endearingly cut in, "Phoebes, I can feel we're getting somewhere here. What's written next?"

"It's a quote. Must be what the chief was telling him. 'Take this root. Give it to the woman of your heart. Tell her to take this special root as a symbol of your love. Make sure she keeps it close to herself always, and you two will be together through the ages. But be warned that such a wish comes with a heavy price. You will remain living in the same year you give her the root. That won't ever change. She will be with you, but for her, you always die at the end of that year and she will go on living her regular life until her natural death. At that moment – either she, or whoever destroys this magic root, will travel back in time…and their soul will enter your loved ones youthful body. For you, it will always seem as if you have gone to sleep, until the cycle starts over once more.' – Oliver, this is awful! This can't be real! Can it?"

"Calm down Sweetie. I am sure we'll get to the bottom of this. I've called Leo a few times, and left urgent messages on his cell phone. I'm certain he will get back to us when he turns it on and sees that we have attempted to reach him." Oliver was anxious, and tried his best to stay patient and not let his fiancé see how worried he was.

Phoebe kept on summarizing, "When Sebastian heard that, he knew he couldn't follow through with it. He couldn't bear the thought of his young bride thinking he was dead and then having to live a life of solitude and sadness. He was a gentleman at heart and decided to return home without her. The morning before leaving on his journey he met the lady of his heart one last time to bid her adieu. The maiden handed him her hand stitched cloth to remember her by, and sadly bid him farewell."

She paused for a moment, and then continued, "On his passage back to France, he met a businessman from Montana who told him he could use his matador skills on a large cattle ranch. He accepted, and less than two years later he married the businessman's daughter and they had one son. He had kept the root, along with his first love's hand stitched linen, hidden in his son's toy puzzle box. His son's name was Walter."

"Sweetie, you know what this means?" Oliver excitedly asked. Before Phoebe could get a word in, he said, "Remember, Walter Dudley wasn't the original owner of Briarwood Mansion – Sebastian Dudley was. Walter must have found his father's diary, read about the magical root, and gave it to his wife Agatha the day of their marriage proposal. Now it makes sense. I suggest we get it tested. I'll bet that it is the Moloka'i koki'o!"

The couple got into their car and drove to down the road to Phoebe's office. Luckily one of the arbor research lab technicians was still there and gladly offered to help. Quicker than expected, they found out that it indeed was a piece of the mentioned tree.

"Now there is only one thing to do. I have to go. Give it to me. I'll destroy it, travel back in time, and find my uncle."

"No Phoebe! If you do that, you'll turn into Mrs. Dudley, and I'll lose you, too. But I have an idea. How about we will **both** get rid of the root *together* and see what happens?"

Uncertain, Oliver and Phoebe held each other tight; their hands firmly gripped the smoldering root that was slowly burning away over the flame of a candle.

…Blackout…

…Complete Blackout…

Oliver and Phoebe woke up in rather tropical surroundings. Neither was Mrs. Dudley, and the ugly root was back in once piece, resting peacefully next to them. Lethargic, the pair began walking across a field. They were greeted by a farmer who was happy to answer where they were. Yes, Phoebe and her fiancé were on Molokai.

The man gladly led them to the royal vacation ranch, which was so beautifully described in the diary. There, they were welcomed by the Hawaiian chief who couldn't wait to hear their fascinating tale.

"What you say is terrible! I warned him. I told Mr. Sebastian that his wish came with a very heavy price. He should have guarded the root *and* its secret better! Now, both of you claim that you are from the future – the year 2010?"

Oliver and Phoebe nodded as the chief carried on, "Well, if you must know, we are in the year 1835, actually just a few days after I handed him that twisted piece of root. If your words are true, and you really wish to save your uncle, then you must hurry! There isn't much time! Only 175 years *after* the original celestial event – a partial lunar eclipse – when the root is given to the one who desires infinite love, can the spell be reversed! We can only hope that it isn't already too late!"

The young couple listened intently, and held on to every word.

"Here, take this, but before you drink this juice made from the flowers of the enchanted Moloka'i koki'o, let me give you instructions. On the night of a summer lunar eclipse, you must go to the tree where the puzzle box was hidden. Stand beside it, and hold your hands forming a circle. The luminosity of the moon during the eclipse is very powerful. Make sure the root is kissed by this moonlight. Position it into the middle of your circle. Then, with your eyes closed, chant this rhyme at least three times throughout the entire eclipse: Wiggi Wiggi Mulu Kali'i…Wiggi Wiggi Mulu Kali'i…Wiggi Wiggi Mulu Kali'i. By the time you open your eyes, the root will have vanished, and in its place will be your uncle."

They thanked the chief, drank the juice, and fell into a deep slumber.

It was dark when Phoebe and Oliver woke up and found themselves on the unkempt lawn of Briarwood Mansion.

"What date is today, Babe?" she inquisitively wondered.

"According to my cell phone, it is Saturday June 26th 2010. It is almost time for the lunar eclipse to begin. Quickly, hold my hand!" Patiently they formed a circle and closed their eyes. Their bodies felt tingly and warm as they stood there, repeating "Wiggi Wiggi Mulu Kali'i" over and over again in the moonshine.

That's when a light breeze stroked lovingly through their hair, and a voice softly echoed like ancient whispers,

"Only true love can break the spell ... you did it, dear Phoebe McDowell."

...Bright Flash...

After Oliver and Phoebe opened their eyes, they saw that everything seemed to be back to how things were when they first arrived at the manor. The gardeners were pruning and raking, just as if nothing ever happened.

Even Uncle Leo was there. He was leaning against the grand stone wall by the front entrance of Briarwood Mansion with his eyes shut and snoring loudly. Phoebe sprinted over to him and eagerly woke him up. Uncle Leo rubbed his eyes and said: "You won't believe what I was dreaming. I felt as if I had time travelled back to the 1860's, and that I was trapped in the body of a woman – Mrs. Dudley. How bizarre! I am very relieved that it was just a very bad dream."

Oliver winked at Phoebe, and both agreed that it was nothing more than an unpleasant dream.

The little unusual tree that once guarded the secret of an old and very ugly root now stands proud with stunning blood orange colored blossoms. Beside it, a gold engraved bronze plaque reads:

**'Dedicated to Walter Dudley
and his beloved wife Agatha.
May your undying love live on in all of us.'**

Each year hundreds of people flock to Pennington for the annual autumn festival. It never fails that some daring lovers, in hopes for everlasting love, wander off to carve their initials into Briarwood's

The Fallen Leaf Anthology

Moloka'i koki'o and break off a piece of its root as a souvenir – ***only to never be seen again ...***

The End!
(Pssst – would *YOU* dare?)

Raising More Than Cain
Cynthia Roberts

Maybe moving here won't be a disaster.
Ben had given his parents such grief about moving to a small town right before his senior year just because his mom had been accepted to graduate school here. Didn't they have graduate schools in California? Couldn't she have waited one more year? He'd never admit to his parents he'd changed his mind about the move, but he could be nice to them for a while. They'd figure it out.

He whistled as he walked, practically skipping. He couldn't believe he'd been invited to Sam's house to hang out with the cool kids from his new high school. The in-crowd at his old school hadn't known his name, but Ben's interests in NASCAR and hockey were much more acceptable here in Indiana than they'd been in California.

This group of kids had a reputation for pranks and daredevil stunts. One boy was hobbling around in a cast from their attempt to ride one of the bulls at a local farm and they had dismantled one teacher's car and hung some of the parts from a tree like a huge children's mobile. Everyone knew they were responsible, but nothing could be proved. When they invited him, the other boys had made Ben swear not to tell anyone what they did. He didn't know what to expect that afternoon, but he thought he was ready for anything.

The scenery matched his mood as he walked through the city park in the September warmth. To one side sunlight glinted off the river, highlighting jumping fish and a flotilla of ducks. On his other side, brightly-colored birds hovered at the edge of the woods and squirrels came out from between the trees watching with interest, chattering happily as he passed by. Ben laughed to himself that he half expected Disney characters to show up and start singing.

When he arrived at Sam's house, half a dozen boys were already milling around the front lawn talking. After listening for a few moments, he realized they were discussing the best way to organize a séance. Ben assumed it was a theoretical debate, like arguing whether the Green Hornet could win a fight with Batman, until they began disagreeing about specifics as if they were deciding on a plan.

Half of the boys wanted everyone to chant, half wanted one person to lead. The boy wearing the cast from the bull riding incident suggested they do both. They took a vote and agreed they should have one person lead while everyone else chanted. Sam was elected as leader since it was his house. Unsure what to do, Ben hid behind another boy through the whole exchange and didn't vote. No one seemed to notice.

Ben thought the séance was a joke, 'razz the new guy', but he was relieved they were doing a prank instead of a stunt. He'd been worried the group might expect him to leap off a cliff or chase some poisonous creature. Instead, it looked like he just needed to be a good sport and play along.

Sam handed Ben a smudged copy of a page from a book before unlocking the storm doors on the side of the house and leading everyone down to the basement, a large open space with cement walls and floor containing a hodge-podge of mismatched furniture and stacks of old boxes.

Everyone else seemed to know what to do, as if they had done this many times before. Ben stood to one side, out of the way, while the other boys pushed a round table into the center of the room and placed a long purple cloth over it. He used the time to glance at the paper. It contained a sort of poem in verses, but the words weren't English except the title at the top. The title said *'Séance Spirits'*. Ben smiled as he folded the paper and put it in the back pocket of his jeans. They had obviously gone to some trouble to set this whole thing up. He wondered how many other people had been in his position. Maybe this was a standard initiation into the group.

When everyone started grabbing chairs, he took one too and expectantly found a place. Everyone set their hands on the table and the other boys began chanting. Ben smiled to himself when Sam started mumbling what seemed like random nonsense sounds.

No one else reacted when the table shook or the lights flickered, so Ben decided the whole thing must be a test to watch his response. He could see everyones' hands still in place, but he assumed they had rigged these effects for his benefit. Pleased with himself for not falling for the trick, he was disappointed afterward when no one congratulated him on his sophistication or explained how it had been done. Instead, they all wandered upstairs to raid the kitchen.

"You've done this before?" Sam asked, around a mouthful of oatmeal cookie.

Ben didn't know how to reply. If he said no he might seem inexperienced. If he said yes they might be less impressed with his lack of fear. He decided on non-committal.

"Just the usual stuff."

Sam nodded and finished his cookie, and Ben sighed inwardly with relief.

After the snack, one of the boys suggested they try to raise a demon and the others enthusiastically agreed.

"Is this what you usually do?" Ben asked. He was getting bored with the charade. He thought they'd be on to something else by now, but apparently his initiation wasn't over yet.

"Sometimes," Sam answered. "We've been doing this for a while. We haven't got this part to work yet, just the séance spirits."

So they aren't admitting to the trick, Ben thought. Fine, he could play along a while longer. "What are you going to do with the demon when you raise him?"

"See if we can get him to do stuff." Sam shrugged, then calmly chugged the rest of his can of Coke and followed the others back to the basement stairs.

At the bottom of the stairs, Ben peered cautiously into the darkness. The lamps were turned off and the only light came from tall white candles set about the room.

Very 'Haunted Mansion,' he thought, while he did a mental eye-roll.

The table and chairs from the séance were pushed to one side. In the middle of this open space on the cement floor; one of the other boys was drawing a chalk outline of a five-pointed star with a circle around it. Ben thought the boy's name was Brian, but he wasn't sure. His concern about making a good impression kept him from asking. The other boys took seats on the floor around the edge of the chalk circle, so he did the same.

Here we go again, he thought, looking around the room trying to figure out what would happen next. At first, he didn't notice when the other boys started chanting, but he pretended to follow along, still glancing around furtively. His mission was to monitor the room and puzzle out whatever trick they had planned. The others would be impressed with his cleverness, and Ben would be accepted as a permanent part of the group. This would result in a new social standing at school, more get-togethers, maybe even a date with Debbie Reller, the cute girl who sat in front of him in history class.

Ben was distracted from his musings by a breeze that began blowing his hair into his eyes. He looked for the source of the wind, but the only window was closed, and he remembered Sam shutting the door at the top of the stairs.

Ventilation system, he decided. Next he noticed a faint, noxious odor.

Dead animal in the ventilation system, he thought. Then he felt as much as heard a low humming that seemed to come from all directions.

Suddenly, all the candles blew out at once.

Ben wondered what he was supposed to do next, just as the other boys began whooping and cheering. Sam turned on the lights, and Ben saw everyone giving each other high-fives and punches in the shoulder.

"Was that cool or what?" Sam asked, putting his hand up for a high-five.

Ben slapped hands with Sam for lack of a better response and groped for something to say.

"So what happens now?" he finally asked.

"Now that he's here somewhere, we figure out how to talk to him. I've got a book. It probably says how in there." Sam casually picked up a rag and started wiping away the star on the floor. The other boys began moving the furniture back into place.

"Where'd you get the book?" Ben asked. His cockiness turned to nervousness as he realized he may have misunderstood what was going on.

"My uncle brought it back from Ireland. It shows how to talk to spirits, how to raise demons, how to keep fairies away. According to the book, fairies are mean little critters. I'm glad we don't have them here. We figured out the spirits, and then started trying demons."

Demons are less scary then fairies?

Ben nodded numbly, searching Sam's face for some sign that he was joking, but his host appeared to believe they really had been trying to raise a demon.

His thoughts bounced back and forth between disappointment and uneasiness. The disappointment was because his new friends were apparently crazy. He didn't think he believed in demons, but no sane person would try to keep one as a pet. The wonderful senior year he'd pictured was probably not going to happen. He'd have to find some other way to get Debbie Reller's attention because he would not be hanging out with this bunch anymore. Meanwhile, his uneasiness grew as he thought over all that had happened. If they were serious, then no one was trying to trick him. This might not have been a test after all.

This wasn't a prank. It was a daredevil stunt, literally.

The other boys roamed around the basement talking excitedly together, and Ben decided to get out of there before they started something else. Still trying to make sense of the afternoon's events, he said his distracted goodbyes and started home.

If no one was playing a trick, had spirits really lifted the table and made the lights flicker? Had they really raised a demon? If so, where was it now?

Ben kept telling himself he wasn't afraid. There was nothing to fear. He hadn't been frightened earlier and this was the same path home. He remembered the snappy, whistling walk on the way to Sam's house in the early afternoon. Now on the way home with the sun setting behind the woods, long shadows were draped across the path, and the river looked like cold, molten metal.

He wished he hadn't argued with his mother about bringing a coat as he trudged along in his short-sleeved t-shirt and jeans with the knees ripped out, hands in his pockets, trying to ignore the chill that raised goose bumps on his bare arms.

All the happy animals were gone, replaced by unexplained noises and half-observed movement between the trees at the edge of his vision. Instead of jumping fish, the river now produced vague plopping and sucking sounds. Something in the river glided to the surface and went back under, something awfully big for a fish. Ben fought the impression that whatever he'd seen in the river was pacing him, watching, waiting. Now he could hear something slithering along the muddy bank of the river slightly behind him to his left. He didn't dare turn around and look. Instead he picked up his pace.

This is silly, Ben thought. It's just my imagination. I'm just spooked.

Something was in the trees. He noticed movement out of the corner of his eye and decided to ignore it. At least the slithering noise along the bank of the river had stopped, but now he was certain something was watching him from the woods. He mustered the courage to glance in that direction and thought he saw two eyes glaring back at him. He quickly looked away and decided to focus on his feet and the path directly in front of him.

Just one of the squirrels, he thought. The eyes were too big for a squirrel.

OK, it was a deer. They were glaring. Do deer glare?

Maybe he's rabid. Ben decided to ask when he got home about rabid deer and what other animals might live in the woods. Meanwhile, he picked up his pace again.

Head down, he trudged around a turn to the right and could now hear traffic noise in the distance. Looking up, he saw cars darting across the end of the path only a hundred yards away. Ben had always thought it corny when people kissed the ground, but he was seriously considering planting one on that pavement. No, that was silly. This was a small town. He had to watch his step or risk trashing his reputation. And there had never been a reason to be scared. He slowed his pace and started whistling. The knots in his stomach began to release. Why had he been so tense?

Then he heard a faint rumbling noise. He paused with hands still in his pockets and stopped whistling. The noise came again, a low growling from the trees at the edge of the woods. Without thinking, Ben looked in that direction and definitely saw glaring eyes, this time much closer and more menacing.

Reputation be damned, he took off running. He sprinted for his life toward the cars, toward civilization, toward normalcy. Behind him to his right, he could hear something running through the woods toward him. The clopping noise it was making sounded like a horse galloping.

Just before the street, the woods converged with the path. Ben was sure that whatever was in the trees planned to get there first and grab him as he ran by. Adrenaline kicked in, and he ran so hard his lungs burned. He didn't dare slow down as he reached the end of the path for fear of ambush, and he deliberately avoided even a glance toward his pursuer. With enormous relief, he made it to the end of the path and didn't begin slowing until he reached the pavement. He tried to stop then, but two flailing steps took him across the sidewalk and into traffic. The impact registered somewhere in his mind as he lost consciousness.

Ben woke in a bed with railings, wearing only a backless gown and a thigh-high cast on his left leg. He quickly realized he was in a hospital. Looking around the room, he saw his parents and a man in a police uniform. They all came forward when they saw he was conscious. Ben was nervous when he saw the policeman, wondering what trouble he was in.

"Ben, you're awake!" His mother said.

"Hi Mom. Dad," Ben said, smiling lamely. He glanced at the policeman, waiting for someone to explain his presence.

"What were you thinking, running into a busy street like that?" his mother asked. "You could have been killed."

He didn't have a good answer, so he said nothing. *I thought a demon was chasing me* didn't seem like the right response.

The policeman stepped forward. "Ben, I'm Officer Reynolds. I have a few questions for you, if you don't mind."

'If you don't mind,' that was a good start. Ben might not be in trouble after all, and the man looked vaguely familiar. He smiled and nodded.

"Were you running away from something? Did something frighten you?"

Ben stopped smiling. He had no idea how to answer that so decided not to, at least not until he could come with a reasonable-sounding story. "I don't remember. Why? Did something happen?"

Officer Reynolds blew out a breath before replying. "Do you know a boy named Brian Granger? He's in your class at school."

Ben nodded. He remembered this was the name of the boy who had drawn the chalk symbols on Sam's basement floor.

"Brian was found dead on that same path about two hours ago," Officer Reynolds said.

Ben and his parents gasped.

"I thought you wanted to ask about the car accident," his father said. "What happened to this other boy?"

"That's what we're trying to figure out. From what we've pieced together so far, it looks like someone or something chased him into the river and he drowned. Except Brian was on the swim team, and the current in the river isn't very strong. He also had some strange bruises and fresh burns on his body. Since Ben was picked up in the same area…" He let the rest of the sentence hang and looked pointedly at Ben. His parents followed the officer's gaze and stared expectantly at him also.

Now on the hot seat, Ben felt somehow responsible for what had happened to Brian. He couldn't think of a reason why the events of the afternoon were his fault, but felt culpable just the same. He tried not to squirm or do anything else to look guilty, but he didn't think he succeeded.

Trying to get his mind around what he'd just heard, he suddenly remembered the séance paper in his pocket and wondered how much the officer knew. "Brian and me and some other boys spent the afternoon at Sam's house," he said, as he started to perspire. "I don't know what happened to him. He was still there when I left."

Then he realized why the policeman looked familiar. "Sam's last name is Reynolds, too. Do you know him?"

"I have a nephew Sam that lives near the other end of the park. It must be the same boy." Officer Reynolds nodded. "I guess I'll be heading there next."

"Sam mentioned an uncle," Ben said coldly as he met the man's eyes. The adults seemed surprised by his change of tone, but if this was the same uncle that had supplied the occult book, then this was the person he thought should be held responsible. He wondered whether Sam's uncle had given him the book as a joke or whether he intended the boys to experiment.

Maybe the boys had pulled a stunt after he left that resulted in Brian's death. Maybe there really was a demon. He wondered how the town would react when the whole story came out, and then realized he didn't want to know. Either way, this place was a disaster.

He wondered how long it would take to hitchhike back to California with a broken leg.

A Change of Plans
Neil McCabe

Henry parks his company truck in the equipment yard and clambers out, his sweat-drenched shirt clinging to his back. He wants to go straight home and take a shower. But he needs to swing by Raley's to pick up enough groceries for dinner tonight and breakfast and lunch tomorrow.

At least his car, an old AMC Pacer, has AC. He needs it now. He needs it in the company truck, too, but his boss, Rocky, is such a tightwad! He says Henry doesn't need AC in a truck he's jumping in and out of all day. That's easy for Rocky to say, sitting on his butt in the air-conditioned office.

With the Pacer's AC set on high, Henry drives to Raley's. There aren't any shady spaces in the shimmering parking lot. He knows he can't blame that on Rocky, but he'd like to. It would be like Rocky to save money by not planting trees.

Henry hasn't adjusted to grocery shopping by himself. Mom had always made the decisions, based on menus she'd planned for a week. He just pushed the cart and stood beside her while she chatted with the checkers. He'd nod as she explained her recipes and ingredient choices. When eyes began to roll in the line behind them, he would gently touch her arm. "Mom," he would say, to sighs of appreciation.

Henry's father dropped out of sight when Henry was ten, but he and his mother stayed together for protection until she died two years ago. Henry is forty-seven now. He still gets angry and fearful when he thinks about his father. What if he's still alive? What if he shows up again? Henry tells himself such questions are ridiculous after all these years. But he can't shake the old feelings.

Halfway across the parking lot Henry notices a woman in his path attempting to park. The space is blocked by an abandoned shopping cart. He waves, signaling his intention, and hurriedly moves the cart out of her way. She rolls down her window and says "Thanks! What a gentleman!" He can't think of a reply. His face flushes, and he shrugs.

As he pushes the cart towards the store, he realizes, too late, that a petition circulator is directly ahead. He chides himself for not noticing her sooner. He's usually alert to avoid solicitors – girl scouts selling cookies, kids giving away puppies, Lions Club members with miniature white canes, and Salvation Army bell-ringers. He skirts them or eases his passage by folding a dollar bill and having it ready to squeeze into the kettle slot. But the circulator is already moving toward him. He tries to avoid eye contact, but she thrusts the petition towards him.

"Can I have your signature?"

"Uh," he says, feeling trapped and clumsy. "No."

He steps around her, waits to allow a young mother and child to enter the store ahead of him, and pushes his cart inside.

He puts bread, cereal, milk, and cheese in his cart. A woman stocking shelves asks if he's finding everything. He says yes, but her question makes him wonder if he looks lost and confused.

He dreads checking out. The checkers always ask questions like, 'How's your day going?' Could he say, I've been outnumbered and surrounded by the enemy, but I gave 'em hell, told 'em to Bug Out! Ha ha? No way. He couldn't attempt a joke about his exterminator job with Bug Out, Inc.

What if the checker asks if he has plans for the weekend? He wishes he could wink and say, I sure do, but they can be changed. How about you? The truth is, he'll just be cleaning his cat's litter box and doing laundry.

He steers his cart to the shortest line, bracing for the inevitable questions. When it's his turn, the checker glances in his direction and says, "Did you find everything OK?"

Henry's mind races, and he stammers, "I won't know until I get home."

It's true, but did he have to admit it? He wishes he could be glib. He tells himself he'll be ready for the bagger's question, Paper or plastic?

He swipes his debit card and enters his PIN.

The bagger turns to him. "Is it hot enough for you?"

"Paper," Henry says.

The bagger gives him a "What the hell?" look before reaching for the paper bags. Henry's ears burn and he wishes he were invisible. It's too late to say, 'It's a scorcher.' He declines help out with his groceries. He doesn't want to struggle with conversation in the parking lot.

The steering wheel feels like the business end of a branding iron. He alternates hands to keep from burning them until the AC cools things down. He avoids traffic by driving around to the back of the store, past a delivery truck backed up to the loading dock, out the rear exit and then to Bruce Road. He turns north on Bruce and cruises through the parched golden-brown fields on the east edge of town.

As he passes Humboldt Road and prepares to stop at the Highway 32 signal, he tunes in the news. A Cal Fire spokeswoman is announcing that the fire danger is extreme. There's been no rain since late February, and, although it's early June, the danger is as high as in August. Henry wonders how quickly a fire would burn across the hills and what Cal Fire's response would be. How would the war be waged against the flames? His home is in the flight path from the Municipal Airport, and he never tires of watching the fire-fighting planes. He pictures a spotter plane orbiting overhead, strategically directing air tankers and ground crews.

No lightning storms are forecast. If there's a fire, there will be a human cause. Someone might toss a cigarette out a car window or park over dry grass and ignite it with the car's catalytic converter. Or someone might leave a campfire unattended. Or hit a rock and strike a spark while mowing weeds. It could be accidental. Like it was when he was a six-year old, before his father disappeared.

He sees himself playing with the book of matches. He tears off a match, strikes it, and drops it before it burns his fingers. A small tuft of dry grass catches fire, but he easily stomps it out. He tears out another and strikes it. He holds it too close to the open book. The book explodes in a flash, and he drops it. The grass around him bursts into flames, too fierce to stomp out! He runs home calling, Mom! Acres burn before the fire trucks come and put the fire out. He cowers in his room until his father comes home and finds him.

"What the hell did you do this time?"

Silence.

"Stand up, you stupid little son of a bitch!"

Henry stands, head hanging, knees shaking.

"Answer me, damn you!"

"I – I didn't know a little fire could turn into a big fire," Henry says.

His father backhands him in the mouth, knocks him to the floor, his cut lip bleeding, swelling.

"That's a sample of what you'll get if you pull a stunt like that again!"

A horn honks. The signal has turned green. Henry lurches forward; embarrassed he's been inattentive, lost in memories.

A week later he's in Raley's again, filling his cart, looking for ingredients for Mom's vegetarian pizza. He locates the tomato paste near a checker stocking shelves and maneuvers his cart past her, hoping she won't speak.

She looks up and smiles. Her uniform shirt and pants don't flatter her pear-shape. She wears no jewelry and no makeup, but her smile makes her almost pretty. He returns it, glances at her nametag, "Marylou," and continues down the aisle.

The next ingredient, canned, quartered artichoke hearts, isn't on aisle 7D where it used to be. He searches all the aisles, crisscrossing the store and passing several employees. It's irritating that things aren't laid out logically and as soon as he learns where an item is, it will be moved to a different aisle. He resents management's manipulation, forcing him to look all over the store so he might see something he hadn't considered and buy it on impulse.

He searches the aisles again, including the one where Marylou is still stocking shelves. She glances up and smiles. Something about her makes him feel comfortable.

"Can I ask a question?"

"Yes, you can," Marylou says, standing. "Whew. Feels good to straighten up. I was getting a crick in my back." She smiles again.

"Where are the artichokes? The canned ones. They aren't in the usual place."

"They've been moved to 8A. Don't ask me why," she says, shrugging. "It's a new brand, too. Different color can. I'll show you."

"Oh, you don't need to do that."

"It's no trouble," she says, starting toward aisle 8.

Another week has passed and Henry is looking for Marylou. She isn't stocking shelves or checking. He's surprised to feel disappointed. When he's ready to check out, he sees her helping another checker bag groceries. He gets in that line, agonizing over what to say if the checker asks questions. He wants to catch Marylou's eye. But he fumbles with his debit card and has to enter his PIN twice. He feels like a klutz and avoids looking at her. He intends to grab his cart and hurry out, but she starts pushing it towards the door.

"You don't need to –"

"I need some fresh air. Which way is your car?"

"Over there," he says, pointing. "It's a –"

"I see it. That tan car, right? I remember you and your mom driving that old car. Kind of a classic, isn't it?"

"Yes, well, I guess. It's a '75 Pacer. Caramel Tan," he says. "It was Mom's."

"You don't see them anymore."

"It's probably the only one in town. The last year AMC made them was 1980. Now AMC doesn't even exist."

"There's something about its shape that makes it look friendly," she says.

"Rounded, overweight, and shiny on top," he says. "Kind of like me," he adds, patting his balding head and immediately feeling embarrassed.

When they reach the car, Marylou looks at him and says, "Henry, you don't have –"

"How do you know my name?" he says, scratching his head.

"We're encouraged to call our customers by name. It comes up on the computer when you use your debit card."

Henry watches as she loads a bag into the car. She isn't really much overweight. And her smooth, round face looks pleasant, even when she isn't smiling.

"Anyway, what I was going to say is you don't have to answer those questions in the checkout line. No one will be offended. It's just a script. We're supposed to act friendly. We speak our parts. Your part is to come back and buy more groceries."

They reach for the last bag at the same time, each saying, "I'll get it," then pulling back. They smile at each other as he takes the bag and she turns the cart toward the store.

He thinks her eyes are green like his. He wants to take a closer look.

When Henry reports for work the following Friday, Rocky waves him into his office.

"Take a look at this," Rocky says, shoving a handwritten letter across the desk.

Henry quickly reads the letter:

Dear Bug Out, Inc.,
    Here is my payment for your services, and I want to thank you for your good work. Your man, Harry or Henry? did above and beyond what I expected. He even repaired the trellis on my front porch. So, I wanted you to know you have a good employ there,
                                    Sincerly,
                                      Harriet Stockton

"What's wrong with this picture, Henry?"
"What do you mean, Rocky?"
"I mean, what's wrong with this picture? You do understand English, don't you?"
Henry feels his face getting hot.
"Well, there's a couple of misspellings. Is that what you mean?" Henry says.
"No, that is not what I mean," Rocky says, wagging his head from side to side in rhythm with his words. "You were not hired to fix trellises, and I was not paid for your work fixing that trellis. Was I?"
"Well, I guess not, but – "
Rocky waves Henry to silence. "I don't want you doing extra work we aren't paid for," he says. "I want you to hustle your fat ass to the next job we are getting paid for."
"But it only took a couple of minutes, and she's a nice lady –"
"I don't give a damn how nice she is," Rocky says. "Nice doesn't pay my bills."

Henry feels a rush of anger. He barely stops himself from saying, 'You wouldn't know anything about being nice, you son of a bitch!' He stands mute. Rocky rifles through papers on his desk as if Henry isn't in the room. Henry is horrified when he realizes he is clenching his fists. He has to control himself. Rocky could fire him, and he needs the job. He has to take the abuse. To keep taking it. Like he took it from his father. Rocky even looks like his father, with his puffy red face and ham hands. He unclenches his fists, backs out the office door, turns and hurries outside.

The wind feels like a blowtorch. Gusts rock the truck as he drives to his jobs. He finishes several termite inspections, but one of his service calls is to spray a previously inspected home. He can't complete that job. It's too windy. Rocky will be pissed if he finds out, but there's no way Henry is going to jeopardize his customer or the neighbors with chemical drift. He'll squeeze that job into his schedule somehow, on a calm day. He'll work through his lunch hour if necessary.

Henry turns on the radio as he drives to the next job. Temperatures are near one hundred, and the fire hazard is extremely high again, especially in the Town of Paradise, on the ridge above Chico. That's where Rocky lives, in the manzanita and pines, in the "castle" he's always bragging about.

For years there have been fears fire would roar up the canyons to Paradise. There isn't a good escape route if a fire closes The Skyway, the main access road. Thousands of people could be trapped. It would serve Rocky right if he were trapped and his castle was incinerated. It's too big a house anyway, a mansion, compared to the two-bedroom, single-bath house Henry has always lived in. Of course, a major fire could be tragic for everyone else in the area. But if the fire started in the right place, maybe off Humboldt Road, and the wind were from the north, like today, the fire would go directly toward Rocky's isolated area on the outskirts of the Town. It would probably be put out long before it reached his house, much less anyone else's house, because Cal Fire would immediately throw everything it had at it. But Rocky would have a big scare.

Rocky thinks he's so invincible! He probably hasn't cleared the recommended "defensible space" around his house. He probably still has a shake roof! Henry laughs as he pictures Rocky frantically spraying his roof with a puny garden hose.

When Henry finishes his service calls and starts back to the equipment yard, he decides to pick up a few groceries. It's against the rules to use company trucks for personal errands, but so what? Raley's is right on his route. It would be stupid to just drive right by. On the other hand, if he stops, and Rocky finds out, there'd be hell to pay. Rocky might fire him.

He changes his mind and drives straight to the Bug Out yard, parks the truck and gets in his old Pacer. It burns him up to kowtow to that jerk and drive the extra three miles back to Raley's, wasting time and gas.

He sees Marylou when he enters the store, but she doesn't acknowledge him. There's a long line at her register, typical for a Friday evening. Maybe she didn't see him.

He decides to barbeque on his Weber grill. Sit in his folding lawn chair in the backyard. Have a beer. Or two. Or the whole six-pack, if he wants to.

He picks out a New York steak, Sierra Nevada Pale Ale, lettuce, cherry tomatoes, a cucumber and green onions for a salad. He's not sure he has enough charcoal briquettes. He puts a bag in his cart. His eye is drawn to the starter fluid. Maybe he should get a can of that, too. And a box of kitchen matches, the long ones with sturdy wooden sticks. The kind you can strike on the sandpaper on the side of the box, or almost anywhere else. Even on your Levi's. Bend your knee and pull your leg up so your pants are tight on the underside of your thigh. A quick flick, and Poof! That was a little macho trick of his father's that Henry secretly imitated. He puts the starter fluid and matches in the cart.

There aren't enough baggers to help Marylou at her register, and she still has a long line. He considers using the quick-checkout but decides to wait for Marylou. He watches as she sweeps groceries across the scanner, smiling and chatting with customers, ringing them up, and bagging their groceries.

When it's his turn, she gives him a smile but says nothing and goes right to work. When she finishes scanning, she says, "I know. Paper."

As she loads the heavy items first and puts the produce gently on top, Henry confirms she isn't wearing a ring.

She leaves the bag of briquettes in the cart, and nods toward it. "Do you have plans for the weekend?" she says.

He feels strangely bold.

"Yes," he says, "but I could change them."

She gives him a questioning look but says nothing.

He thinks he sees her raise an eyebrow.

She looks down and takes out her ballpoint pen. She marks something on the receipt. Henry wonders if she circled his "savings" or wrote, "Thanks for shopping at Raley's." She drops the receipt in the bag without a word.

He assumes her silence and raised eyebrow are disapproval of his dumb remark. He picks up the bag, takes the briquettes out of the cart, and leaves it behind. He hurries out the door and through the parking lot with thoughts swirling in his lowered head.

What was I thinking? That she was interested in me? That she was interested in my plans? She seemed different, but now she's used one of those scripted lines. I fell for it. She smiles at all her customers. She's like all the rest of them, following orders. Screw orders!

He puts the groceries on the passenger seat and tosses the briquettes on the floor. He jams the Pacer in gear and short-cuts across the parking lot instead of up the row. He bounces out the rear driveway onto his normal route and up Bruce Road. Then, almost before realizing it, he veers onto Humboldt Road.

Humboldt is only lightly used. It runs roughly parallel to the newer Highway 32 through the rock and oak-studded hills a few miles until the two roads merge. The Pacer rattles and shakes as Henry winds up the road, with 32 sometimes in view on his left and sometimes not. He stops a half-mile before the merge, where he can't be seen from the Highway.

He leans across the seat to roll down the passenger window, eases out of the driver's seat, and walks around the car. The hot wind takes his breath away. He looks up and down Humboldt. No cars are in sight. He reaches through the open window and lifts the fluid and matches out of the bag. He takes a match out of the box. He crosses the bare shoulder and walks to a patch of dry grass. He squirts fluid on the patch and in a line back to the shoulder. There are still no cars in sight. He strikes the match on his Levis, touches it to the end of the line, and jumps into his car as the flames snake away. He drives uphill to the merge with 32 feeling exhilarated, his heart pounding. He stops at the merge intersection and looks both ways.

A Highway Patrol cruiser is coming down the hill, headed towards Chico. He tells himself to act natural. Don't panic. The officer couldn't have seen him setting the fire. The fire can't be seen from this location. He waits for the cruiser to swoosh past. He turns in behind it, keeping his distance and driving the speed limit. He has a sick realization the Pacer itself might draw attention, but he reminds himself its color is an inconspicuous tan. He keeps glancing to his left, towards Humboldt. He can't see any smoke, not even when he's nearly adjacent to the place he'd set the fire. Maybe it hasn't caught.

Yes, it has! There it is. A thin plume of smoke you wouldn't notice unless you knew exactly where to look. The officer hasn't seen it. The cruiser continues straight down 32 toward town. Henry relaxes his grip on the Pacer's steering wheel and grins, thinking how panicked Rocky will soon be. When he gets back down to Bruce Road, he turns north and resumes his normal route home.

He pulls the Pacer into his carport, suddenly wishing he had a garage he could close. He takes his groceries inside. He'll unload them and then watch for smoke and planes while he barbeques in the backyard. When he lifts the Pale Ale out of the bag, the receipt flutters to the floor. He stoops to pick it up and sees Marylou's handwriting next to his thumb.

He sags as he reads her note, and then stiffens.

He rushes to the backyard hoping he won't see smoke, hoping the fire hasn't really caught. But the plume is darker and bigger than he expects, more ominous than he wants now. He hears sirens in the distance and the familiar twin-engine drone of the spotter plane passing overhead.

Henry sinks into his folding chair. He doesn't look up at the plane. He re-reads the note. It is a phone number followed by "Call if you want to change your plans."

Section VII:
Canine Companions and Feline Friends

If I have any beliefs about immortality it is that certain dogs I know will go to heaven, and very few people.

James Thurber

Do Dogs have Souls?
Melanie Johnston

I am keenly attached to my dogs. One is a large female—a nine-year-old, Bernese mountain dog, named Abby. The other is tiny—a five-year-old, clownish, femme fatale, pug named Floyde. They are about as opposite as they can be except when it comes to the importance of food. On that subject, they unequivocally agree.

Sometimes someone will ask me if I believe my dogs have a soul. It causes me to pause. I do believe my dogs have a soul, I think, I guess, I bet. I mean, well, they both have personalities, they both communicate albeit not in verbs and pronouns and they both love, truly, deeply love. Does that constitute a soul?

What is a soul, exactly, anyhow? Is it something that lives, breathes, feels pain, joy, reproduces and dies? Or? If there's one place that will know how to define souls, it's the Bible, so I dig into the oldest book not knowing where to begin except with the elusive word: soul.

Job tosses out this, "Ask the animals and they will teach you; ask the birds of the air, and they will tell you; ask the plants of the Earth and they will show you; and the fish of the sea will declare to you. Who among all these does not know that the hand of the Lord has done this? In His hand is the soul of every living thing." I ask my dogs to teach me as Job instructs, they say only with their eyes, "Feed me."

I search scholars. Albert Schweitzer says, "Hear our prayer O Lord…for animals that are overworked, underfed and cruelly treated; for all wistful creatures in captivity that beat their wings against bars; for any that are hunted or lost or deserted or frightened or hungry; for all that must be put to death…and for those who deal with them we ask a heart of compassion and gentle hands and kindly words." Hmm. Now it would appear without reading too much into that paragraph that Schweitzer believes animals feel more than just pain. Maybe?

Perhaps it starts to address the soul argument or perhaps it depends on your state of mind. If you're connected to your animals, like I am, well, of course that logically leads you to conclude, Schweitzer agrees with the "Soul Theory." But others might argue, "He just wants people to treat animals kindly." They have a point.

In fact, the English word animal is derived from a Latin word 'anime' that means, what else: soul. Did animals come to be called "animals" randomly, accidentally, whimsically? That's a little too coincidental, wouldn't you agree?

The author Anne Tyler once said, "I've always thought a hotel ought to offer optional small animals…I mean a cat to sleep on your bed at night, or a dog of some kind to act pleased when you come in. You ever notice how a hotel room feels so lifeless?" If something feels lifeless, couldn't that be thought of as soulless? Or is that splitting dog hairs?

Even Napoleon at the end of his days, when he was exiled to St. Helena, wrote in his final book that he was most moved when he saw a dog loyally licking a wounded soldier on a battlefield where other humans had left the soldier to die. This is Napoleon, one of the bloodiest generals in history rhapsodizing about a steadfast canine. Maybe only a devoted animal could touch the soft side of his warrior soul?

St. Francis of Assisi surely believed that animals have a soul. In fact, many churches hold a formal blessing for all vintages every October in his honor. Those churches must believe there's something to bless, right? No? My mind battles.

I dabble back into the Old Testament. Isn't the entire Bible an argument about what happens to souls? In Ecclesiastes, I bump into a passage that reads, "For the fate of humans and the fate of animals is the same; as one dies, so dies the other. They all have the same breath. Humans have no advantage over the animals; for all is vanity."

Ahh, that's clear, mostly, sort of, somewhat. But does that mean rats have the same soul that a dog has? Are cats in the same league? Or elephants, whales, polar bears – all the cute, popular animals the same as all the ugly, unpopular ones? Do we have the same soul that a dog has just a different brainpower? Do we all end up in the same sphere once again somewhere else in the Universe? It seems to me to say, yes, rats, dogs, mice and men are all the same. They live, they breathe, they die and they have souls while they're doing it. Possibly?

My heart palpitates. I'm getting a headache thinking about Abby's big soul and Floyde's tinier one. I'm tired of reading the Bible – did you notice that it never seems to end – besides my dogs are imploring me with soulful eyes that it's time to put that book down and go for a walk. I put Soul Train on my iPod and grab the leashes.

As I gaze up at the powdery sky while they sniff the bottom of a straggly bush, I'm glad I put that dog soul question to rest, kind of, sort of, somewhat, who knows?

You see, a year ago, I came close to dying of encephalitis. No, I don't know how I got it. Yet, even in my semi-conscious state, I kept hoping I'd see everyone I loved again, somewhere, some time, in some form, in this world or another. And one difficult afternoon, when words were too puzzling to speak, somehow through the fog I heard the click of tiny claws from small paws on the hospital linoleum floor and then felt them lying next to me, in the ICU bed which managed to bring me back to Earth and reminded me not only of the people I love, but of the souls.

Real life never lets you down.

Farewell, Thompson
Lorilyn Parmer

Last Thursday afternoon, our beloved black lab departed this world. Thompson's head rested in my lap as he breathed his last breath. Ten years with us, then gone in a moment. As I hugged him one final time and left his still body behind, I felt the familiar emptiness that comes with loss. I also was filled with love and gratitude. It wasn't until he had left us that I fully appreciated all we had learned from him. Our lives had truly been enriched by his presence.

Thompson had lived with cancer for the last four months, but you would never know it. He pulled through emergency surgery, and, defying his bleak prognosis, continued to revel in excursions to the beach and the snow, romps in local fields, and walks in our neighborhood green belts. We all knew his time with us was running out. Even as he slowed down, he remained upbeat, inquisitive, and affectionate. We cherished his noble, goofy presence even more, and took note of the lessons he was teaching us.

Thompson was no ordinary dog. An un-neutered male, he had a dream job as a stud for Guide Dogs for the Blind. He mated with dozens of dogs over his career. At home this alpha male was mellow and sweet; he would purr like a cat when we stroked his head and scratched behind his ears. He embraced his contradictions: he was genteel and rambunctious, attentive and oblivious, independent and totally devoted. He took great pleasure in this world and seemed linked to another. At a favorite beach on Monterey Bay, he would sometimes stop at the surf's edge, stand with his nose in the air, and gaze out over the water, as if he were connecting with something over the horizon. As we watched him we often had a sense he knew something we didn't know.

Until the day he died, Thompson continued to live in the moment, fully engaged with the delights and mysteries of the world. He relished his favorite activities--nuzzling his dearest humans, lapping up juice from tuna cans, and of course sniffing and peeing on every rock, shrub and lamppost he encountered. No doubt about it, he left his mark on the world.

Thompson was bred and raised to be a service dog, to partner with visually impaired people and help them lead active, fulfilling lives. He was trained to provide guidance and companionship to the blind. He never served in a harness because he was selected to work in the Guide Dogs breeding program, to pass on his sterling attributes to future generations. Yet even though his gifts and talents led him to another job, he was still **our** guide dog. With sensitivity and compassion, Thompson saw us through failures and successes, joys and disappointments, hilarious and harrowing adventures, and illnesses and deaths.

He connected with others easily and eagerly. Every time the doorbell rang, he would leap up and bark excitedly about who or what was coming his way. Wherever he went, this dog expected the best from everyone he met. With tail wagging he would seek attention, affection, and tasty treats. He often got all three. When he met up with someone he knew and cared about, he'd show his enthusiasm by dancing a distinctive jig, whimpering, and wiggling with abandon.

Thompson's love was unconditional. When you were with him it was clear that he accepted you for who you were. He didn't care about what you did or didn't do today. He didn't get mad or hold grudges, and he was a master at letting go. If he did something he thought might displease you (like sneak a snack of cat poop), he would creep back and grovel for forgiveness, then happily accept it and move on.

"Tommy Tom" Thompson was a legend at Guide Dogs for the Blind, not just because of his impressive production (270 puppies and innumerable grandpuppies), but because of his handsome face, his easy-going temperament, and his capacity to bounce back from adversity, ever sunny and eager to please.

When Thompson collapsed at home that morning, I feared the worst. With heavy hearts my twelve-year-old son Quinn and I gently loaded him into the car for the trip to the Guide Dogs veterinary clinic. The two of them shared the back seat, with Thompson wrapped in blankets and nestled against Quinn's side.

I wasn't surprised when the vet told us his prospects looked grim. Still, it's funny how you can be prepared for bad news, and still be shocked by it. Thompson was dying, and she recommended that we ease him over the threshold by administering drugs. Tears streaming down my face, I asked her, "Is there really nothing else we can do, no other way?" I asked myself, who am I to make this decision about when his life will end? Maybe it is the right thing to do…yet how can something so right feel so wrong? The word spread through the Guide Dogs campus. In his final hour, there was a stream of visitors who came to comfort us, pet him, and bid him farewell. Clearly Tommy Tom didn't belong to us alone.

Quinn and I were with him at the end. As we joined Thompson in an exam room, his tail thumped the floor – his way of saying, so glad you're here. Revived a bit by IV fluids, he eagerly gobbled the food we offered. It was excruciating to serve him what would be his last meal. How can I have agreed to end his life this afternoon? My head said it was the right thing to do, but my heart wailed, Noooo. As the vet came in with the syringes, Thompson seemed calm and loving as ever. He gazed at me as he laid his big head in my lap, his brown eyes full of trust and understanding. Quinn leaned down for a nuzzle and Thompson licked his face. Quinn caressed him and whispered, "It's OK, buddy, I love you forever."

It was heart breaking to say goodbye. Quinn was a toddler when Thompson joined the family and can't remember life without him. "I love him so much," he sobbed. "He understands me better than anyone else ever has and ever will…Why, why, why does he have to go?"

There are no easy answers for such profound questions. Death is an indisputable part of life. Love almost always leads to loss, and loss brings pain. Our family is fortunate that we had Thompson to teach us that love also brings solace and joy. He showed us the art of opening up and letting go. I'm sure he would want us all to move on, tails wagging. We'll cherish our many memories of the big guy and nurture a new place in our heart for Aqua, a lovely young black lab who joined the family last fall.

After we left Thompson that final day, Quinn and I walked down to the puppy kennels. We spent half an hour romping with a litter of his grandpuppies: adorable, eight-week old black labs. Soon they would be leaving the kennels and going to families who would raise them, love them, and let them go. This is also Thompson's legacy: hundreds, then thousands, of dogs who will guide, comfort and teach their human companions.

So farewell Thompson, rambling explorer and stud extraordinaire, faithful companion and loving playmate, wise teacher and understanding friend. We will honor you by living as you did – with curiosity, compassion, and unbounded enthusiasm. And we will pass on the lessons you taught us: to live in the present, appreciating each day as if it's our last…to give generously and delight in serving others…to greet every stranger as a potential friend… and to practice giving and receiving the gift of unconditional love.

We're grateful for the years we had with you. And we'll miss you. As we move forward in our lives, we will remember to lift our heads, sniff the air, and look out to sea, wondering what's over the horizon.

Girl with a Secret Comes Home
Laura Kaufman

The vet looked perplexed. "Would you please hold out your cat, tummy up, like this?" she gestured. She did a quick tail-end exam, then kept looking the cat over from stem to stern. She still appeared puzzled. "Hold your kitty out again, please," she said, and I did. My anxiety grew. Kitty stayed remarkably grounded.

What was ailing my beautiful silver-haired writing buddy, my lovely muse, my giant Maine Coon, best friend of my son? She had been with us for nearly eight years, and was always as healthy as a very small, fluffy horse. But today, she didn't feel like herself. I didn't feel too great, either.

Since the day we met, this animal had been an indispensable member of our family. We adopted Sterling right after I bought her a place to live – when we moved from our downtown apartment with the huge deck to my condo in the tall pines, a few miles away.

It was love at first sight at the Pet Grocery store on cat adoption day. This was a momentous occasion – my son was a third-grader and we had been pet-less for a couple of years since the divorce. My parents got custody of our cats, which happily relocated to Seattle. There, they got to go outside, eat bugs, and throw them up again.

So, this was a fresh beginning. I even brought my camera in case we had a "first meeting" photo for the album.

And we did. Looking at the beautiful kittens in the cages from Community Concern for Cats, we were mesmerized. I was almost afraid to bond with any of the little faces peering out from their wire cubes because I knew I would want to take all of them home. But this was to be Teddy's cat.

John, the gregarious owner of that place, now out of business, watched us ponder. He held forth on the virtues of a kitten vs. a grown cat. But then he said, "Now, for a great pet, that one up there, that would be a great housecat." He pointed to the other side of the store, where all the carpeted cat trees were growing like a beige, maroon and blue forest. On the tallest one was a proud gray longhaired tiger, uncaged, with a studded red leather collar, presiding over the store. He called her over, wiggling his fingers, and inviting, "Sterling! Come on down." Apparently, it was Sterling's forest.

My son's head rotated to the cat trees and froze.

She leaped down, with an agile downhill grace, and sauntered over. They locked eyes. Cat flopped over on her side to be petted by third-grader. I got this on film, and the orange skateboard logo on the sleeve of my son's T-shirt reflected the light of the flash. Sterling's thick, soft coat was about a dozen shades of frosted silver, with faint stripes, and felt like warm silk. Her green eyes were wide and intelligent, and she clearly had a sense of humor. She regarded Teddy approvingly. She was so cool.

You guessed it. "Can we really have this one, mom?" asked Teddy, in that kind of voice that strains with monumental importance.

I was surprised that this cat was adoptable, figuring she was on the store payroll, and probably had work to do in the back. And though I had planned to take home a kitten, I could see that the decision was out of my hands.

Yes, the big fluffy gray girl could come home with us. We looked at her paperwork: spayed female, approx. 2 years old, feral, from Martinez. Has shots. I signed a check, and the excitement that followed was enhanced by choosing cat dishes, the litter box, just the right food for a two-year-old, and a couple of sparkly toys that even I found attractive. We were on our way.

I felt as if an important foundation was being laid in our family – not one that would make up for the divorce, but one that was full of promise, excitement, and the potential for a bond that would make coming home from school such fun for my son. Perhaps this cat would absorb some secrets, and maybe some tears.

Being a cat person already, I knew Sterling would also provide moving sculpture in our new place, probably an ample dose of humor, and definitely some comfort.

Sterling was soon the "it" factor in our house, doing interesting things and creating mysteries all the time. What would she eat? Where would she choose to sleep? She investigated all of the brown U-Haul moving boxes, and sought the top floor of any stack. She helped find stuff in closets, and shot toy mice under the old avocado-green fridge. She liked workmen and visitors, especially the UPS guy.

I bought her a wicker "in" box for my desk so her tail wouldn't drape over the keyboard. We began what would be years of a great working relationship. This has endured even since our second kitty arrived, with her own veil of mystery and elegance, punctuated by hairballs.

Seven contented years went slowly by, and the third-grader entered middle school, and then became a freshman in high school. Sterling was still his baby, and I have a series of photos that show how he grew while she looked remarkably the same. Now, she can sit on his lap, instead of overflowing his little-boy legs and filling an entire chair.

So when the day arrived recently that Sterling didn't feel well, it was a shock. She circled around and mewed, and would lie down, then get up, then lie down again. She clearly didn't know what to do with herself.

I decided it was time to get a new vet, and chose a group nearby. Loading Sterling into the blue plastic and wire travel cage upset us both, but we made it and were welcomed by an earnest-faced Dr. Lee, a sweet and professional vet in a white coat. Dr. Lee explained that she liked to take a long time examining each new animal, and she handled Sterling expertly, running her hands over her neck, chest, under her ribs, feeling her abdomen, and checking the cat's temperature from the south end, producing an interesting expression.

After I held the cat out upside down for the second time came the unexpected diagnosis.

"Laura, your cat...is a boy."

I had to sit down. My first thought was that this probably wasn't fatal. Then I dissolved in laughter and disbelief. "You know, sometimes, volunteer cat agencies don't get it right," she said gently. But Sterling was wearing her favorite collar, turquoise with yellow daisies! She had long eyelashes! She couldn't be a boy, not after seven years of being a girl. Could I have a transsexual cat? Sterling beamed at me.

"Yep, I can see where he had surgery, long ago. He's definitely a boy, neutered," she said. She suspected he had some crystals in his bladder, making it harder for him to urinate, and causing his recent distress. "It happens a lot to male cats, and can be serious," Dr. Lee said. The plot had thickened, now we had boy cat issues. Sterling was whisked off for an X-ray, which indeed showed crystals. This was a lot to absorb in an afternoon.

I got prescription food and other instructions, and drove home slowly, with my new cat. How could he have changed his stripes, all of a sudden? The good news was that his name could go either way. I felt uncomfortable about how I had raised him, immediately thinking of the expectations and assumptions I had made about her. Er, him. How beautiful he was, and how loving, and how smart, and how we had thought he was a bit aggressive as a female, sort of an Amazon, really. Hmm.

I called Teddy when school was out. "Ted," I said. "Sterling went to the vet." "Yeah? What does she have?" he asked in his deep, teenager voice.

"Well -- she's a boy." Complete silence from the other end. "Whuut?" He thought I was kidding. "Yep. He's got crystals in his urine, and he's going to be OK. But he needs a new collar." Ted tried to absorb the news, and I'm sure a few amusing text messages circled the campus. We went directly from school to the pet store, and he chose a black nylon collar with iron crosses on it.

It took about three weeks to stop calling Sterling "she" and switch to "he." We were amazed at how much difference it didn't make -- *at all*. Everything was the same. The cat didn't have a complex, and we didn't change our treatment of him. When you think about it, we put a lot of silly assumptions (and sometimes silly outfits) on our pets, which they don't care a fig about.

Several months later, it's no big deal. It is, however, a little weirder to have him stare at me getting out of the shower.

Sterling is now sitting out on top of the patio fence, checking out the cul-de-sac for any news, and exchanging cool recognition glances with other cats on our block. He knows exactly who he is.

So much for this cat's secret. And that's why I said Sterling had a sense of humor.

But I am never changing vets again. Not sure I can handle any more news.

Section VIII:
Drama

Ordinary riches can be stolen,
real riches cannot.
In your soul are infinitely precious things
that cannot be taken from you.

Oscar Wilde

Taban
Will Harrison, MD

My name is Taban. At least, that's what the other boys call me. I think I might have another name; all the other boys do. I remember a long time ago, someone used to call me a different name. But I can't remember who she was, or what that name was. I know she was a grown-up, and she used to carry me places, and give me something warm and sweet to eat. But it's been so long ago, I'm not sure if she was real, or if it was just a dream.

I have a lot of dreams. Some of them are good dreams, like dreaming about the woman who gave me porridge. Some of them are about a place where there are lots of big white cows, and I get to go with other boys to chase the cows with a long stick. But mostly I have really bad dreams. Mostly, they are about big men with light-colored skin and big guns, who are chasing me. There is always something burning where they are, and lots of noise. I don't like those dreams, but I always have them.

Anyway, I was going to say that I don't know why the other boys call me Taban. That word means "Trouble" in the language that the soldiers speak. I try not to be trouble for anybody. When we all lived with the soldiers, I always went out to help the bigger boys gather firewood for the cooking fires. I couldn't carry as much as they did, but I always went. And sometimes they'd laugh at me, but other times one of the biggest boys - his name is Karbino, and he has a really nice smile - he would put me on his shoulders, along with my sticks and his sticks, and carry us all back to the soldiers' camp.

I'd like to have a name like Karbino, or Joseph, or John. But I'd really like to be called Mabior. I remember one of the soldiers who was called Mabior. He was bigger than most of the other soldiers, with broad shoulders and strong arms. When he saw me in the camp, he would always pick me up and throw me over his head, and then catch me before I came down. He was my favorite soldier. He went away one day, when there was a lot of loud noises near the camp. It sounded like the thunder that comes with the rainstorms, but it was not as loud. It made the ground shake, and all the soldiers picked up their guns and ran towards the sounds. They told us to go the other way, into the brush and trees, and wait until they came back. After a few hours, they came back, but I never saw Mabior again.

I guess I always lived with the soldiers, until the White Truck people came and took us away, to the boys' camps. Sometimes, when I dream about the nice woman, I can see some other children playing outside the hut where she is. There is a lot of tall green grass around the hut, and some goats. The goats are all different colors. Some of them have so many colors; it's hard to tell exactly what color they are. The sun is warm on my face, and I feel good. I'm not hungry, and I like watching the other children. They are all bigger than me, and I think they are girls. I'm not too sure. We didn't have many girls in the soldiers' camp. Only when somebody's family came to visit. Otherwise, it was just the soldiers, the women who cooked for them, and us boys. I wonder why there are girl-children in my dream, but not when I am awake.

When the White Truck people came, everything changed. Us boys called them "White Truck people" because they came in white trucks with big blue markings on them. All of the army trucks were either brown or other colors, but the colored ones were so dirty and faded it was hard to tell what color they were. But not the White Truck people. Their trucks were so white; it almost hurt your eyes to look at them. And they had big blue letters on the sides and top. My friend William Deng said that they did that so that the Horses from the North wouldn't drop bombs on them. I don't know. We never had any bombs dropped on us, even though the Horses' airplanes flew over our camp many times.

We call the enemy soldiers "Horses from the North." That is part of a song we sing about them when we are marching. William told me that they used to ride horses to fight us a long time ago, but now they have trucks and tanks and airplanes to fight us with. I don't know exactly what a 'horse' is. William says that it is a big four-legged animal like our cows, except with no horns. He says the enemy soldiers used to ride on them when they came to burn our homes and kill our cows. I can't imagine anybody riding on a cow. They are sort of mean if they don't like you. I have seen a lot of dead cows from after the times that the enemy came down into our land. In some of my bad dreams there are lots of dead cows, and dead children, too.

But William says the Horses won't do anything to us now that we have come with the White Truck people. They made all the boys from our army camp get into their trucks, and take all our things with us. That wasn't hard to do. All I had was my shirt and my shorts, a pair of old slippers, and a piece of a blanket. The White Truck people gave me a backpack and a new shirt with pictures of children on the front of it, and we drove for a long time. I had gotten to ride in the army trucks when we moved our camp a few times, so being in a truck was nothing new. But what came next was!

When the trucks stopped, and we got out, we were beside a big airplane with two motors. I was really scared then, because I thought only the Horses had airplanes. But Karbino came up to me and said,

"Don't worry, little Taban. This is not one of the *gelaba* airplanes. It belongs to the YouEnn. The White Truck people are going to take us to a safer place."

When Karbino told me that, I felt better. He always told me the truth, and he never teased me, the way some of the bigger boys did.

We all climbed into the airplane, through a big door in the back. The White Truck *kawajas* made us all sit down on the floor of the airplane, and hold on to straps that were attached to the floor and walls. Then the big door closed, and the motors started. The airplane shook and rattled, and then it started to move. I began to be afraid, but then I looked over at Karbino. He smiled at me, and shouted something. I couldn't hear what he said, because of the noise of the airplane, but it made me feel better. Then, we began to go up into the sky! I could see a little bit out of the window next to me, and the trees began to get smaller and smaller. Then all I could see was blue sky and white clouds.

"This is fun!" I thought. I looked around. Some of the bigger boys looked really scared.

"Well, maybe they are not so tough after all," I said to myself.

Then Joseph Kuec began to get sick. He threw up all over the big boy next to him, and then HE threw up. Pretty soon, several of the big boys were sick. But not Karbino. He looked like he was having a good time. So I decided that flying in an airplane was OK, if it made bad boys sick and good boys happy.

After a while, we began to go down, and pretty soon we were on the ground again. There were some people there who looked like they were from my tribe, and they spoke my language, so I decided we were still in my country. 'New Sudan' is what the head soldier had called our country. There were more White Truck *kawajas* there, too, and they had us pick up our backpacks and follow them.

We walked for about half an hour, and then came to a lot of old buildings that looked like they had been bombed by the Horses. Some of them had been partly fixed up, and there were some long huts in the spaces between the buildings. The tribesman who had met us told us to find a bed in one of the repaired buildings or one of the huts. He said that food would be ready in an hour or so. I looked for Karbino, and went with him into one of the buildings. There were bamboo beds lined up along both walls. Karbino found a bed near the door, and I put my things on the bed next to his. William Deng came in and took the bed next to mine.

"What kind of *tukul* is this?" I asked Karbino.

"This is the kind of house that the *kawajas* build for themselves," answered Karbino. "This was a school that *kawajas* from a far-away land made to teach our people about many things, so that we could have a better life. But the *gelaba* dropped bombs on it many years ago, and drove out the *kawajas*. So now we have no school here."

"Why did the White Truck people bring us HERE," asked William. "Do they want us to get bombed, too?"

"No," answered Karbino, "They brought us here so that we could get better food and clothes than we had with the army, and maybe find our families again, so that we can go back to our homes."

"But the *gelaba* are fighting where my village is," cried Santino Bol, who had been listening to Karbino.

"My mother and sisters are down in Yei at a refugee camp, and my father and older brothers are all up north, fighting the *gelaba*," chimed in Marco Malek. "How can I go home?"

"I don't know," answered Karbino, who was almost fifteen, and had been just starting Grade 4 when the *gelaba* destroyed his home village.

"The Commander at the army camp told me that was the reason all of us boy soldiers are being demobilized."

"Well, I guess we better find out whether the food is any better here than with the army," Marco responded, and we all went out of the building looking for the kitchen.

We stayed at that first camp for a while. It was very crowded. There were over two thousand boys there, at least that's what William Deng told me. There were boys from several different clans there, and there were a lot of fights between the bigger boys from different clans. Sometimes boys were beaten with sticks by other boys, and had their heads cracked open. The grown-ups who were supposed to be our caregivers were nice to me, but there never seemed to be enough of them. Things were always getting stolen. My backpack and my new shirt disappeared the first week that we were at Agot. I got half of a new blanket; Karbino actually was the one who got the blanket. But he tore it in half and gave me part of it. William Deng was always having his food taken away from him by bigger boys. I never had that problem, because I always found Karbino and ate when he ate.

One day the White Truck people came again, and began to separate the boys into smaller groups. We were going to go to smaller camps, where there would be fewer boys. They were also going to separate boys from different clans, so there wouldn't be so much fighting. I thought that was a good idea.

When the *kawajas* came and told me to get in the truck, I was happy. At least at first. But then I saw that Karbino and William were not leaving. I tried to ask the *kawaja* where we were going, and why Karbino wasn't coming, but she didn't seem to hear me. The truck drove away from the camp. I wondered if I would ever seen Karbino again.

We drove and drove. The rains had started, and the roads were very muddy. When we got to a river - one of the other boys said it was called the Crocodile River, because there was a huge old crocodile that lived there that ate little boys - the driver almost couldn't get across, because the water was so deep. But we made it across. And no crocodile. I think the big boy was teasing me.

It was beginning to get dark when we stopped. Everybody got out, and looked around. There were some small *tukuls*, and some bigger ones - long and narrow, like the ones at Agot. There were some different tribesmen there, and they told us to find a place to sleep. I went in to several of the long *tukuls*, but they were all full of big boys, from a different clan. They told me I couldn't sleep there. Finally, I found an empty bed in one of the smaller huts. The bamboo was all broken at one end, but it was big enough for me. I was so tired, I just curled up with my blanket and went to sleep.

The next morning, the roosters began crowing, even before the sun came up, so I couldn't sleep any more. I went outside and looked around. There were a lot of huts scattered around, with chickens and goats here and there. I saw a boy carrying a water jerrycan, and asked him where the borehole was. He told me, so I went there and pumped some water to wash my face and hands. The borehole pump was surrounded by a big mud puddle, so it was hard to get there and back without getting all wet and muddy.

Then I went to see where the food was. There wasn't any. The cooks were just getting started, so we didn't get our porridge and beans until the sun was beyond the middle of the sky. And there was only one meal that day, because they ran out of cornmeal and oil. I was pretty hungry the whole time I was at that camp.

After a while - I don't know how many days, but it was quite a few - I saw Santino Bol.

"Where did you come from?" I asked him.

"I'm at a camp just a few kilometers down the road," he answered. "It's really nice. They have a bamboo fence all around it to keep out the village boys who try to steal our blankets, and they kill a bull once a week, so we get meat. But the best thing is that we get tea with sugar once a day!"

"Who else is there?" I asked him.

"Joseph Kuec, Santino Deng, John Garang, and Karbino Yirol are probably the only ones that you would know."

"How did you get here?" I asked.

"I walked. It's only about six kilometers down the road. There are a couple of villages along the way, and some farms, so there really isn't any danger from lions. At least, not during the day."

I didn't know if Santino was telling me the truth or not. I have never seen a lion, but some of the bigger boys told me once that the local people here could change into lions at night, and attack strangers. I wasn't sure I believed that either.

After Santino left, to walk back to Maleng Agok before it got dark, I began to think. Nobody that I knew lived in this camp. It was mostly bigger boys, and they weren't very nice to me. We didn't get food twice a day on some days, and we never got tea, or meat. And I really missed Karbino and William. William was only a couple of years older than me, so he was like my brother. And Karbino was more like a father. I guess I had a father, someplace. Everybody has a father. But I never had anybody tell me that I had one, or that they knew who my father was, or what my family name was. So I guess my father had gone away, or been killed in the war. Lots of boys' fathers had been killed in the war. I just didn't know.

But, what I did know was that I didn't like living at this camp.

As the sun was coming up, I rolled my piece of blanket up, went to the borehole and washed my face and feet. Then I looked around in one of the kitchens, to see if there was any food left. The cooks were all still asleep on their bamboo beds at the sides of the kitchen. I found a pot that had a little bit of cornmeal porridge in it, so I ate that as quickly as I could, and then went out to the road.

"Which way did he go?" I thought. "I think he went towards the north. Anyway, six kilometers isn't too far. If I don't find the camp, I'll come back here."

The road past the camp and into the little village on the other side was good. It was solid dirt with some small red rocks on top, and it looked like two trucks could go side-by-side. I went as fast as I could walk, because I didn't want anybody to make me go back to the old camp. Some dogs barked at me from the marketplace in the village, and a boy a little bigger than me came out to the road to watch me go past. He didn't say anything, and I didn't say anything.

Pretty soon the road got narrower, and there were big trees on both sides. The branches hung out over the road, and it was cool and green in there. The bushes were pretty thick on both sides, and I began to think about the lions. Santino said they didn't come out in the daytime, but it was dark underneath the trees. I walked a little faster, and then I ran for a little while.

It was hard to run on that road, because there were big holes full of water every few feet. Karbino told me once, when we were watching the White Truck people's truck splash through these mudholes that they had been made by the Horse Soldiers, with things they put in the ground that exploded when a truck ran over it. I was careful not to run through any of the mudholes.

After a while, the trees got thinner, and there were farms on both sides of the road. The dura and groundnut plants were beginning to get big, and I knew that pretty soon there would be more to eat than cornmeal, at least for those families. A little girl about my age was digging in a garden beside the road. I stopped and looked at her for awhile, then said "Hello." She said something back that I didn't understand, so I walked away.

I was beginning to get tired, when I came to another village. There were boys playing in the water around the borehole there, and another market with some tea shops, and a school with a big football field.

"Hey!" I called to one of the smaller boys at the borehole, "Is there a boy-soldier camp around here?"

"Yes. It's just up the road. Do you see that bamboo fence? It's right there."

"Thank you," I said, and started walking again.

The bamboo fence went on for a ways, and then turned away from the road. I couldn't see any holes in the fence, but a small path went away from the road, alongside the fence, so I followed that. Pretty soon I came to a gate in the fence, made out of white metal with bumps in it. While I was looking at the gate, some boys came along the path, stopped at the gate and yelled:

"Malek! Malek! Open the gate!"

An old man with no teeth and a really dirty green *gamisa* opened the gate. I walked in behind the other boys. The old man looked at me, and

I could see he only had one eye. He winked it at me, and smiled. No teeth at all.

Inside the fence there were many long *tukuls* with grass roofs, in two lines along a wide flat open space. I could see some kitchen buildings beyond the long buildings. There was a big flat space with a kind of net up on poles in the middle of it. Under the trees, between the long buildings and the fence, there were groups of boys, sitting in rows, looking at a man. Behind each man there was a big flat black thing with white markings on it. I couldn't decide what they were doing for a minute, but then I realized that it must be school. So that's what 'school' looks like. I was going to go over and take a closer look, when somebody yelled "Taban!"

I looked around. It was Karbino.

"What are you doing here, little Taban?" he asked me.

"I don't like the other camp. I came here to live with you and William and Santino."

"Good. I'm glad you're here. I was worried about you. I have to go to school now, but you go over to that second *tukul* there. You see it?"

"Yes."

"That's where I live. There's an empty bed next to mine that you can have. It's the third one on the left. You do know which side is left, don't you?"

I started to say something, but then I decided that Karbino was teasing me. I walked over to the hut he had pointed to, and went inside. It was empty, except for two rows of bamboo beds, one along each side. I counted to three, and stopped. There was no blanket or backpack on the bed, like there was on the other ones, so I decided that it must be the right one. I climbed up on it, put my rolled up blanket under my head, and decided to take a little rest.

The next thing I knew, William Deng was shaking me.

"Taban! Taban! Wake up! It's time to eat!"

I couldn't remember for a minute where I was, and then I did.

"Hello, William. Where do we go to eat?"

"Right outside. Here's a bowl, a cup and a spoon for you to use. They belong to Mattias, but he's in Rumbek in the hospital right now, so you can use them until he gets back."

We went outside. There were about fifty boys standing around one of the kitchen *tukuls*. When I got in line, I saw some boys that I had known from before. They all smiled and pointed at me.

"Look! There's Taban! Good old Taban."

A very tall woman in a pretty dress filled my bowl with porridge, and then put some beans on top. Another woman poured tea into my cup, and a short little man with a crooked back dumped three spoonfuls of sugar into my tea. I thought I must be still asleep and dreaming.

William and I walked over to a log lying on the ground and sat down. I was really hungry, so we ate for awhile, and I sipped at my tea. I don't think I had ever tasted anything as good as that food and that tea.

Finally I said, "William, why is this camp so different from the other ones?"

"Well," he said, "As far as I can tell, this camp is run by *kawajas* from a distant land, who believe in Jesus. And they do this because they believe that Jesus wants them to help boys like us, who don't have homes or families."

I had heard of Jesus before. My soldier friend, Mabior, sometimes sang a song about 'Jesus Loves Me'.

"Who is Jesus?" I asked William.

"I'm not really sure, but there are some older *kawaja* boys who live here that tell us stories from a book they call 'The Bible', every night. They know more about Jesus. Let's ask them tonight."

So I lived in the new camp for a few days, and had enough to eat, and heard stories about Jesus and other great warriors from the *kawaja* Bible, and everything was good.

Then, one morning, the little man with the crooked back came to where I was sitting near the P-1 classroom. I was listening to see if I could understand what 'school' was all about. There was a *kawaja* lady with the man.

"This is the small boy I was telling you about," he said to the lady.

She sat down on the ground next to me and smiled. She had the most beautiful eyes that I had ever seen. I can't tell you what color they were, but it looked like she had candles burning inside them.

"Hello," she said to me in my dialect. "What is your name?"

That really surprised me. I didn't know that *kawajas* could speak Dinka. None of the White Truck people did.

"Taban," I said.

"Where did you come from, Taban?"

"Don't know."

"How did you get here?"

"Walked."

"From where?"

"Back down the road."

"Why did you come here?"

"Karbino was here, and William. They are my friends."

Just then another *kawaja* came up to us. He was a big man with a red beard and no hair on his head. The woman with the beautiful eyes said many words to him, but I didn't understand them. Then she sat down beside me again. She smiled at me, and I thought it looked like the sun coming up. Maybe she had gotten something in her eyes, because there was water coming from them.

"Little Taban, you can stay here until we find out who your family is, and where your village is. Then we'll decide if it's safe for you to go home."

She put her arms around me and squeezed me very hard. I didn't think I was going to like that, but it was nice. Then the little man with the crooked back gave me a new blanket, patted the top of my head, and went away.

The new camp was good. I was with my friends again, I had enough to eat, and I got to sit on the ground at the edge of the P1 class and begin to learn things. But the best part of camp was in the evenings. A younger *kawaja* man would come to our *tukul* and tell us stories, or read to us from the *kawaja* Bible. They were really good stories, about men named Daniel, and Joshua, and Moses. I think they must have been Dinka men, because a lot of the men in the army camp had those same names. But the best stories were about Jesus. I really liked to hear about Jesus, especially the stories about Jesus and the children. One day I told Nate - the young *kawaja* who read to us - that I really wanted to see Jesus, and where did he live? Nate told me that Jesus lived in a place called Heaven, with God, but I could have him live in my heart, if

I really wanted to. I didn't understand how somebody could live in my heart, but Nate always knew what he was talking about, so I said yes, He could come into my heart.

I didn't feel any different after I said that. Nate showed me how to talk to Jesus - he called it 'praying' - and then he told me some more stories about Jesus and small boys. When I went to sleep that night, I prayed to Jesus to stay in my heart while I was asleep. I didn't dream about the Horses from the North that night. Instead, I dreamed that I was in a place with lots of other small boys and girls, and a very big man with a nice face was with us. We laughed and talked and sang songs, and it was nice. I was almost sad to wake up. Since that day, when I go to sleep, I always try to remember the big man's face, and it helps me go to sleep.

One day, there was a lot of excitement in the camp. The White Truck people were there again. They said that the boys were going to go back to their own villages, because the rebel army had driven the Horses from the North out of our land. I packed up my clothes and blanket in a new backpack, and got ready to go. The nice lady came over to me and gave me another big hug. I was really beginning to like hugs. She said,

"Goodbye, little Taban. Always remember that Jesus will be in your heart, no matter where you go."

She looked like she was crying, but I'm not sure, because she got up and walked away very quickly. Nate saw me, and said,

"Taban! You can't read yet, but you will learn. Here is a Bible that is written in Dinka, so that you can read all about Moses and Daniel and Jesus, all by yourself, whenever you want to." Then he walked away very fast, too.

We got into the trucks, and drove for awhile, then stopped by the big airplane. I was ready for the trip this time. I got in next to Karbino, and found a place right beside a window, so I could see everything on the ground when we flew up in the air.

We flew for a long time. I could see lots of trees and rivers. Then the trees disappeared, and it was just grass, and more rivers. When we began to come down, I could see many *tukuls*, and round cattle pens, and lots and lots of cows. When we landed on the ground, I got the biggest surprise of my life.

The first person I saw when I got off the airplane was Mabior! I ran up to him and put my arms around his legs, and gave him a big hug, just like Christina had given me. He picked me up, and said,

"Welcome home, Taban. You and I are going to go home now. I am your father's brother. I am out of the army now, so I can take you to my home, and we can live together until you grow up."

"Where is my father?" I asked.

"He went away to fight the Horses from the North, and never came back," Mabior said. "And your mother and two sisters were taken away to Khartoum by the Horses. We don't know what happened to them."

"Will they ever come back?" I asked.

"I don't know," said Mabior. "Only God knows that."

"I know about God. And Jesus!" I said, and I showed him my Bible written in Dinka.

"You have a Bible! That's good. Now we can read it together every night."

We walked for a long time. After a while, Mabior picked me up and carried me. I fell asleep while we were walking. When I woke up, it was getting dark. Mabior set me down on the ground in front of a *tukul*. A woman came out of the *tukul*.

"This is my wife, Rebekah. She will be your mother until we can find your real mother. Would you like something to eat?"

I said yes, but the next thing I remember is waking up in the morning. I went outside to wash my face, and look for Mabior. He was looking at a big red bull with a white face.

"This is Mayom," he told me. "He is going to be the start of my string of cows."

I said hello to Mayom. He just stared at me. There were three white cows nearby. Rebekah was milking one of them. We had milk and porridge for breakfast. Then Mabior read something from the Bible.

"Mabior, how old am I?" I asked him.

"Well, I think you are five years old," he replied.

"Mabior, what was my father's name?"

"His name was Malual Deng Garang, and he was a very brave man," Mabior replied.

"Mabior, from now, on, I don't want to be called Taban. From now on my name is Malual Nate Garang. OK? And I want to grow up to be as brave as my father and as kind as you."

Epilogue

The civil war in the Sudan has gone on for more than 25 years. The people most affected by the war are the Dinka, who live west of the White Nile, and the Nuer, who live to the east.

The Dinka call the Muslim soldiers from Khartoum "Horses from the North," because in earlier times, they would attack the Dinka settlements on horseback, stealing cattle and children, whom they sold into slavery. In modern times the Muslims, or *gelaba*, use tanks, helicopter gunships, and aerial bombardment to decimate the Dinka and other non-Muslim peoples in the south.

Taban's story is true; his words and thoughts have been recorded as well as possible. His story is similar to that of more than 10,000 other Dinka, Nuer and Bari children, although he is younger than most. When their villages are destroyed by the government forces, the children flee into the bush. If they have family - fathers, brothers or uncles - in the rebel army, the boys gravitate to the army camps for food and protection. The women and girls migrate to the refugee camps in the far south, in order to keep from being enslaved.

The United Nations/Unicef staff in the Sudan have made a great effort to have the rebel army "demobilize" these boys, calling them "child soldiers." In fact, most of the boys - ages five to fifteen - have never carried weapons, never fought. They have lived in the camps, carrying firewood and water to the kitchens, primarily as a means of obtaining food and safety. For older boys, being a soldier is essentially a rite of passage. The Dinka have always been a warrior race. Being a man amongst the Dinka means being a warrior, whether to protect the cattle - their chief resource - from predators, or from rival clans or Nuer raiders.

Taban is now living safely with his family in "New Sudan." Hopefully, the fragile peace accord will endure, and these "child soldiers" can grow up in peace.

Fresco-1
Prolog and Chapter One
Will Harrison, MD

Prolog

THE EARLY MORNING SUN filtered through the blinds of the hospital room and played across a form on the bed that seemed too frail to be a body. It stirred slightly and a thin, pale hand reached out from under the sheet. The man sitting next to the bed grasped the hand and strained to hear.

"... Son..." she whispered faintly.

"Yeah, Babe. The sun is coming up. Time for breakfast soon," he replied.

"No...Son..." and her voice trailed off to nothingness.

The man held her hand tightly, and bowed his head onto the bed. The woman breathed a long sighing breath. Then nothing. Seconds passed. A minute. Another long, deep, sighing breath. He found himself straining, mentally forcing her to take another breath. She breathed again, a shuddering sigh. He relaxed slightly, then began projecting his strength into her body, willing her to breathe. A minute passed. Another minute. He felt her hand cool perceptibly. He grasped her wrist and felt for a pulse. Nothing. He willed there to be a pulse, a breath.

Nothing.

He moved closer and laid his head on her chest. He listened. No sound. No breathing. No heartbeat. Nothing. He closed his eyes and groaned from the bottom of his gut. He sat like that, half-leaning across her body, eyes closed, bleeding into his soul. He waited for the tears.

Nothing.

Finally, he moved away from the bed, looked one more time at the woman he had loved beyond all loves, and walked out of the hospital room. As he passed the nursing station, he spoke:

"She's gone. About fifteen minutes ago," and kept walking.

The nurse sprang up from the desk.

"Oh, Mr. Tucker, I'm so sorry. Can we do anything..."

But Ethan Tucker was already outside the small hospital, walking swiftly toward his silver-and-green Viper. He slid behind the wheel, started the engine, and then sat there. He had no place to go. Nowhere that wouldn't remind him of her. As he sat behind the wheel, the oncologist who had been his wife's doctor came up to Ethan's car.

"Captain Tucker, I know you must feel terrible right now. Would you like to come back inside and we can talk for awhile?"

"Thanks, Doc. What would we talk about? How you quacks couldn't do anything for her? How your miracles of modern medicine weren't worth squat? How even the magnificent specialist from L.A. was useless?"

"Ethan...you're upset. We've been friends for a long time. It will do you good to talk about it. Get it off your chest."

"Sorry, Doc. I know you tried. It's just so unfair and rotten! Look, I know you mean well, but there's only one place left for me now."

With that, Ethan put his car in gear and moved out of the parking lot. He headed east, toward the small airport and fixed-base operation that he had poured his life, energy and money into. Now, just when things were getting really rosy, this had to happen.

"God! Why now? Why this? Why her? If you wanted to kill somebody, why not me? I'm not a quarter the Christian she is. She deserves to be alive! Why? God!"

Ethan was howling at the top of his voice now, spitting the words out the open top of the car, challenging the God he thought he believed in to give him some answers. Without thinking he had pushed the Viper up to 130 mph. As he saw the turn for the airfield ahead, and began to slow, he heard a siren behind him. Ignoring it, he turned left into the airport road, then right into his hangar area.

✷✷✷✷✷✷✷✷

Mary, Daniel and Santino waited patiently in the hot sun of the African mid-day. There was no shade here in the open field where the Operation Lifeline Sudan trucks were distributing bags of maize to the villagers. There were many people gathered here, but Mary could see that there would be food when their turn came. She could carry two bags on her head, and Santino could manage one. Maybe there would be a smaller bag for Daniel to carry. After all, he was only five.

The Antonov, when it came, made only a faint buzzing sound in the air that gradually grew louder, until everyone was looking to see where it was going to fly.

"There it is," cried Santino. "It's coming this way!"

As the bomber came closer, some people began to panic, dropping their bags of maize and running towards the trees, or rocks, or anything that would hide them from the bombs. Others stayed in line, but shifted nervously, like rabbits aware of an approaching jackal, ready to bolt in an instant.

The Antonov came steadily onward, heading directly for the OLS feeding station. The twin turboprop engines trailed faint lines of grey-black exhaust in the clear blue sky. As it flew overhead, Santino yelled:

"The door isn't open! It's not going to drop bombs!"

And he was right. The Antonov bored steadily westward, further into rebel-held Sudan. The people who had run away began to come back to the feeding station. The OLS workers, who had run fastest and furthest, slowly came back to the trucks and resumed their distribution. There were some squabbles about who had been where in line, but not many.

With a ripping noise that paralyzed the villagers, two government Mi-24 helicopter gunships popped up over the low rise of hills to the east and bored directly in on the feeding station. Each one fired several salvos of 57mm rockets into the crowd, carefully avoiding the UN trucks. As they came within range, the gunners opened fire with their 12.7mm machine guns, spraying the periphery as the villagers tried to find some sort of hiding place. The gunships passed over the feeding station, looped up and around, and flew back in the direction they had come. There was silence again, broken only by the cries of the injured.

Mary raised herself from the ground and looked for her sons. As she got to her knees, a man ran screaming past, knocking her down again.

"The soldiers are coming! The soldiers are coming!"

"The Horses from the North! They're here!"

"They are going to make us slaves!"

"Run! Run!"

As the crowd of villagers panicked yet again, Mary caught sight of Santino, being pulled along by a man she didn't recognize, running towards the village across the river. She began to run after him, but stopped when she saw Daniel lying on the ground.

Daniel had been hit by fragments of one of the rockets. It had exploded against a large rock several yards away, but bits of shrapnel had slashed Daniel's right leg, and mangled his left arm. Mary could see a white bone sticking out of Daniel's arm. He was bleeding, and he was unconscious.

She looked around for help. Everyone who could run was gone. The OLS workers had taken their trucks and gone. There were dead people lying all across the field, and some injured who were crying for help. There were no government soldiers, either. That had been a rumor, started by a panic-stricken villager.

Mary could see no one she knew. She ripped long strips of cloth from her skirt, and bandaged Daniel's leg. He had a long gash on the side of his head, but it had stopped bleeding, so she left it alone. She found a bundle of sticks that someone had dropped, and used them to splint Daniel's arm, the way she had seen the village healthcare worker do for her husband when an angry cow had broken his arm. When she had done as much as she could, she sat back and wondered what to do next. She breathed a little prayer: "God, please don't let Daniel die. And help me find Santino."

The first thing was to find some water. When she had done that, she washed his face and gave him a sip to drink. Daniel was awake now and crying a little from the pain.

"What happened, Mama?"

"The government helicopter came and shot bombs at us."

"Where's Santino?"

"He went away to the village."

"I want some more water."

Mary thought Daniel needed medical help. There was no one in the villages around who could help his arm; it was too badly injured. She had heard of an old church hospital further south that had been reopened by some *kawajas* – foreigners. Maybe they had someone who could help. It was only sixty miles away. She would go there. If she could find it, they would surely help. Santino was old enough that he would be all right until she could come back and find him.

****

The sheriff pulled in beside Ethan and walked over to the driver's side of the Viper.

"Little emergency out here, E.T.? You was goin' a bit over the limit back there."

"Sorry, Mike. She just died. I'm not sure what I'm doing right now."

"Awwww, gee, I'm sorry, E.T.! I knew she was bad, but...aww, that's terrible. We just had special prayer for her last night."

"Mike, what good did it do? Where's God when you really need Him? She was about as strong a believer as anybody. Look what God did to her! Look what happened! How could there possibly be a loving God, when this happens!"

"E.T., I just don't know..." and the sheriff turned and walked slowly back to his patrol car.

Ethan walked to the hangar doors, slid them open, and moved the airplane out onto the apron. He climbed up and raised the canopy, then walked around the airplane, doing a cursory pre-flight check. Even as angry as he was, the brief check was complete. He climbed back into the cockpit, and fired up first one, then the other of the two Allison V-12 engines. Then he taxied the P-38 out to the runway, did the remainder of his pre-flight checks, and took off into the bright Arizona morning.

"OK, God! I'm coming. Now, talk to me! Why? Why?"

Ethan opened the window in the canopy and yelled as loud as he could into the slipstream. Surely he'd find some answers here. He had always found clarity and common sense up here. Things were simple here. There were rules, and if you obeyed them, you lived. If you didn't, you died. It was that simple. But now...

She had followed the rules. She had never been outside the envelope. She believed. Why her? Ethan screamed at God until his throat was raw. But no answer came. Finally he decided that there would be no answer, that God was just up here somewhere laughing at him. He could see only one solution.

Ethan pointed the nose of the P-38 out toward the empty desert, and climbed to maximum altitude. All he had to do was fly around up here with no oxygen mask until he passed out. Then time and gravity would do the rest. If God wouldn't come to him, he'd go there. One way or another, if there was a God out here somewhere he'd be knocking at His door soon.

Even as he flew, Ethan began to have intruding thoughts. Suppose he didn't pass out. Could he consciously dive the plane into the mountains? Suppose he passed out, and the airplane turned back towards town? Suppose it crashed into a school? And the plane. He had restored it to pristine glory, mostly by himself. Did it deserve to die, just because he had to? Should he be as unfair to the bird he had, truly, created from junk, as her Creator had been?

Ethan Tucker landed the plane and put it back to bed in the hangar. Then he drove to the nearest liquor store and bought a liter of Courvoisier.

"Might as well go in style," he muttered.

****

"Who's next, Joel?"

"We have a Dinka mother and two babies, Doctor Kate. They're twins, I think. They are about one year old," answered Joel Oliver, who was translating for Katherine Mary Stuart MacKenzie, MD. He moved to the door of the clinic office and called to the tall, slender woman who was sitting under the thatch roof of the waiting room.

The woman strode gracefully into the office, ducking her head automatically as she came through the door. She stood more than six feet tall, and was as graceful in her movements as a ballerina. She held two sleeping babies, one in either arm. They looked like they had been carved out of ebony. Joel spoke to her in Juba Arabic. She smiled and replied in Dinka.

"Ah, she doesn't speak Arabic. We'll need to get Mabior to translate," said Joel.

"Mabior! Mabior! Here, in the clinic! We need you!" Called Joel. The large Dinka watchman who was manning the gate to the hospital compound came lumbering over to the clinic.

Doctor Kate watched with mixed amusement and tenderness as the tall watchman spoke softly to the twins' mother. As tall as the woman was, Mabior towered over her. They spoke rapidly back and forth in the Bor dialect. Then Mabior turned and said a few words in Arabic to Joel.

"Mama says the babies have been sick for three days, and haven't been eating anything," Joel relayed to the doctor.

Kate drew in a breath, and silently reminded herself that this wasn't Melbourne, and she shouldn't expect sophisticated patients who could spin off a list of signs and symptoms so fast it made your teeth rattle.

"OK, Joel, ask Mama how the babies have been sick. Have they had a fever, diarrhea, cough, fits...just what kind of sick."

Kate watched, torn by frustration and amusement as Joel and Mabior talked back and forth in Arabic. Mabior was a good, kind, solid man, but his knowledge of anything beyond simple pastoral tasks was nil. He needed a lot of help with medical terminology. Finally Mabior turned to the twins' mother. They spoke back and forth for what seemed like an eternity, but was more like a minute. Mabior spoke at length to Joel, who finally said,

"The babies have had fever and cough. They don't feed at the breast, but they don't have diarrhea."

"All that palaver for two little symptoms! No wonder it takes me all day to see fifty patients," Kate though to herself. "Ah, well, now I know a little more."

She gently began to examine the first baby, letting him sleep on his mother's arm.

"Lungs: clear. Heart sounds: normal but rapid. Belly: Oops! Large liver and spleen. No sign of dehydration. Fingers and toes: OK. Oops! Shouldn't have tweaked his bladder like that!"

Kate stepped back as the little one urinated on the concrete floor. Joel waited until he was finished, then brought out the mop that stood in the corner, for just this purpose, and mopped up the puddle.

Kate went over to the second little boy, who woke up just as she began to listen to his heart. He took one look at Kate, grabbed for his mother's neck and let out a yell that could be heard for a mile. Howling at the top of his lungs, he tried to scramble away from Kate, almost causing his mother to drop the other twin. Joel took the other baby from his mother, so she could attempt to calm his frightened sib. She said something, and Kate caught the word *kawaja* – foreigner. Her guess was verified in a few seconds, when Joel said,

"He's never seen a *kawaja* before, so he's a little afraid."

Kate smiled and nodded, then attempted to finish her exam. Listening to the chest was out of the question. All she would hear would be his screams. She palpated his belly, in between the shrieks, when his belly muscles relaxed. Same as the other twin: moderately enlarged spleen and liver. She could tell by the babies' skin temperature that they had fevers, probably about 39°.

"Now what would that translate to in Fahrenheit?" she thought. "Probably about 101°. Too bad the Americans hadn't converted to the metric system like the rest of the world." But they had funded the resurrection of this hospital, so most of the equipment was American, which meant that she had to think Fahrenheit, and not Celsius. Jerking her thoughts back to the patients, she quickly scribbled some notes on the 5x8 inch card the clinic used as a patient record, then said to Joel:

"These babies have malaria, most likely. Let's send them to the lab for thick and thin malaria smears, and then admit them to the Pediatric Ward. While we're at it, might as well test Mom's blood, too. If they have it, she probably does. Tell Mama we want to keep them here for a few days, to give them some good *dawa*, and make them better."

Joel spoke to Mabior, who spoke to the mother, who countered with a long statement. She and Mabior talked back and forth. Finally Mabior said something to Joel, who said,

"She wants to know who will take care of her daughter while she's here. They all came down from Tali Post, by footing."

Kate knew that "footing" meant "on foot," so she knew they had walked about forty miles to get to the clinic.

"Let's test the daughter's blood, too. She can stay with the rest of the family. If there's a spare bed on the ward, she can sleep there.

Otherwise, she'll have to sleep with the twins." Kate knew that the mother would sleep in the same bed as the twins, so four in a bed wouldn't be that much different than three. It would be a small improvement over the bamboo mat and dirty blanket that they probably shared in the cattle camp at Tali Post.

Chapter One

    Ethan could see the glow in the sky ahead of him long before he crossed over Railroad Pass and began the descent into the wide valley. Las Vegas was like a huge glowing candle in the middle of the desert, attracting all sorts of human moths to its flame. Some would burn, others would escape. He wondered idly, as the Viper slowed to a non-trooper-attracting speed, whether he would die in Vegas, like the drunk in the movie he had watched on late night TV during one of his many sleepless nights. He hoped to die. The pain of living was so great that he felt he couldn't bear it any longer.

    It had been almost a year since she died. A year that he'd like to forget. He hadn't awakened once, even after nights that had been totally anesthetized by alcohol, without the sharp gut-thrust of pain that reminded him. She was gone. God had taken her. God wasn't fair. He hated God. He'd make somebody pay, if he couldn't get through to God. He had tried, several times, to find God in the sky, but the clear blue stratosphere of Arizona was as empty of God as it was of clouds. He had talked to his friends, the sheriff's captain and the doctor. They had listened sympathetically, prayed for him, brought him food when he hadn't eaten, 'been there for him.'

    "Been there for me! What does that mean? They can't be there. They can't understand the pain. They just don't know. They've never lost somebody like her. Sure, Doc's lost a lot of patients. But it's not the same, losing a patient as it is losing a wife. He's not alone at night when he goes home. He doesn't have things pop up in front of him that remind him of how much he's lost. They just don't get it!"

Musing savagely to himself, Ethan drove slowly north along The Strip, the kaleidoscope of flashing lights and colors from the huge electric signs battering his senses. Maybe he could lose himself here, forget about things, at least find something to distract himself from his wound. He wasn't here to gamble, that was for sure. He had enough Scots blood in him to resent the very idea of giving money to someone on the off chance that they might give him more money back. And to drop it into a machine! The idea was laughable.

No, he was here to see a wealthy casino owner who wanted to buy his Lockheed P-38J. He had put it carefully back in the hangar after he had been unable to crash it and die. He hadn't flown it much since then. He'd kept it maintained, fired up the engines once a week, done all the necessary things. But the joy of soaring above all the dust and dirt and hassle of earthbound life was gone. He had taken the old-style vacuum-tube radio equipment out of the cockpit and put a jump-seat behind the pilot's seat, so that she could go flying with him. Every time he sat in the cockpit, he seemed to feel her presence behind him. At first he thought it was just imagination, but the feeling became stronger over time. Finally he decided he just wanted to get rid of the airplane. It was too painful a memory for him.

So he had put out some quiet statements, in the circle of warbird owners and pilots that he was thinking of selling it. He'd had several offers, but this was the most intriguing. A man who didn't fly wanted to give him twice what the airplane was worth, just to put it in a private museum. He'd have to meet this man, just to see if he could figure out what made him tick. The man was "too busy" with his casino operations to come to Ethan, so Ethan had come to the mountain.

He reluctantly turned the Viper over to the pimply-faced valet in the massive entry drive of the Florentine, his prospective buyer's flagship casino, and went to the registration desk. As he took his place in the line of tourists, gamblers and thrill-seekers waiting to check in, a well-dressed man in a gray suit approached him.

"Captain Tucker?"

"Well, I used to be."

"We've been expecting you. Leave your bag with Lester, here, and I'll take you up to your room."

Bemused, Ethan followed the man, who had introduced himself as Mr. Faulise, the assistant front desk manager. They entered one of the elevators, and Mr. Faulise put a key into the control plate and pushed an unmarked button at the top of the row.

"You'll have a key like this to access the VIP suites. You won't need one for your room."

'Room' was an understatement. As they stepped off the elevator, a butler in a dark morning coat and gray pants met them.

"This way, Captain Tucker. My name is Blake, and I'll be here for whatever needs you have. Whatever," he added with a smile.

Blake opened a door for Ethan, and he stepped into a room that was the size of his service hangar at home. The wall was entirely window, stretching two full stories. There was a magnificent view over The Strip toward the mountains beyond. The furnishings were a combination of soft beige leather, chrome and glass. A full bar with a mahogany top stood along one side of the room. A kitchen that would suffice for Bobby Flay was visible across a low island on the other. Turning around, Ethan saw that there was a balcony above him, with several doors leading from it.

"There is a master bedroom on this level, as well as a master bathroom, and a guest bathroom. There are two more bedrooms upstairs and two baths as well. Unfortunately, the building code wouldn't permit an elevator from this floor to the next, so you'll have to use the stairs. There's a supply of edibles there in the kitchen, if you get hungry, and, of course, the bar is fully stocked. If you'd like something more than a snack, just ring, and I can make you just about anything. The kitchen is really very nice. You won't need to worry about room service. If you'll be entertaining guests, let me know a few hours ahead of time, so that I can have a decent meal ready. The wine cellar up here is adequate, but if you want something special, I can have it brought up from the dungeon."

So saying, Blake scurried about the room, showing Ethan where the electronic controls for drapes, curtains, TV, stereo, DVD player, lights and air-conditioning were located. Ethan fumbled in his pocket for his wallet.

"Oh, no, Captain. I'd be embarrassed to accept a gratuity. This is all part of our service to you," Blake said.

"Well, don't you really make your living on tips," Ethan said without thinking.

"Captain, I am extremely well-compensated by the inn. I never accept gratuities from guests of the inn."

Thus saying, Blake marched from the room.

"I hope I didn't insult him," Ethan said.

"You did, but he'll get over it," answered Mr. Faulise. "Mr. Black would like to see you in his office tomorrow some time, whenever would be convenient for you. If you have pictures of the airplane, he'd like to see them."

"OK. That would be fine. Whenever he's got time. Can I ask you, how did you pick me out from all those people in the registration line?"

"Very simple. Even though there are many wealthy and famous people who stay here, not too many drive up in a brilliant silver-and-green Viper with Arizona plates."

****

"SAF-011 rolling. Departing Runway 126 at 0800 GMT." The Sudan Air Force Antonov-32 picked up speed as it moved down the runway, its two Ivchenko AI-20 turboprop engines leaving a trail of greasy black smoke behind. With its massive engines mounted above the wing and its beetle-browed cockpit, it looked like some prehistoric flying carnivore, off on a hunting trip.

"Well, Mohammed, here we go, off to kill more of your countrymen," said the Ukrainian contract pilot.

"I tell you again my name is not Mohammed! My name is Achmed," swore the copilot. "And these are not my countrymen. They are ignorant savages who invaded my country from the jungles. They are infidels who simply want to steal our land and our oil."

"I thought all you Arabs were named Mohammed," replied the pilot, who enjoyed bullyragging his employers.

"I am not Arab, I am Sudanese! Why you thick-headed Russian cannot understand that?"

"Since I am Ukrainian, I will ignore that insult. As far as stealing your land, from what I have seen, you probably should pay them to take it," replied the pilot.

"Sudan is great country! We have oil, we have gum arabic, we have Great Nile River! I will not talk to you if you insult my country anymore," said Achmed.

They flew on in silence for twenty minutes, the pilot chuckling to himself. He enjoyed infuriating these little brown men. Once they were insulted, they sulked in silence, which eliminated stupid questions about Russia, the former Soviet Union, Antonovs, and why he, Arkady Nossov, was flying an ugly, slow beast of an airplane like this in a desolate, backward, God-forsaken country like the Sudan, when he should be in command of a PVO Strany squadron of MiG-29s. It was impossible to get even <u>bad</u> vodka here!

"SAF-011. This is Juba Base. Standby for target coordinates." The ground controller's voice broke the silence.

"Standing by."

Once the data had been relayed, double-checked and the course change made, Arkady turned to his co-pilot:

"Ah! Excellent! A hospital, a church and a marketplace. This will do much damage to the rebels' ability to fight!"

Achmed ignored him, instead calling back to the technicians in the cargo bay:

"One hour twenty minutes to target. Make sure the bombs are secure until I give the word. And somebody please rid me of this infidel dog of a Russian," he said in Arabic.

"Watch your tongue, Mohammed. I am Ukrainian. And I speak your archaic language."

Achmed ignored him.

The Antonov droned on toward its target.

****

The view from Mr. Black's office was impressive. The entire wall was a one-way glass window, and looked out over the main casino floor. Ethan looked out over more than an acre of slot machines, video poker machines and table games. At nine AM on a weekday, the floor was crowded. Most of the tables were busy, and most of the machines were occupied.

"What do you think of my little place?" asked Mr. Black.

"It's popular."

"And this is only one of three here in town. There are five more on Indian reservations in Washington, Wyoming and New Mexico. We're doing reasonably well. But, let's talk about your airplane. You were in the Navy, right? Tell me a little about your career."

Ethan thought a moment, and then replied.

"Not much to tell. I flew jets for twenty-five years. I was fortunate enough to have my own squadron, but when the flying time stopped and the desk jobs started, I decided to retire."

"What did you fly?"

"F-8U Crusaders, F-4 Phantoms, F-14 Tomcats, mostly. There were some other types, but those were the big three."

"I understand all Navy pilots have nicknames. Did you?"

"Well, yes. Early on they called me 'Tommy', as in Little Tommy Tucker, but after the movie came out, it was always 'E.T.'"

"May I call you E.T., or would you prefer Ethan?"

"It makes no difference. Whatever you prefer."

"Well, I like E.T. Are you married?"

"No."

"Oh, divorced then, I suppose."

"No. I'd rather not discuss that. We're supposed to be talking about the Lightning. Why do you want to buy it?"

"I'm sorry. I didn't mean to offend you, E.T." Mr. Black looked genuinely contrite.

"I'd prefer to talk business, that's all. I've had several offers for the airplane, but you've offered twice the highest. Why?"

"I have always been fascinated by the World War Two airplanes, but I never had a chance to even get close to one until now. Thanks to all those foolish people down there," he waved his hand toward the casino floor, "I have enough money coming in now to build my own collection, with the finest examples still available. Yours is one. I want it. I'll pay what it costs."

Ethan was struck by Mr. Black's apparent disdain for his guests. "'Foolish people'? You mean the customers in your casino?"

"Yes. They're all fools, chasing the pot of gold at the end of the rainbow. Every one of them thinks he or she will win big. Nobody does. If there were lots of winners, do you think that I, and all the other casino owners, would be building these extravagant 3,000-room hotels? The guest room rates don't come close to paying the expenses. The gaming does. Do you know how much that VIP suite you're staying in costs per night?"

"No," said Ethan, feeling distinctly uncomfortable.

"It has no rate. It's free. Free to our high-rolling guests, and the average Joe couldn't afford it with a month's salary. And the reason I can give away a magnificent suite like that is because even the high rollers lose more than they win. Come over here," and Mr. Black moved to a bank of TV monitors that covered one side of the room.

"See this one? This is our Baccarat room. It's only for invited guests. Are you familiar with Baccarat, E.T.?"

"I vaguely remember that James Bond was a whiz at it."

"Baccarat is a high-stakes game that depends entirely on the luck of the draw. You see the man there, playing alone? He's a publisher from Singapore. He plays against the house. He never bets less than ten thousand dollars a card. Sometimes he bets as much as five hundred thousand. If he loses the draw, he loses the money. One card, five hundred thousand dollars. Zip! Like that! When he wins, he wins big. When he loses, I win big. So far this trip, he's ahead by about two million dollars. He's never quit while he's ahead. In four years he's dropped about twenty-five million here, to say nothing of his losses in Macao and Monte Carlo."

Ethan was almost unable to comprehend what he was hearing. The numbers were so high as to be almost beyond his grasp.

"Don't you wonder where the money's coming from? Who's supporting him?"

"No, and I don't care. I'm providing a service, that's all, just like the liquor stores, the Indian tobacco vendors and the bordellos up in Nye County. If people want to waste their money on something that's unhealthy or immoral, that's their business. I'm just providing a service." Mr. Black wore a smug, self-righteous look that somehow irritated Ethan.

"You take their money and don't worry about how it affects them," he asked softly.

"It matters not to me whether it is that old lady spending her Social Security on bingo, or the man down there losing his company's profits. If they want the action, I'll be happy to provide it. And, take the winnings."

"Well, I think that finishes our business," Ethan said, moving toward the door. "My Lightning is not for sale to you at any price."

"Wait! You can't just walk out on me like that! I made you a legitimate offer! I want that airplane."

"Yes, you made an offer, and I'm turning it down. Good day, Mr. Black."

"No! I want an explanation. Why are you refusing to sell to me?"

"You may be able to live with your actions, but I couldn't take money I knew had come from a business like this. I've done some shabby things in my time, and seen some shabbier ones, but this is the topper."

"What, you think you're better than I am because I'm a gambler?"

"No. I agree with you that people are free to make their own choices, and they need to live with the consequences of their actions. But I find your attitude toward your customers to be intolerable. You pander to greed and avarice, put it in a spectacular, appealing, billion-dollar package, and then say it's all their fault? Sorry, Mr. Black. No sale."

****

The clinic was getting busier these days. Kate had come to the Sudan four months earlier to work in a hospital that had been reopened by an American relief organization. The hospital had been in operation since the 1920's, in one form or another, but with the coming of war to the area in the 1960's, it had been shelled, bombed, burned, and finally abandoned. The staff who had worked in the hospital had been killed or had fled as refugees to Kenya, Ethiopia, Egypt or Chad. The entire southern Sudanese school system had disappeared with the war, so there were no younger medically-trained staff to serve the community as the war front moved northward and people began to filter back to their old homes.

Thus it was that relief organizations from Europe, South Africa and the United States began to help the local people restore what had once been a reasonably stable country. Of course, the war still went on, in fits and starts, mostly during the dry season. But the rebel forces had succeeded in driving the government troops northward, so that the southern third of the Sudan, in landmass the largest country in Africa, was under rebel control, and the people began to resume a more normal existence.

In this one small part of southern Sudan, the hospital had once been the major treatment facility for dozens of miles, not an insignificant distance when the only mode of transportation was by foot. Now it had been cleaned up, rebuilt, and staffed with a mix of Sudanese, Kenyans, Ethiopians, Americans, and one Australian. Kate felt proud to be a part of something as useful as the hospital. In Australia she had been near the top of her field, a board-certified internist with a subspecialty in infectious diseases. She had even gone to the University of Washington for special training. But she had felt bored, cramped and generally unsatisfied with her university praxes in Melbourne. When a friend she had dated as a college student returned from the Sudan talking about the need and the opportunity there, she couldn't put it out of her head. She tried to ignore the subject, but everywhere she turned, it seemed, there was some other news or information about southern Sudan. Finally, she began to pray about it, asking God if there was something that she was supposed to do.

The answer came the next day, in the form of an e-mail from a doctor in Kenya she had never met. He had been told about Kate by her friend, and felt that she might be able to help, not only with patients at the hospital, but also in training the Sudanese staff, most of whom had had no formal education, only what they could garner in bits and pieces from wherever. She pondered the message, prayed about it, and decided she couldn't go. There was no way. She had too much to do. She had teaching responsibilities. She had patients who relied on her. She had two cats. What would she do with Puck and Bottom? She decided to ask her department chairman about a leave of absence. He'd undoubtedly say no, and then she could e-mail back to Kenya, saying that she couldn't get away.

Two days later, her chairman told her that, not only could she have a leave of absence, she'd be allowed to stay on staff at half-pay, her teaching clinics would be covered and all she had to do was bring back interesting cases to present to the students and staff at Grand Rounds. Two weeks later she was on a Qantas flight to Nairobi, her cats and apartment being cared for by a friend of a friend of her former boyfriend. Kate marveled at how swiftly and smoothly everything had fallen into place.

"I suppose I'm supposed to be here," she had thought. "No whineging now!"

****

"Juba Base, this is SAF-011. Approaching target area."

"SAF-011, Juba Base. Target confirmed. Commence your run."

Achmed looked expectantly at Arkady. By the provisions in his contract, the Ukrainian was permitted to turn over the controls of the aircraft to a Sudanese co-pilot during the bombing runs. Arkady had insisted on this. He had no qualms about being a chauffeur for these people, especially at the salary they paid, but he didn't like the idea of bombing civilians. He had seen enough of that in Afghanistan. When he reflected on it, he could see that there was little difference between carrying the rifle to the execution, and actually pulling the trigger, but the provision made it possible for him to get to sleep most nights without too much vodka. Nonetheless, he delayed in the turnover, just to annoy Achmed.

"Well, Russian?"

"I am relieved. Co-pilot's airplane."

"Co-pilot's airplane." Achmed fiddled with the controls. The airplane was perfectly on course, at the proper altitude. There was nothing that needed to be done. In the time-honored tradition that no pilot was as good as oneself, however, such fiddling was mandatory. It wasn't even that Achmed felt superior to the Ukrainian. It was just something that you did when you assumed control.

"Bomb Crew. I am opening the cargo door. Stand clear."

"Standing clear."

The Antonov had been designed as a cargo airplane, with powerful engines mounted above the wings, ideally suited for operating in primitive, high, hot climates. It had a large cargo door and ramp at the tail, that lowered down to allow cargo and small vehicles to be loaded straight into the long axis of the fuselage. The Sudanese government had originally been given a fleet of these aircraft by Iraq, to move troops and military equipment from one part of the country to another. But someone discovered that ordinary iron bombs, 'dumb bombs', could be rolled off the end of the cargo ramp in flight, turning the Antonov into a bomber. The accuracy of these bombs was nil, especially since the Antonov had to fly above 15,000 feet to avoid the Stinger missiles that the rebels had. But the load that the plane could carry, the relatively low cost per flight-hour (compared to the MiG-21 and Mi-24 attacks), and the terror that such indiscriminate bombing caused among the southern civilians had made the Antonov the favorite weapon of the Government of Sudan.

"I have visual on the target. Prepare to release three 200-kilo bombs at two second intervals on my command."

"Standing by."

The Antonov droned on, straight and level at 17,000 feet. The bomb crew fused the bombs with simple impact detonators, rolled them to the ramp, tightened their security tethers, and waited.

"Stand by. One minute."

"Standing by."

"Release weapons."

"Number one gone. Number two gone. Number three gone! Death to the rebels!"

"Death to the rebels," replied Achmed.

"And to any women or children who happen to be foolish enough to live in this area," added Arkady.

The Antonov droned on. The bombs fell, describing a graceful spiraling motion through the air. In two minutes there would be casualties on the ground.

****

"The Antonov is coming! The Antonov is coming!"

Kate was tempted to ignore the warning shouts and the blast on the little hand-held air horn that the watchman carried for just such a purpose. It reminded Kate of football games back home. She really resented the interruption in her clinic. These airplanes flew over two or three times a week, and always, it seemed, when the clinic was busiest. They had never dropped any bombs on the village, just droned on and on, to some other place. She started to tell Joel that she wasn't going to run to the cave in the rocks where most of the staff and patients hid when the Antonov flew over, but he took her hand and said:

"Doctor Kate, please come and hide. This one is coming straight over the hospital!"

Kate wondered how he could tell. She could hear the irritating sound of the engines, but she couldn't see anything up there.

"Please, Doctor Kate. Come to the cave!"

As Kate ran toward the granite outcropping that stood at the southern edge of the hospital grounds, she was aware of a new sound. It was a high-pitched warbling noise, something that she had never heard before.

"The bombs are coming! Run faster!" shouted Joel.

Kate looked back over her shoulder at the clinic area. She was horrified to see the Dinka mother she had just treated struggling with her twins. She was yards and yards from the shelter of the rocks. Kate turned and ran back toward her, as the warbling sound became unbearable. Then blackness.

Editor's note: this section is an excerpt from a novel in progress.

Hark the Herald Angels Sing
Bernd Kutzscher, MD

The Middle Fork of the Salmon River, known to all whitewater guides as "The Middle Fork," flows from south to north, in the midst of Idaho's enormous Frank Church-River of No Return Wilderness. This is the largest wilderness area in the U.S. outside of Alaska. From small streams in the high meadows that meander in the shadows of the mighty Sawtooth Range, the Middle Fork carves its way 104 miles north to its intersection with the Main Salmon River. On the last day of most commercial raft trips, groups face the sheer cliffs of "Impassable Canyon" and its spectacular rapids that come in swift succession. Near the start of Impassable Canyon, tucked into a small bend on the left side of the river, is a sandy and forested camp by the name of Elk Bar. A day that I will never forget started at Elk Bar.

June is often cold on the Middle Fork since its location in Idaho puts it far north and because the Middle Fork is truly a mountain stream, with the starting point at Boundary Creek at an elevation of 5,800 feet. I was lead guide on this trip, a reward of sorts for quite a few years of guiding experience in Idaho and especially on the Middle Fork. Fortunately, I was surrounded by a group of exceptionally experienced and talented guides, five boats and five guides in all.

This morning in mid-June was cool with a light drizzle that coated the vertical granite slabs above Elk Bar. Guides prepared for a cold and wet day, tucking green thermos bottles with silver stainless steel lids into their loads. They could anticipate that their passengers would appreciate a sip of hot, sugary tea or warm cocoa once they entered the rapids.

The passengers were a bit restless, since they had not been on the water in over a day. Because the river was flowing so rapidly, our group of twenty-five passengers and five guides had easily reached Elk Bar at the entrance to Impassable Canyon in four days. This left the fifth day for a "lay over day" – a passenger's chance to relax, read, hike, fish and socialize. Instead of breaking camp the morning of the fifth river day, the group could sleep in and make camp a home for another twenty-four hours.

I especially enjoyed the Mahoneys. The Mahoney family was out west for the first time. John and Carole were in their 40's, with a young boy and girl. This summer vacation was well-earned, a celebration of selling a scrap metal company that John had built from scratch and which made him, for the first time in his life, financially independent. Their son, Steven, was 12. He had the young swagger that growing up in the blue collar parts of Boston provided. Except, he had never been in the wilderness, and he was very impressed by how wild and remote these surroundings felt.

During the introduction to the trip, as lead guide, I had given the usual warnings and precautions. The river was swift and cold, and grew in volume as we floated downstream. Life jackets were mandatory, and safety always the first priority. Falling in the water might be fun, but only for a moment until the cold and overwhelming power of the Middle Fork made one feel very small and even helpless. In addition, for this trip, I had an additional matter of safety to discuss.

Yellowstone National Park in neighboring Wyoming was having bear problems. Not only were the bears feeding on garbage and breaking into cars. These bears had become aggressive and dangerous. The park rangers had a plan. When a bear misbehaved, it was sedated, given a large ear tag and driven far away from populated areas. If a bear with an ear tag reappeared and misbehaved, it was sedated, given a large ear tag on the other ear and driven far away from populated areas. If a bear with two ear tags returned and misbehaved, it was designated a "three time loser." It was given the royal treatment including sedation, a stripe of red paint down its back and a helicopter ride to the deep wilderness in the mountains surrounding the Middle Fork, its new home.

During my lead guide orientation talk, I had mentioned the various dangers on shore – slippery rocks, poison ivy, rattlesnakes and red-striped bears. I could see that Steven and his 10 years old sister, Erin, were quite impressed, especially the bear part. Both Steven and Erin looked confident and relaxed, and I sensed they would stay that way, at least while the sun was shining and the whitewater looked friendly. Impassable Canyon would prove to be a challenge of a different type.

As the lay over day moved along into late afternoon, the Mahoney family returned from a hike on which they had a view of a few of the early rapids they would be facing in the morning. They were clearly impressed, both by the size of the whitewater and by the quick succession of one large rapid after another. This was no longer a narrow mountain stream. This was a large river with an ominous growl.

Rapids are formed in a number of ways. Some rivers, such as the Colorado through the Grand Canyon, are nearly flat with only a slight drop in elevation. Rapids there are formed because large boulders have been washed down side canyons during flash floods, producing a dam over which water cascades and drops. Mountain rivers, however, are different. Rapids on rivers such as the Middle Fork are formed by a combination of gradient, boulders, constriction and water flow. Gradient is the drop in elevation that pulls the river downstream by gravity. The steeper the gradient, the faster the river flow. Unlike the Colorado which drops around 10 feet per mile on average, the Middle Fork drops 25 to 30 feet per mile. Boulders are strewn everywhere in the Middle Fork. When the boulders are large enough to withstand the current, they can clog the main channel and create an ill-defined path that zig zags its way through the rapid. When the river constricts, the water accelerates through the narrower channel, and this speed is another element in creating a rapid. Water flow on the Middle Fork is related to the winter snowpack and the daily temperature. When the snowpack in the Sawtooth Range is deep, more water is ready to rush down the Middle Fork. When the days in the spring and summer turn warm, the snow melt turns from a trickle to a flood, and the water volume on the Middle Fork can rise within hours.

High water on the Middle Fork is a sight to behold. Familiar beaches on the shore are underwater. Trees that are usually anchors to tie a raft are instead within the current. Branches and occasionally entire trees can be swept downstream. The water in the main river channel is white with froth and pushed into standing waves by the boulders deep below. When the boulders are large but the water is high enough to flow over them, the downstream side of the boulder will become a "hole," a vortex of chaotic water coming in from all directions to fill the vacuum behind the boulder. These holes are where even the largest rafts can flip like tiny bathtub toys. When steep gradient, large boulders, constriction and high water flow all combine, a raft is at the mercy of the river, with a guide making small adjustments using long and heavy oars. These small adjustments are the difference between success and potential disaster.

At the Elk Bar campsite, it was clear on the lay over day that the warm temperature was making the water rise. The current looked faster, with small waves appearing in current that had been smooth only hours before. As hikers returned from their adventures, they were hot and thirsty. Even when the temperatures fell over night, there would be high water in the morning just as we were entering Impassable Canyon. A quiet tension began to build as the rising water level created a new visual image of the river, accompanied by a rumbling sound of water churning over rocks.

Impassable Canyon earned its name long before recreational rafting came to the Middle Fork. The Sheepeater Indians who lived in this canyon gave it the name because the steep cliffs made it impossible to pass easily up or downstream on foot. The name was perfect for early rafting guides in small wooden row boats who often did find the river impassable. As whitewater rafting grew more sophisticated with the introduction of rubber rafts and other specialized equipment, the steep canyon portion of the Middle Fork was still a challenge to whitewater guides, but no longer impassable. At high water, however, it was more than just a fun ride.

The Mahoney parents approached me in the evening, after putting the kids to bed in their sleeping bags. The warmth of the day had faded, with clouds and drizzle moving in. They were a bit concerned about their young children who would be challenged in the morning by a less friendly river. They asked if I, as lead guide, would take the family on my boat. I told them "yes," but I knew something that they did not know. By tradition, the lead guide's boat takes the lead position in more challenging water. If the lead boat flips, there is no one downstream to pick up the pieces. To make matters worse, people float faster than rafts.

Guides share a light-hearted camaraderie and, in many cases, deep friendship. Mutual trust is the essence of the relationship, followed by nearly blissful shared experiences and the sure knowledge that they have the best job on the planet. The light-heartedness of the friendship is genuine, but just beneath the surface for any experienced guide is a serious side based on the pride of having hard-won skills, a respect for the danger in such powerful water and the sobering knowledge that guests are entrusting their lives and the lives of their family members. As a young and adventure-seeking person, every guide faces the gulp moment when a CEO makes it clear that the safety of a spouse and children is a matter of the utmost importance.

Despite their frequent devil-may-care moments, guides are highly trained and chock full of the hard-won knowledge that comes only with experience. In high water, each guide has a job on the water, determined in large part by boat positioning. The lead boat sets the pace and chooses the best route or signals the boats behind if there is a better route. The second boat, especially in high water, is responsible for the lead boat since the lead boat is very exposed. Like every other boat, the second boat is also responsible for the boat behind it. The third boat is the back up boat for people who need rescue from the first two boats. The second to last boat is in charge of gear. If it sees any rafting items from the yard sale of a flip, the second to last boat picks up the pieces so that the trip can be reassembled downstream. The last boat, the sweep or safety boat carries the key safety items such as advanced first aid supplies, communications if available and numerous safety lines and related gear needed for swift water rescue of people and boats. The last boat is also responsible for keeping the entire trip in front of it. If a person is on shore or in the water, the sweep boat has to deal with that person so that no one is left behind and no one is unaccounted for. In high water, especially on a cold and challenging river, each experienced guide will know the number of people and the names of the passengers in the raft in front and behind. These rules, seriously taught and rarely needed, are the gospel for skilled guides. They define the relationship of total trust amongst guides in a highly professional crew.

By habit, the guides are awake in the morning well before the guests. By the time the coffee is brewing and the fresh fruit is sliced, the guests are usually starting to emerge from their sleeping bags and tents. On a drizzly morning after a moist night, the start up ritual takes a bit longer. Guests are encouraged to dry their sleeping bags so that they will be ready for use in the evening. This, however, was the last day of the trip, so the sleeping bags could dry in a warm motel room in Salmon, the town where the guests would be taken by bus from the take out point close to where the Middle Fork of the Salmon merged with the Main Salmon, the first point where we would see a road after 104 miles of floating downstream.

I prepared a warm, extra rich and extra large serving of hot chocolate for the kids. I poured scalding hot water right off the fire into the thermoses to warm them and then replaced the water with hot chocolate, two thermos bottles full to the brim. Steven and Erin were a bit nervous at breakfast, but the French toast was a hit and the maple syrup reminded them of their New England home. By the time they came down to the boats with their gear, they were well prepared for the morning ahead.

Before the advent of synthetic cold weather gear, guests on potentially cold trips were asked to bring various items of wool. Once dressed in wool from the cap past the sweater to the socks, and if covered by rain gear, even a child with little body fat could stay warm when wet. Once the wool was wet, though, it would stay wet. But a warm and wet child was so much better than a cold and wet one. Steven and Erin were barely recognizable in their gear, but they were set to go.

Guides are proud of how they secure their gear to their raft. Each guide has developed a system of making sure the raft could flip in rapids and still be righted with every item secure and accounted for. Starting with webbing used by climbers, each passenger's dry bag, food box, passenger's day bag and any other incidental item needs to be lashed down with a line through some handle or ring so that nothing can float away – even if the boat floated upside down through rapids and struck underwater rocks. This morning, I was especially careful to double-check each item. The last pieces to be stowed were two lime-green thermos bottles, filled to the top with hot chocolate.

Distribution of weight is one of many arcane topics that guides discuss, and it makes a difference in how a raft behaves. Having the entire Mahoney family in the front of the boat gave it more momentum going into large whitewater and could help push the raft through the most challenging waves and holes. In a guide's mind, large whitewater was an adrenalin filled thrill. The honest truth was that the whitewater brought many guides to the job. What kept them, though, were the beauty, freedom, tranquility and friendship. On a big water day, however, guiding took on an extra meaning. Here was a chance to test skills refined over hundreds of trips and thousands of miles.

Big water is always a challenge. Waves higher than most people ever see in the ocean stand in the main channels through a rapid. The tops of the waves are dynamic as each wave builds and collapses on itself. A smooth run one second can be a collision with a breaking wave the next. Waves in the best channel might be angled so that they not only rock the raft but also apply torque which can twist a heavy raft up, sideways and over – like a spatula lifting and then depositing the over-matched boat back into the current upside down.

Waves, though, are the easier part of a run through a large rapid at high water. What can stop a boat and make it a mere plaything is a large "hole." As water flows downstream, it passes boulders. The water needs to fill in the empty space downstream of each boulder by flowing back upstream, creating an "eddy." Looked at from above, a large rapid with numerous boulders is a chaotic mix of currents going in many directions, usually with a most desirable route where the main current flows between the rocks. In higher water, the same boulders are covered by the current. At just the right level of flow, the swift current as it passes over a barely submerged rock breaks back on itself, creating a vortex or "hole" just downstream of the boulder. Such a hole can hold a large raft and can suck it back upstream where the water pouring over the boulder instantly fills the raft with water or flips it in an instant. When whitewater guides talk about rapids, they talk about the holes and rarely the waves.

The Elk Bar campsite usually has a gentle current flowing past it. This morning, the current was powerful and fast. The Middle Fork of the Salmon is completely wild. There are no upstream dams to regulate flow levels. The current we were about to join was recent melt from the enormous snow and ice fields of the spectacular Sawtooth Mountain range a few miles upstream. We would have just a few miles of floating downstream in swift current before starting a long section of nearly continuous large rapids. Usually, a few miles mean a nice long break. At high water, however, a few miles translated into a few minutes to prepare. We were in Impassable Canyon. Since the start of our trip, huge and rushing creeks had increased the volume of water in the river by nearly ten-fold. The sky was gray, a light drizzle fell, the huge granite cliffs on either side were slick and dark gray, the air temperature was cold, and the water was much colder. It was a set up for a great ride or a very long morning.

As we were swept downstream, I kept up a steady conversation with the Mahoneys. I wanted to keep them from becoming fearful. Though tense, they seemed ready – except for young Steven who began to cry. He was inconsolable, even with his mother's arm over his shoulder. "Steven," I shouted out over the deep rumble of the approaching rapid. "Come back and sit near me." That did the trick. Quickly, Steven clambered up and over the gear to where I was sitting with the oars in my hand. I gave him a hand as he worked his way past me, to the mostly empty back space in the raft where I had set up a tight line for a passenger to hold on. I turned to look back, and his crying had stopped. As I looked downstream, I saw the gentle bend to the right which led into Redside rapid, the start of the biggest water on the Middle Fork. Just then, Steven again started to cry.

Many rapids begin on a turn in the river. For a guide, the bend was critical. Water sweeps to the "outside" of a turn, just as a car is pulled to the left on a bend to the right. One of the many commandments for a guide, especially in high water, is to stay to the inside when approaching a rapid, especially an unfamiliar one. It is always relatively easy to move to the outside, even in powerful water. However, once on the outside, there is no chance of moving back to the inside against the full force of the current. I knew Redsides rapid well. I had run it successfully over fifty times. I knew that there were two main runs. At normal water levels, the run through the middle was exciting, challenging and beautiful. The main current passed between two enormous boulders that stood out clearly from upstream. On the right, there was a sneak channel close to shore that was the safety run in high water. In usual water levels, the same right side channel was clogged with rocks. There was little time left to choose my route as the water pushed me to the left, the outside of the turn. I had a few seconds remaining to choose the safety run on the right which I would be able to reach only with a very determined effort. In front of me, the Mahoneys framed the approaching rapid.

Usually, an experienced guide can look downstream and "read" the rapid, even one that he had never run before. The rocks, the holes, the current direction and sound and the most favorable current to run are all "visible" despite being unseen, based on an instinct developed over hundreds of similar runs. As I glanced ahead at the rapid, it was not at all clear to me that the usual middle channel was safe. I could only see a maelstrom of exploding white waves and the froth that could only be a large hole in the usual channel. The two old familiar house-sized boulders that marked both sides of the main run had, in this water level, created holes that joined together to create one huge hole in the middle of the river, exactly where I was headed. In that instant, I looked right and realized I had waited too long. The safety channel on the right was no longer attainable. I was headed into trouble, and there was no turning back.

I glanced back to see where the other rafts were positioned. I planned to point with my hand to the right, following the iron-clad rule amongst guides to only point to the "positive," to safety. I felt even more exposed when I saw all four rafts behind me neatly lined up in position to take the safety run on the right. It was my good fortune that my fellow guides had ignored my lead. In high and dangerous water, rafts stay in close formation so that they can watch and help each other. My friends in the other four boats were following this rule to perfection. As I looked back, young Steven began to cry again. He must have looked at my face and sensed that there was trouble ahead. Over the din of the approaching rapid, I yelled to him, "Sing a song." He hollered back, "I don't know any." With other problems on my mind, I suggested, "Sing a Christmas song." As we dropped down the last few yards before the froth and chaos now directly in front of us, I heard a sweet and surprisingly steady voice singing, "Hark the Herald Angels Sing…"

In an instant, I was underwater in a dark space. Hundreds of times, I had told our guests during pre-trip safety talks that coming up under a boat would be frightening and disorienting. It was. The immediate goal would be to remain calm and "crawl" along the raft in any direction to get clear and into air. An overturned raft added an additional challenge, the many items now underwater creating a barrier and a potential source of disastrous entrapment. I calmed myself long enough to follow the rule, and soon was out from under the boat. I immediately looked around and saw three heads bobbing in the water, held high by their life jackets and their own efforts. Young Steven was missing. Holding onto a strap on the side of my overturned boat, I pulled myself back under the load and immediately found Steven motionless beneath the raft. I yanked on his life jacket and pulled him into the light of day, keeping a hand grasped to his jacket. The raft was still in huge waves, but I could see from the peak of each wave that there was a large eddy just downstream along the shore on the left. This was the chance I needed. With all my strength, I pushed Steven to river left and watched him rise over a submerged boulder and into the eddy where the water moved back upstream and toward the shore. I screamed at Steven to swim for shore, and he followed instructions perfectly until he was in knee high water on the left bank. I looked downstream and saw Carole in the current but on the left side. She glanced back at me, expecting help. I gestured wildly for her to swim to the left shore and the same eddy, and to my amazement, she was soon also safe. Erin was close by but flailing in the water, and I grabbed her life jacket and pulled both of us toward the left shore. I pushed her decisively into the safety of the eddy and glanced downstream once more. More than a hundred yards away and in the middle of the current, Dad was bobbing along and seemingly not making any effort to fight his way to the side as he approached Weber Rapid, even larger than Redsides. For an instant, I thought of getting back into the current to chase him, but I knew I was already exhausted and would end up just adding another body to be saved in the rescue effort. I looked to my right, into the current, and there was Guy, the number two boat, positioned exactly where he should be. I thought I saw a hint of dismay in his face regarding my ill-advised run into the center of the river. As we had all been trained, he knew who had been in my boat. I hollered and gestured to him that three were safe but that John was downstream and in the main current. In an instant, he gave chase. We both knew that John was already exhausted and about to enter a series of enormous rapids with little chance of self-rescue. His life jacket was his best friend, it and the guides behind him who were speeding downstream through the rapids in a desperate attempt to save John whose life was clearly in imminent danger.

Life jackets are jokingly called "personal flotation devices" by the guides because that phrase, or PFD, is government lingo. Any whitewater trip, even if the whitewater is a barely moving trickle, includes mandatory Class 5 PFD's. A Class 5 PFD is designed to keep an unconscious person on his back with his head out of the water to allow breathing. At this moment, John was being kept afloat only by his Class 5 PFD. As soon as the average person is thrown into cold, churning and overpowering whitewater, there is a natural and healthy tendency to physically react by fighting the current and moving toward shore. In virtually all cases, guides remind their guests to float in whitewater on their backs with their feet downstream. This position allows a swimmer to see what is coming, breathe between waves and protect the head from on-coming rocks and other obstacles.

After a very short time in the cold water of the Middle Fork, however, most people have their energy sapped to the bare minimum, enough to keep breathing and to keep closing their mouths enough to prevent swallowing large amounts of water. That was the only effort John was still capable of as his head bobbed up and down in the middle of the current. Below Redsides rapid were more large rapids. In lower water levels, there was a clear cut break between rapids, enough to get to shore. At high water, John could barely tell that one rapid had ended and another was about to begin. To the extent that he was still thinking, his only conscious effort was to keep breathing. He did not have the strength left to swim toward shore or even to look upstream to see whether help was on the way. Had he managed to turn his head, the large waves would have prevented him from seeing Guy and Jody who were in pursuit. In most rapids, especially in high and fast water, a guide rowing a raft will face downstream while pulling the oars to slow down and maneuver. This gives the best control, the best view of approaching danger and the most time to find the best route. Guy and Jody had both made the decision to ignore that approach and to instead row with their backs to the upcoming rapids to increase their downstream speed. Only a quick glance over a shoulder could tell them what was coming. Fortunately, both knew the rapids of the Middle Fork so well that they also had experience and instinct on their side. The passengers in each boat were now on the upstream end of the raft, but they had been instructed to help by looking downstream, looking to find John whose head would be nothing more than a black dot on the white waves.

Upstream, Tim in the number four boat moved along trying to catch every eddy he could to give him some time to scan the river for gear. His passengers helped pick up any floating pieces, throwing them into the bottom of their raft. Just upstream, David knew his job as the sweep boat well. David was young, confident, a sailor and a perfectionist. He exuded competence and expected the same from his fellow guides. He could be seen as brash by the more veteran guides, but no one denied that he could get the job done. Fighting the fast current in the middle of the river, David moved in toward shore where I was standing, trying to help stabilize the swimmers. Knowing that there was a poorly defined path over the boulders along the shore, David made the decision that he could leave passengers behind. He needed to keep his boat light to speed downstream to help. He gave instructions to his passengers to jump to shore one by one, and he quickly untied his expert sailing knots to release gear and throw sleeping bags toward shore. As he started to move back into the current, I jumped into his raft and shouted brief instructions to the passengers from David's boat. "Warm up the swimmers. Use clothing. Use the sleeping bags. Use anything you've got."

Hypothermia is the killer in cold and fast water. With a life jacket, a swimmer can stay afloat and keep breathing. As the body's core temperature drops, all basic functions quickly grind to a halt. Strength, clear thinking, orientation, even the will to live are soon erased. The treatment is to warm the body's core. As instructed, I could see the passengers on shore pull off the wet and cold clothes of the three swimmers and cover them in warm gear. As we started to round the next bend, I could see the brightly colored sleeping bags being pulled out of their stuff sacks and wrapped around the swimmers. I knew they would be ok. Now several miles downstream, John's body was in a desperate fight to stay alive. His nervous system had shut down all non-essentials, including the muscles he could have used to get to shore. The blood vessels on the surface of his body clamped down to preserve the remaining warmth of his body for his heart, lungs and brain. He was still alive, but helpless. He was in the main current and headed downstream with no chance of fighting the still fast-moving river enough to reach the safety of shore. He had a few more minutes of life in him.

Guy's passengers kept a watch for John. "Look at the top of waves. He has to be there. We have to be getting close." Just then, a passenger in his boat screamed, "I think I saw his head in the next rapid." Guy glanced quickly over his shoulder to remind himself how the rapid needed to be run. Now was not the time to put more people into the water. "Keep looking at John. Don't lose sight of him. Hold on tight." Guy's boat dropped stern first into a deep trough, and the passengers in the bow held on with both hands as they were whiplashed into the air. A huge wave washed over the raft as it dove down into the next trough. "I've got him," one of the passengers shouted. "He's in the middle of the current." Guy was short, wiry and strong. He could move a raft. He knew the currents and eddies. He was the right person for John at the right time. Guy felt the waves subside before he glanced back to see a stretch of only green, fast current. He knew the next big rapid was just around the corner. With each stroke of the heavy ash oars, he pulled closer to John who was oblivious to the help coming to him from upstream. With a swift motion, Guy used both arms, moving the heavy oars in opposite directions to spin the boat around. He was now again facing downstream and the passengers in his boat were in a position to grab John as soon as the raft closed in just a bit more. With two powerful pushes on his oars, Guy closed the final gap. In an instant, John was in the bottom of the boat. He was totally immobile, only his eyes showing signs of life and feeble hope. As the passengers in his boat cheered and celebrated, Guy knew that the hardest part was yet to come.

John's body temperature had, by now, plummeted. At 98.6 degrees, our bodies are ready for anything. John's core temperature was well below 95 degrees, and his usual metabolism had all but stopped. He had no idea where he was or what had happened to him. He was beyond fear. He was helpless and below a temperature which would allow his body to replenish warmth on its own. He was severely hypothermic. As quickly as he could, Guy pulled his raft toward the left bank where one of the passengers jumped out and secured the bow line. Along with the other passengers, Guy lifted John out of the raft and onto a small patch of sand between large boulders immediately next to the river. Standing in the front of David's sweep boat, I could see the activity downstream and hollered to David to pull to the left shore. He was already turning and on his way there. At the moment we reached the shore, I jumped out of the raft and scrambled over rocks to reach John. I was the most experienced person on the trip in advanced first aid, and it was my job to take charge. I kneeled down next to John who did not recognize me. His body looked pale with patches of blue. Even to my chilled hands, he felt ice-cold. Trying to remain calm, I gave instructions to pull dry gear from one of the boats. I told one of the passengers from Guy's boat to help me remove John's cold, wet clothing. I glanced up to look at the sky. The clouds had broken, and the warm rays of the sun had already started to heat the dry sand along the shore. Naked, blue, disoriented and completely limp, John looked barely alive. I searched for a pulse at his wrist. Nothing. I reached down to his larger femoral artery at his groin. Still nothing. I placed my index and middle fingers at the side of his throat below his jaw where I knew the carotid artery should still be supplying John's brain with oxygenated blood. Nothing. At this moment, I thought that CPR was the last step available. Just as I was ready to pull away my fingers in a near panic of frustration and despair, I remembered what I had been taught. During hypothermia, the heart rate can drop down to the low 30's. I placed my fingers back on John's carotid artery, and there it was. A pulse, weak and slow – but a sign that John's heart was still beating without help. I placed my ear next to his mouth and heard the faint sound of shallow breathing. John was in grave danger, but alive. I knew that, with proper care, he might be saved.

The passengers helped me pull a thick goose down sleeping bag around John and up to his nose. They found a knit cap and pulled it over his head and down to his ears. John still did not respond to my words to him. The passengers piled more clothes on him, giving him more insulation. But insulation did not equal heat. John could survive only if he was given heat. In an ER, various sources of heat could be used to slowly raise John's core body temperature. The warming therapy would be placed at strategic points on his body, and warmed IV fluids would start to warm him from within. In the wilderness, along the banks of the Middle Fork of the Salmon, we had only two readily available sources of heat. A fire could be built fairly quickly, and small pieces of driftwood would keep the flames burning. But external warmth at this time would risk causing John's most superficial blood vessels to dilate, pulling blood away from his vital organs. The other source of heat was another human body, a 98.6 degree heat producing machine. I pulled off all my wet clothes and slipped into the sleeping bag next to John. I looked up to see the faces of the passengers who had pulled John out of the water. In an instant, they understood that this was the final step, the final effort to bring John's chilled body back to life. After a few minutes, I could hear a low moan from John, and I could hear the sound of his breathing as it became deeper and more regular. I felt again for his carotid artery pulse, and it felt stronger and faster. As the minutes passed, he began to mumble some unintelligible words. Then, as if a switch had been reset, John's eyes opened, and he took in the scene around him. "Erin, Steven, Carole. Are they ok?" "Yes, John, they are safe and fine. They are upstream, and they'll be here soon." After a few more minutes, I slipped out of the sleeping bag and back into my wet clothes, I could see the fear leave John's face, replaced by a tentative smile as he whispered, "That was some set of rapids."

I looked upstream as the other rafts floated toward us. Seeing that John had been rescued, they had waited for the walkers and then floated downstream, filled with all the remaining passengers including John's anxious wife and children. Carole escorted her children out of the raft and looked at where I was standing next to her husband. I called to her to come over. As she neared John, with her children following, she whispered ahead to me, "Is John ok?" "Yes, Carole, he's going to be fine."

    The rest of the run through Impassable Canyon is now a blur to me. Tim had recovered my raft and various pieces of floating gear, pulled the raft to shore and turned it upright. I was pleased to see that the gear had shifted but was, with Tim's salvaging efforts, largely accounted for. The oars were still attached to the rowing frame. I stepped into my raft. I looked at my fellow guides, filled with admiration for the job they had done. I hesitated for a moment, wondering if we should modify our original boat order and distribution of passengers. As I rested, sitting in my raft, all the pieces of the trip came back together. I could only look up at the high cliffs and thank the river gods for their help. When I turned back to look at the passengers on the shore, I saw the Mahoney family headed my way, ready to resume their journey in my boat. I glanced over at Jody, the most senior of the guides. "Lead the way," he said.

    After its course of nearly 100 miles through the high mountains of Idaho, the Middle Fork of the Salmon runs at a perpendicular angle into the Main Salmon, its larger cousin which also begins in the Sawtooth Mountain range. On the far side of the Main Salmon River is a dirt road, the first road we had seen since the headwaters of the Middle Fork 6 days ago. A few miles downstream on the Main Salmon, a boat ramp on the right had been built by the Forest Service to make the take out a bit easier. A school bus was waiting for the guests. This was always a bittersweet moment for me. Friendships fashioned in a concentrated way over nearly a week of adventure were coming to a sudden conclusion. For the passengers, the magic of the Middle Fork canyon was at an end. The smooth elegance of the simple life of river and camp was about to be overwhelmed by schedules, messages and thoughts about tomorrow. And yet, this was also a moment each guide relished. As soon as the passengers rolled off, we could all breathe a sigh of relief and return to the care-free mode that had brought us all to this place and this line of work.

Once we had placed the gear into the back of our open truck, we scrambled up the sides of the truck and climbed onto the load of deflated rafts and other river running debris, looking for a comfortable place from which to enjoy the long ride back to our guides' house. If we were lucky, we would see a few bighorn sheep, some golden eagle riding the thermals along the cliffs and possibly even a mountain goat. As we bounced along, back upstream along the Main Salmon River, we came again to the place where the Middle Fork poured into the Main Salmon. The truck stopped, as it always did as this point, and we looked up the Middle Fork canyon. Along the side of the road, square with the view back up the Middle Fork, the Forest Service had placed a sign that always captured my imagination. "Yonder lies the Idaho Wilderness Area."

I looked at the satisfied faces of my fellow guides who also gazed with an affectionate longing up the free flowing water of the Middle Fork. They had saved me today. We shared a moment of silent reflection, knowing how close we had come to disaster but savoring the skills that had rescued us all. In another week, we would be back in Impassable Canyon with a new group of people. Today's adventure and near tragedy would give us tales to tell them. Some morbid humor was all I could muster. "Hey," I called out. "Let's have some fun tonight in town. I nearly killed the whole Mahoney family, and they just gave me the biggest tip I've ever seen."

My Fish Story
Jeanne Verville

Once upon a time, in the early '90s, I was a green in-house lawyer in the area of transactions. During my first big negotiations, I was the only woman on either team. While I had succeeded in other assignments, I now felt like a fish out of water. I couldn't figure out how to communicate, even during the pre-negotiation phase in the morning.

I understood this coffee time as an opportunity to meet with members of my team and the opposing team to establish rapport. I tried the style I'd used successfully all my life, asking such questions as, "Do you have a family?" and "What do you do for fun?" It didn't take long to notice that, after a perfunctory answer, the man I was trying to make nice with turned and starting talking to another man. I observed the interaction.

"Last time I saw Michael Jordan play he made 30 points," one said, jiggling the coins in his pocket.

"Last time *I* saw Michael Jordan play he made 32 points," the other responded, crossing his arms, spreading his feet and tucking his chin.

Then they turned to boasting about golf scores on particularly steep slope courses in Scottsdale or Palm Springs. "I couldn't believe my drive on that long par 5 on number 8. I hit it three hundred yards!"

I felt lost at sea, surrounded by the pointed fins of one-upmanship. I wasn't in the conversation and didn't know how to get in. For one thing, I had never played the Grey Wolf course in Scottsdale. And if I had, it would never have occurred to me to brag about my score. I was taught *not* to brag. And if I had seen Michael Jordan play, I'm sure I wouldn't have remembered how many points he made.

I would learn later that, for some men, the important thing before starting negotiations is to take each other's measure to see who is smarter and more powerful – who is going to be hard to beat down on the millions of items to be decided around the negotiation table. How they did that by comparing how many baskets they saw Michael Jordan make escaped me.

In the conference room we sat around a large gleaming table made of some exotic, non-sustainable wood and got down to business. An hour into the meeting, after a review of the main issues, I tried to participate by throwing out an idea.

"Why don't we keep a log of what both sides agree on and an assignment list of who's going to work on the unresolved issues?"

No response. Fear that I'd said something stupid was followed quickly by blushing shame that I *was* stupid. My stomach clenched and I looked at the wood grain through a thin veil of tears.

Three minutes later Jerry said, "We need to keep track of issues we agree on and decide who's working on what."

"Great idea, Jerry," the others chorused.

I felt confused. What was going on? Were they deaf?

This continued at the next session and the next. I felt ineffective and second rate. I felt invisible. At night I replayed the scenes of me trying to contribute, noting with chagrin that I just wasn't part of the team. I felt like the clumsy fat kid neither team really wants to pick.

Enough wallowing. I knew I needed help. I called a lawyer friend and arranged lunch. She brought along four experienced female transactions attorneys. At first they all laughed at me when I shared my dismay.

"Oh, that's just the game they play," Gail said. "You know. They're *men*. They always have to be one up. They're going to claim *any* good idea as their own – if they can get away with it. Just don't let them get away with it!"

Back at the conference table, I tried out their advice. Throw out an idea. Wait to see who claims it, then firmly take it back.

"Jerry, I'm glad you like the idea *I* threw out a few minutes ago. Let's build on that."

"Good idea, Jeanne."

It worked! That wasn't so hard. *'Get up, stand up, stand up for your rights...Get up, stand up, don't give up the fight!'*

But something was still wrong. At the breaks and pre-meetings I still found myself alone in left field. I had to find something sporty to talk about. My male secretary's advice to say, with enthusiasm, "How 'bout those Mariners?" just wasn't working. I didn't have any statistics to throw out with it. No "How 'bout that line drive Ken Griffey Jr. hit in the bottom of the fourth." No "Man that Randy Johnson was blazing last night."

But – I finally figured out how I could play the game.

A couple of years earlier I had shamed a law firm into inviting me along on their "special client" fishing trip to the Queen Charlotte Islands. I had noticed my colleague Ted missing in action for a few days and, upon inquiry, was told he had gone fishing with the law firm. I said, elbows akimbo, "Well...Why wasn't *I* invited? I like to fish! And I'm giving them a big piece of business right now – bigger than Ted's."

During the next year, every time I saw a lawyer from that firm I mentioned the business they were getting from me and teased them about the all-male fishing trip. I assumed they thought I was just kidding around, but I really did want to go fishing in the icy waters of beautiful northern British Columbia.

One day in April I got a call from one of the firm's senior partners. "Jeanne, we'd like to invite you to go on the fishing trip this year; *however* you need to know that we get up at 4:30 in the morning and fish until 8 at night and you have to wear a survival suit and there really isn't any place for a woman to go to the bathroom in those two-man boats." Pause. "Do you want to go?"

You bet I did. And I did. And – I caught a 28.5-pound salmon. Yup – cut the bait fish's head off, baited the hook, brought the diving and jumping fish in over 45 minutes of documentary film-like struggle and even bonked the poor thing on the head to end its thrashing – all by myself! It was thrilling.

So, what I figured out in the power plant negotiations was to use my fish story to gain entry into the male locker room of acceptance.

One day on a break, after a particularly good piece of negotiation on my part, I specifically cornered Charley, a young businessman on the opposite team, the one with the slicked back hair like Jon Hamm on *Mad Men,* the one who never met my eye.

"Charley," I said with a little swagger in my voice, "have you ever been salmon fishing in Alaska?"

"Well, no. I haven't," he said, looking at me cautiously.

"Well, *I* went a couple of years ago. It was *great. I* caught a 28.5 pound salmon." As I said these words I spread my arms about a yard wide and shook them up and down a little to indicate the heft of my trophy. "My friends loved me that summer at all those cookouts I threw. Um, nothin' like fresh Alaskan king salmon."

I saw it happen clear as day. As I told Charley about my conquest on the briny deep, I could see respect for me forming in his eyes. Respect. R e s p e c t. I had him. I was no longer just the girl lawyer. I hadn't changed but I *had* learned how to play "mine's bigger than yours." And during the rest of my career, that sorry fish tale helped me establish the rapport I needed to be heard.

Two Toes (Part 1)
Kinsley Earl

The waiting room at the Northwestern Memorial ER felt sterile, mostly because it was nearly empty and smelled like antiseptic. The faces of the few other people in the waiting room were strained – with their own pain or concern for someone else's, I couldn't tell. And I wasn't about to ask.

I limped from the icy linoleum entrance onto the worn, maroon carpeting, and was grateful momentarily for the comparative softness against my one bare foot, stiff with the pain and swelling of what would turn out to be a broken toe. Treading as lightly as I could on the wounded foot, I wondered how often the carpets of an ER waiting room had to be cleaned, and then wondered about the volume and variety of substances that might have been spilled/dropped/poured/projected/leaked onto it over the years.

I had been worried I might end up in the ER that day, but it had never occurred to me that my toe might be the body part to drag me there. I couldn't find my shin guards that morning. In my co-ed, recreational soccer league, shin guards are technically optional, but for me they are a learned obsession. My shins seem to operate with a death wish, seeking out the hardest/sharpest/meanest object in the vicinity and then working their way (and the rest of me) into a head-on collision with said object. I'm quite sure that if you x-rayed my shinbones, they would be covered in tiny nicks and dents, lined up like a prized collection of painful memories between my ankles and knees. Why my shins couldn't develop an unhealthy obsession with, say, pillows, I will never know.

But this wasn't just about my disaster-prone bone structure. It was also about the soccer league I played in. Most of the players in our league fall into one of two, equally dangerous, groups. There are the pseudo-athletes, who used to be good, are desperately trying to relive their glory days, and treat the "rec" league like it's their second coming because they can't qualify for the better leagues. They take the games way too seriously, play with extreme intensity but not a lot of integrity, and wouldn't be caught dead playing defense. Their hard kicks are exactly the kind of thing my shins gun for, like heat-seeking missiles.

The other group of players is totally clueless. They just signed up because it sounded like fun, or their friends were doing it, or some cute girl from the accounting department made a random comment about how "hot" soccer players are. This group kicks spastically at anything that goes past them, and they are just as likely to plant a foot in their opponents' shins as they are on the ball.

So I believe in shin guards. But that morning, I had to play without them. I spent most of the car ride to the game cursing myself for misplacing them, and trying not to imagine the worst-case scenarios. A night in the ER with a broken toe was not among those scenarios.

My friend and roommate, Carrie, had dropped me off at the ER. We had a brief argument as we sat in her car outside of the hospital, each of us cast in a sickly green tint from the fluorescent lighting of the entryway. She wanted to wait with me, but I insisted she go home. I told her it was late and she had work the next day, but the truth was that I didn't want to share whatever experience was waiting for me inside. I hate hospitals (though I don't think I know anyone who actually *likes* them), and I had been dreading this since it had become obvious that some kind of medical attention would, in fact, be necessary for my toe. Before leaving, she extracted a promise from me to call as soon as I had been diagnosed.

I checked in, and then returned to the quiet waiting room where the uncomfortable faces of the other three occupants had not changed. I sat down, careful to keep my throbbing foot off the old carpet, and waited. Leaning back gingerly into the anonymous chair I'd selected at one end of the room, I began to notice how silent and empty the hospital seemed. The lone nurse at the check-in desk was soundlessly absorbed in her own administrative tasks, and there was no sound from the ER itself. There was a TV in the corner, but it was turned off. In the waiting room, the few other people sat without moving in their chairs – whatever shock/concern/pain/desperation had brought us together physically now isolated us each in its absorption.

It took 20 minutes for the triage nurse to call my name. I explained my symptoms, waited, limped back across the maroon carpet to the desk to fill out forms, waited some more, filled out more forms, and then waited some more. I was finally admitted, loaded barefoot onto a gurney, rolled into a curtained-off stall in the ER, and left to wait.

With my feet stretched out in front of me on the cold sheets of the gurney, I looked at my toe. I had nowhere else to look, really. The throbbing sent spikes of pain through my foot – they seemed to fan out from my toe, spreading like rays of something that definitely was not sunshine. I wondered if the throbs coincided with my heartbeat.

That morning, I had thought the toe was just badly sprained, but nine hours later, when my toe had swollen to the size of a ping-pong ball and turned a couple of unnatural colors, I rethought my original diagnosis. I finally asked Carrie to take a look at it. Instead of responding, she left the room. I was concerned the purple ping-pong toe had caused her some form of nausea, so I was surprised to see her reappear a moment later, with her car keys.

"Let's go," was all she said. "Now."

Ten long, silent minutes passed, as I contemplated my injury and strained to pick out the sound of approaching feet, from what little sound the ER produced beyond the white curtain that separated me from the medical help I was hoping to find here. Unlike the waiting room, everything in the ER itself was white or gray, including my gurney and the curtains surrounding it. And I noticed that the pervasive silence of the waiting room had followed us into the ER. Sitting in my blank, curtained stall, I began to wonder why it was so quiet. Where was everyone? Wasn't this an ER? Weren't there supposed to be noisy emergencies being attended to?

Then, without the warning, a guy in scrubs pushed through the curtain. He introduced himself as the x-ray technician – he seemed to fill up the tiny curtained stall, wearing scrubs and a bland smile on his face. He seemed young to me – my age or close to it. He announced that he would be wheeling my gurney into the x-ray room. He was cheerfully casual about the whole thing. And he very cheerfully ran my gurney into every obstacle in the hallway - doorways, garbage cans, wheelchairs. I clung to the rails on my gurney and thought of bumper cars.

"I could walk," I offered, as we careened off a side wall.

"We're almost there," he said, as we bumped into another gurney. I smiled sheepishly at the man sitting on it, clutching his gut wound.

In the x-ray room, the tech pushed one of a dozen colossal machines up to my gurney. The remaining machines gaped down at me like an army of dumb giants, awaiting orders. The tech stretched my leg out, and pulled the x-ray's scope down toward my bare foot. The sheer proximity of the giant scope to my injured toe made me wince in anticipation, the imaginary threat of cold, heavy steel suspended inches above my foot.

Just before leaving the room, he dropped a lead apron into my lap. I doubled over from the impact.

"You're not pregnant, are you?" he asked, without the slightest trace of concern.

"Not anymore," I said, or tried to. It came out as more of a wheeze. That apron must have weighed 15 pounds. I looked down at it, crumpled clumsily across my abdomen.

"Do I need to pull this up over my torso?" I asked. The tech waved a dismissive hand as he stepped out of the room.

"Nah," he said, and closed the door behind him.

Back in my curtained-off stall, I waited for the doctors and an official diagnosis. I didn't want to look at my throbbing toe, but the blank space around me was almost harder to look at - there was nothing to hold my attention, nothing that could compete with the waves of pain still echoing through my foot. I waited, feeling the hard, thin mattress of the gurney pushing back against the underside of my legs.

Thirty minutes passed before I saw another person. This time, it was a timid intern with a slight, untraceable accent and an enormous engagement ring. In contrast to the x-ray technician, she seemed tiny, almost swallowed up by the small curtained-off space we now occupied together. She had dark hair, and she wore a white lab coat that made her seem more official than the tech. In contrast to his cheerful carelessness, she moved precisely, hesitantly, around my toe. She was exceedingly careful as she poked and wiggled it. I did my best not to flinch as her hands set off sparks of pain across my foot. Then she asked me if I was married.

"No," I said, surprised by the question. I looked at her ring. "But it looks like you are." She waved a hand, vaguely.

"Oh, you know," she said. But I didn't know. I had no earthly idea what she meant. Was that a yes? Or a no? Was she just engaged? Was there some kind of unspecified "arrangement"? I gaped at her. She didn't elaborate, and distracted by the pain, I lapsed back into silence.

She ran out of ways to bend my toe after a couple of minutes, and let herself back out, carefully, through the curtains – to do what? I waited. As I sat, I became aware of how cold it was, that the cold was creeping up on me, subtly starting to work its way between the threads of my sweater, with what felt like planned stealth. Even the tip of my nose was becoming numb. I thought about stretching my sweater over my feet to try to keep them warm. But it was my favorite sweater, and even if I could have stretched it far enough to reach my feet, I would only have ruined its shape. And I wasn't about to abandon my upper body to the icebox temperatures of this place. So, instead, I sat. And waited. And wished that the ER had been cold enough to at least numb the pain in my toe.

I mostly tried to hold still. That didn't help with the cold, but it seemed to minimize the pain still flooding through my foot at regular intervals. I could have lain down on the gurney, but I found I was too agitated and restless (despite my self-imposed stillness) to want to lie down. Though I was blocked from human view in my curtained-off stall (if there *were* any humans still out there), I feared that lying down might send the wrong message to the universe – that I was fine here, that I could stick this out as long as they needed me to, that I was okay with the pain and the cold and the isolation. As my agitation increased, I realized that there was someone I would like to share this experience with, after all – the guy who had broken my toe.

I had braved the game that morning without my beloved shin guards, and found myself trying to yank my legs out of harm's way on every encounter with an opponent. I made it through the first half unharmed. In the second half, I was on defense and found myself matched up against a new forward. He was one of the has-beens-reliving-their-glory-days-and-taking-it-all-too-seriously players, and making a drive for the goal (passing is like admitting weakness for this group). Generally, I like to give my opponents the chance to let me outsmart them, and if that fails, then I opt for the time-honored tradition of dropping a shoulder and going in hard. But without my shin guards that day, dropping a shoulder was suddenly a lot less appealing, and there was no guarantee I could outsmart this one. I moved in to stop him, feeling the phantom spasms of pain up and down my shins in anticipation of our seemingly inevitable collision. Then he came down hard on my toe. I felt something pop. And that's when I stopped worrying about my shins.

I was very sorry my aggressive opponent wasn't here now. I wanted to hold my foot up to his face, wiggling the warped, discolored toe at him, and say, *See? Thanks so much.*

Twenty minutes later, a new doctor came through the curtain – older and more weathered than the previous ones. With him were two younger doctors whom he didn't bother introducing. They stood on either side of him like sentries or bodyguards, but were clearly students or interns, soaking up every word he uttered and every gesture he made. They barely looked at me.

Like the timid intern, the older doctor had dark hair. Unlike the timid intern, he was not all cautious with my toe, which he poked at confidently, ignoring my wincing, as tendrils of pain found new areas of my foot to explore. He explained that the x-rays showed a fracture. Then he pulled a ball point pen from his white lab coat pocket and sketched the injury for me on the gurney bed sheet, which Heckle, Jeckle and I all leaned forward to gaze at – like students in a lab, listening to their professor. I wondered how much bleach it would take to erase this illustration from the sheet. The doctor explained that the fracture should heal within three weeks, and that there wasn't much to be done about it in the meantime - no casts, no braces, no crutches, no painkillers, etc. I looked up at him over the ballpoint sketch next to my foot.

"So what should I do for the toe while it's healing?" I asked.

"Limp?" he offered.

In the end, he agreed to "buddy tape" my toe to its neighbor. This would stabilize the injured appendage and minimize the pain by limiting its movement. He said he'd send someone in to do the taping, and then he left, trailing Heckle and Jeckle behind him. *Wait* – I wanted to say – *why can't one of you do it?*

But they disappeared through the curtain, and I sat on the gurney and waited. Minutes crawled by like they had nowhere to be. Then I heard voices, just outside the curtain. Recognizing the voice and accent of the timid intern of undetermined marital status, I leaned forward to listen. Apparently, the intern was asking another doctor for instructions on how to "buddy tape" an injured toe. And the other doctor was not helping.

"Okay, but how does the tape work?"

"What do you mean, 'how does it work?' It's tape..."

"But how do you actually use it?"

"You just - I mean, it's tape - you just tape the toes together...you know, you just...wrap them..."

"I don't get it."

At this point, I lost what little patience I had left. I'd spent the last two hours (mostly in isolation) in an ER that could pass as a refrigerator, just to be told I had an injury for which the medical profession had no remedy or (judging from the conversation going on outside my stall) clue what to do with it. I scooted to the edge of the gurney prepared to shout an offer to the conversing doctors through the curtains: *Throw me the freakin' roll of tape, and I will tape the toes myself.*

But before I could speak, the timid intern stepped through the curtain, alone. She held a roll of fabric tape in her hand and wore an uneasy smile on her face. I'm pretty sure I did not smile back. Without taking my eyes off of her, I reluctantly slid back from the edge of the gurney, resettling onto the cold sheet as she reached for my foot. And then I held my breath.

An hour later, I dropped gratefully back into the welcome warmth of Carrie's car. Glancing at the white fabric bands now striping the first two toes of my left foot, Carrie asked how it had all gone. I told her the story as we drove north on deserted Lakeshore Drive. The sleeping city of Chicago sprawled on our left, stretching away from the dark infinity of Lake Michigan to our right. But I was staring at my toes, now taped and stabilized and prepared for the next three weeks of limping.

As we neared our apartment, Carrie reached for something on the driver-side floor of her car. In the dark, I couldn't tell what she was holding, but then she stretched out her arm towards me. I looked at her, as the grin on her face appeared, disappeared and reappeared in the flashes of street lamp that passed us.

"I found your shin guards," she said, and dropped them into my lap.

"Only a BB Gun"
Fred Michaud

When Donny was ten, he couldn't bear the last four long weeks before the start of summer vacation. The sun was shining; he was ready to find his swimsuit and do cannonballs into the community pool. He was ready to grab his baseball glove in the equipment box in the corner of the room and play ball. He was ready to do anything but sit at his desk all day in school. Although it was still morning, Donny's thoughts raced ahead to the afternoon. When the end of school bell rang, he would run out into the warm fresh spring air to play with his friends.

Donny went through his usual morning routine absent-mindedly. He ate a quick bowl of cereal with milk. He brushed his teeth. He brushed his hair. His crew-cut brown hair didn't need much brushing. On his way out of his room, he glanced at the toy soldiers that had been his father's as a boy and had been handed down to him. He re-arranged one and left all of them lined up on the floor for the next battle. Donny's father, John, had been ordered to active duty in the Army and sent to Iraq in late winter. His last words to Donny were, "You are now the man of the house until I get back."

"Be home by 5:00," his mother, Jane, called to him as he went out the door on his way to school.

Donny hurried to catch up with his curly-headed blond neighbor, Joe, a big boy of twelve. Joe was smart and all-boy, lots of fun and usually willing to let Donny tag along. Joe wore "muscle shirts," T-shirts with the sleeves torn off, and Donny had started tearing the sleeves off his T-shirts too. All the boys wore jeans and didn't care if they were dirty or had holes. Their neighbors down the street, Brad, also twelve, and Kenny, nine, joined them, joking and pushing and jostling their backpacks.

Brad said to Donny, "Yah, yah, your mother wears army boots."

Donny replied, "You're crazy, my mom doesn't, but my dad does; he's a real soldier with a rifle and everything."

Before they reached the schoolyard, they made a plan to meet and go to the creek after school.

Joe said, "I think I can get my big brother's BB gun out of the house when my mom is at my brother's football game."

All the boys were thrilled with this plan and told Joe they would meet him right after school. They were normal kids and good boys, full of adventurous spirit but enjoyed the sneaky feeling of their plan for the afternoon.

Sitting in class, Donny daydreamed about how he would join the Army and go help his Dad with his own rifle as soon as he was old enough. He sat tapping his fingers on his desk and looking at the clock over and over. He hoped his older neighbor, Joe, would give him a chance to shoot a genuine BB gun.

Finally, the end of the school-day bell rang. Joe, Brad, Donny, and Kenny grabbed their backpacks and took off together toward Joe's house, eating their snack bars on the way. When they got to Joe's house, he turned to his friends and said, "Brad, come on in with me. Donny and Kenny, you guys play basketball on the driveway."

Joe and Brad went into the house and once inside checked to see that no one was home. Then they went into Joe's brother's room and opened the closet and moved a chair for Joe to stand on so he could reach the shelf over the hanging clothes. Joe grabbed a pack of BBs and tossed it to Brad, saying, "Catch." Then he took the BB rifle off the shelf and handed it to Brad before he stepped down from the chair. Brad hefted the gun and sighted it on himself in the mirror before handing it back to Joe. Before going out of the house, Joe stuck the rifle into the leg of his baggy pants. He had to walk stiff-legged, but that did not keep him from making it to the creek, two blocks away on the edge of the park. He tried to look cool all the way. Donny walked behind Joe, copying Joe's stiff-legged gait.

When they got to the creek, the water was only a foot deep, but enough to keep them out on the bank. Eager to try out the pilfered gun, they looked around for something to shoot at and chose a nearby tree with a hole in it.

"Yeah, that will make a great target," Brad said, "Just like the bulls-eye on the dart board in our family room."

Joe brought out the BB gun from his pants where he had hidden it. The boys all admired its long gunmetal black barrel with sights on the top and its handsome brown wood stock. Donny could hardly wait to get his hands on it and start shooting, but the rifle was Joe's, so Joe got to shoot first. "Pop," he shot at the trunk of the tree, and it made a "Crack" sound as the BB hit the dry bark of the tree. Joe handed the gun to Brad, the eleven year old, who shot at the tree and heard his own satisfying "Crack."

Donny's heart pounded as Joe handed him the weapon. The BB rifle felt heavier than he expected. Donny aimed carefully and pulled the trigger. He heard the "Pop," and the "Crack," relieved and proud he hit the tree, though off to the side.

Kenny, only nine, missed the tree with his shot, the BB making only a little "Poof" as it hit the dirt on the opposite bank.

Joe said to Kenny, "I'll show you how to do it," taking back his gun. A blue jay landed on the tree. Joe said, "Watch this," as he took aim. Just as he pulled the trigger, the jay flew away squawking, as though to say, "You missed," leaving that BB soundless in the air.

Bored with shooting at the motionless tree and frustrated at missing the taunting jay, Joe came up with a new idea. He told Donny,

"Hey, you get up on the rope swing and I'll try to hit you."

Donny said, "I don't want to get shot!"

Joe replied, "It won't hurt; it's only a BB gun. The BB will just bounce off your clothes. You're not chicken, are you?"

"No, I'll do it," said Donny, wanting to be accepted but secretly wishing Joe had chosen Kenny to be the moving target. Brad thought shooting at the little kids on the rope swing was a great idea and said, "It's my turn to shoot next."

Donny climbed onto the small plywood seat held up by many knots, and straddled the thick rope hanging down from the tree branch overhead. Joe hollered at him, "Go on one: five…four…three…two…one!" As Joe aimed at where he thought Donny would be swinging, Donny pushed off. Joe pulled the trigger, expecting the BB to make a direct hit on the side of Donny's blue jeans.

"Aagh! Aagh! My eye! It hurts! It hurts!" Donny cried out as he fell from the rope swing. Joe, Brad and Kenny all rushed to him.

Joe said, "What happened? I couldn't have hit your eye. I was aiming for your leg. It couldn't be too bad. It's only a BB gun."

"It's my eye, my eye!" said Donny as blood started to run down from his eye onto his cheek.

"Oh-my-God! I'm sorry! I didn't mean to hurt you," said Joe.

"Just get me home. It hurts so much I can't see!" said Donny.

"Yeah," said Joe. "Come on, we'll help you. Let's go. Brad carry my gun," as they scrambled up the dirt bank and across the field. "What're we going to tell our parents? How about if we just say Donny fell? They'll be so mad at us if they find out what we were really doing. They'll take this BB gun away and never let any of us shoot it again."

"Okay, okay, let's go," they promised and headed toward home.

On the way, Donny was holding his face as tears streamed down from both eyes. "This hurts so much I can hardly stand it. Hurry! Hurry!" He wanted to call his Mom in the most desperate way, but he was afraid she would find out how he really got hurt.

When they reached Kenny's house, Joe and Brad made him promise to say nothing about what happened unless asked directly. In that case, Kenny was to say that he was looking the other way and didn't see Donny get hurt, and only saw him after Donny "fell on the creek bank."

Joe and Brad took Donny into Joe's house where Joe put the BB rifle away right where it had been in his brother's closet. Brad washed off the dust-streaked tears from Donny's face and made him a cold washcloth with ice to put on his eye. Then Brad went to his house, promising to tell the same half-baked story that Donny "fell on the creek bank."

Joe and Donny sat together in Joe's room, Donny moaned from the pain and Joe said over and over, "I'm sorry. I didn't mean to hurt you."

Donny answered, "I know, I know."

Joe said, "Let me look at your eye again," hoping it would look better, but wished he hadn't when he saw it up close and bloody. He turned away saying, "I'll get you another piece of ice."

As five o'clock approached, they went over the story one more time and both walked next door to Donny's house to wait for his mother who would be home soon.

Joe was feeling confused inside. "Should I stick with the story or tell Donny's Mom what really happened?" Back and forth in his mind, he was afraid to tell the truth, so he decided to stick with the story that all four boys would be telling. Confessing would not undo the injury to Donny's eye. What would help would be for Joe to urge Donny's mom to take him to the doctor to fix it.

As they waited to face Donny's mother, Joe watched the clock on Donny's nightstand by his bed: 5:01…5:02…5:03…they counted until 5:13, when Donny's Mom finally came home. Those thirteen minutes before she came seemed endless.

"Hi Donny, I'm home," she called out as she came through the garage door to the house. "I picked up a pizza on the way; sausage, your favorite kind."

"Great Mom," Donny called back from his room, but she detected the whimper in his voice.

"Come on into the kitchen for pizza. I'll pour you a big glass of milk. I know pizza always makes you thirsty." "How did school go today?" she asked, reaching into the refrigerator.

"Oh, okay," Donny answered walking into the kitchen with Joe.

Turning to pour the milk, she saw Joe first and said, "Hi Joe, I didn't know you were here, but this is a large pizza so you can have a piece with us. I'm sure your mom won't mind."

Then she saw Donny's face with his eye closed and his face red. Alarmed, she asked him, "What happened to you?" Then, half-joking, she added, "How does the other guy look?" Pausing to look more closely, she asked, "Seriously, have you been in a fight?"

"No, I fell on the creek bank," Donny answered.

Joe chimed in, "Yeah, I was there too, but I was looking at a bird and didn't see him fall. He must have hit a rock or something because he really yelled. It must have really hurt a lot. Donny's no cry-baby." Finding the courage to say what he knew he had to say even though he was afraid it might get him into big trouble, Joe puffed his chest a little and went on, "I think you'd better take him to the doctor."

"Let me look at your eye closely," she said, moving to Donny. "Here, sit under the light." He winced as she held his eyelid open. She tried to stifle her gasp when she saw that his eye was all bloody. "You're right, Joe. We do need to get a doctor to look at this, right away."

Donny said to her, "It hurts real bad, Mom; like there's a big rock in it."

"I know, Donny, I know," she said, holding back her own tears and doing her best not to panic as she dealt with her wounded little warrior alone. Wishing Donny's father was there to help her deal with this crisis, she went to the refrigerator, took out the blue-ice soft-pack, wrapped it in a kitchen towel and handed it to Donny saying, "Here, hold this against your cheek and eye. It'll help keep down the bruising and bleeding. You boys go ahead and eat some pizza while I figure out where to go. We need an eye doctor for this; I'm going to call our family doctor first for his recommendation."

She was lucky the office was still open and Doctor Bob himself came on the line. As soon as she described Donny's eye, he recommended an ophthalmologist and said he'd call the eye doctor himself and get him to stay late. He called right back and told Donny's mom to keep the ice pack on gently and take Donny immediately to the eye specialist, whose office was only a few minutes away.

"Let's go Donny, get in the car. Keep the ice pack; we're going to the eye doctor right now. Thanks for bringing Donny home, Joe. You're a good friend. I'll call your mom later."

Joe felt terrible about hurting his little friend Donny. He felt half relieved that Donny's mom seemed to believe their story about Donny falling, but he was still half scared that Donny's eye could be wounded bad and that the blame would come back to him.

During the short drive to the eye doctor's, Donny and his mom didn't talk. He kept both eyes closed and held the ice pack against his face, trying not to whimper too much. His mom drove as fast as she could. Once they arrived, they rushed into the office. The nurse ushered them into a small examining room, taking the ice pack and dropping it into the sink. Then she wiped his face clean around the eye, talking kindly to him in the nurse way, "You're a brave soldier, Donny."

The doctor in his white coat joined them; speaking in a soothing tone and opened Donny's eye with a touch so soft that Donny could barely feel it. After completing his examination, the doctor asked Mom to step outside.

He explained, "The eye itself was penetrated and the impact even tore the iris. I'm sorry to have to tell you, but there is nothing we can do to restore the sight in this eye."

Donny heard his mother whisper, "Blind?" He saw her shoulders sag.

"Yes, in this one eye," the doctor replied with his soft voice, "but the other eye is unharmed so far. What is important now is for us to protect the good eye from infection and over-reaction to the injured eye and the foreign body in it."

"Can't you take the rock out?" asked Donny's mom.

The eye doctor answered, "Rock? No, it's round and smooth; it's a BB."

Donny's mom wondered how she would explain this to her husband, so far away. Donny shrunk into the seat on the ride home. His eye throbbed with pain deep inside. He'd overheard the doctor saying how bad his eye was going to be forever. He knew he'd let Mom down and even Dad. The lie was out. It was a BB not a rock that had blinded his eye. He'd probably lose Joe as a friend and maybe Brad and Kenny. "It just isn't fair," he thought. "I've done my part; I didn't rat on Joe." Almost the worst thing was the metal piece with the holes in it that the doctor had taped over his eye. Now all the other kids would know that he was the little kid who got shot.

Joe felt a guilt that he would carry the rest of his life. Brad didn't think it really was such a great idea, after all, to shoot at little kids. Kenny had nightmares that he was the one who got shot. As the months unfolded, their friendships faded, smothered by the enormity of what they had done and by the lie. Donny stopped tearing the sleeves off his T-shirts.

Donny, Joe, Brad, and Kenny would never again say, "Only a BB gun."

Their parents were changed, too. Joe's parents were mad at Joe at first, asking him, "How could you be so stupid?"

But later in the privacy of their bedroom, his mother nodded agreement as his father said, "It's partly our fault, too, for having any gun in the house without giving both our boys one of those gun safety courses that the NRA and the Boy Scouts offer. We never should have left the gun unlocked with our young boys in the house. What were we thinking?"

Brad's parents reacted to their own shock by telling him, "You are forbidden from playing with Joe all summer."

Kenny's parents sighed with relief, saying to each other in private, "Thank goodness our little Kenny wasn't hurt. It could have just as easily been him."

Donny's Mom, Jane, was reeling from this trauma. It was yet another low blow in her struggle to maintain normalcy while raising their son without his father at home. She had had to go back to work because with Dad away there just wasn't enough money to pay all the bills without their usual income. Donny was the most important thing in Jane's life, and when she wasn't working she was with him trying her best to keep his life as normal as possible despite his father's absence. Once a young beauty, she looked harried by the routine of getting through each day balancing her low paid job, the house, and most importantly, their boy, Donny. Now this! She felt her own guilt for not seeing that he had more adult supervision after school until she got home. She silently cursed the "dreadful war" and sobbed alone in her bed.

Donny's dad, John, in Iraq, did not get shot that night. Still, he couldn't sleep when he received the news that Donny had been blinded in one eye even though it was,

"Only a BB gun."

The Good Driver
Jerry Thrush, MD

For many in the bustling metropolis, today would be absolutely unforgettable, for some, the last day on earth. Inhaling fantasy and exhaling fury, the living, breathing, gears of the city ground onward. People here, like the teeth of the gears in a great machine, marched ever forward toward their unknown destinies, oblivious to the enveloping chaos and simmering entropy around them. Until that is, one well functioning, good intentioned sprocket freezes the mechanism.

In the emergency room at City Heights Receiving Hospital, Doctor Webster picked up a chart for the next patient. For him, a day at the office meant stopping bleeding, attenuating psychosis, diagnosing strokes, and delivering humorous diatribes intended to get his patients to stop smoking. He repressed the little boy inside of him, *Josh* Webster, to defer gratification, skip meals, and save as many lives as he could.

Across town, Dale Yawk, a nauseous mouse of a man whose employment was unemployment was on his way to a rendezvous at the corner of Maple and Vine. Today his greatest decision was to risk of strolling a block outside of his gang's turf for a better price. He adjusted his crimson bandana and spindled a twenty-dollar bill as he walked. He coolly planned to elevate himself from purveyor of goods to consumer thereof.

A half a block away in the tenement building at the corner of Mr. Yawk's intended meeting place, five-year-old Katie Simonds hummed to herself as she played with her tattered one-eyed doll. The song she made up was one familiar to her alone. She sang it whenever she retreated into her private little world that was far removed from the chaotic environment outside her broken screen door. Little Katie knew that today would be different than most. She would be getting a visit from someone very special who lived across town. To celebrate her excitement she threw her doll in the air and let out a whoop of joy.

Between little Katie and Dr. Webster at City Heights Hospital three men wearing bandanas of a different sort sat drinking liquid courage in a lowered 1964 Impala. Bored with life and lack of opportunities, they marinated themselves in booze contemplating how to dissipate, misuse and squander the remainder of their day.

In a more manicured area, Marjorie Tuttle thought of her granddaughter as she rigidly adhered to her exacting daily routine. At precisely eight A.M. Mrs. Tuttle left her pristine neighborhood to see Katie. She glanced at a note reminding herself to spend a few minutes teaching the little one proper table manners – beginning with the correct way to say grace. The girl had stumbled over a few words the last time they shared a meal. Mrs. Tuttle worried that there were errands that she had to complete without Katie. She was relieved that there was always a teenager willing to help in Katie's building, because the child would probably not be dressed well enough to accompany her anyway.

Marjorie Tuttle could assure herself that her principles were high. Certainly higher than most! In spite of a shiftless husband who had sought consolation in a bottle, she had worked to raise their daughter and give her a college education – before the girl took leave of her senses and ran off pregnant and unwed.

White haired, widowed, and living alone in a respectable neighborhood, Mrs. Tuttle was pleased to give her energies to the poorer communities, even if time with her family was sacrificed. She could dismiss the bitterness of her daughter's withdrawal when she filled her days with chores and exactitude. She would take no time off even when it was her day with Katie. The tearful objection of her granddaughter notwithstanding, it was not proper to miss work, especially not important work.

She smiled to herself as she recalled the words of her last lecture to her daughter: "One should not use pleasures as excuses. I hope Katie will learn to do the right thing from my example – even though others in her life have failed."

Marjorie Tuttle carefully parked exactly six inches from the curb at the intersection of Maple and Vine. Such attention to the detail of driving had made Mrs. Tuttle the invariable choice as driver for the Helping Hand Club. It was an accolade of course, but it meant that whenever there was a carload of kids to be ferried to a picnic, a softball game, or the junior matinee at the movies – she was elected. She had never suffered the indignity of a traffic ticket in her entire life.

Today, besides dropping in on her granddaughter, Mrs. Tuttle would call on Helping Hand volunteers who had sewn cuddly toys for the annual party at the Children's Hospital. After her errands she could spend some time with her granddaughter. The little girl would understand the need to follow through with obligations before fun by her example. Marjorie was sure to impart this most important of lessons to Katie. She tried with her own daughter, but such instruction seemed to pass her by.

After exiting her car, Mrs. Tuttle paused to wipe a dead insect from her windshield and waved to her granddaughter as she approached the decaying building. Mrs. Tuttle's smile faded when she saw the image of her own face minus thirty years appear in the doorway behind little Katie.

"Hi Katie," she said, ignoring her daughter.

"Hello mother," the younger woman replied.

"Hi Grandma!" interrupted the beaming kindergartener.

Mrs. Tuttle stooped down and gave Katie a pat on the head.

"You can give her a hug mom. She won't bite."

Mrs. Tuttle reluctantly gave Katie a squeeze, holding her at arm's length so her favorite scarf wouldn't get soiled from grimy little hands.

"I'm glad you came, I need to run. Thanks for watching Katie."

"Another boyfriend?"

"That's none of your business."

"Like her father was nobody's business?"

"I have to go."

"About that, I was wondering if I could watch Katie a little later. I have –"

The little girl's mother exploded, "You always do this! Say you're going to babysit, then do some God-dammed do-gooding for someone else. Perhaps if you spent half the time with dad when he was alive, he wouldn't have drunk himself to death!"

"Enough! And no taking the Lord's name in vain."

"I'm leaving. If you don't want to take her with you like you *promised*, maybe one of the neighbors can sit for a little while. There's a teenager next door, Sasha, who often helps. I don't care. And another thing, Katie's had a runny nose. If it gets into her chest take her down to City Heights ER. If you can't I'm sure Sasha could find the time," she added, sarcastically.

"You don't understand. It's not that I don't want her to come, and of course we'll take care of the runny nose. I'll need all the room in the car to pick up the stuffed toys. Katie understands. Don't you darling?"

A crystalline tear silently rolled down the little girl's cheek. She squeezed the bundle she held even tighter.

That dirty, ragged, one-eyed thing Katie held burrowed deeper into Mrs. Tuttle's awareness. She did not approve of the doll. It was entirely unhygienic. Her daughter should have known better than to let her family be represented by such a shabby toy.

Mrs. Tuttle suddenly had an inspiration. Bending down she said, "Katie, dear, may I see your dolly?"

The little girl shook her head and backed up.

"Bye mom," called her daughter as she ran out the door.

Katie watched her mother strut down the walk. She hoped that when she got big she could make her hips sway just like her mother's. Her grandmother's voice interrupted her thoughts.

"But why Katie?" An edge of disapproval sharpened Mrs. Tuttle's voice. Her daughter should have instilled obedience. "Let Grandma see."

The little girl thrust a grimy thumb into her mouth; to Mrs. Tuttle it was a detestable and most unhealthy habit that should have been corrected years ago. Katie clutched her doll like a vice. "Uh – Ua."

"Now, Katie, don't disappoint Grandma! We've talked about good manners, and how you must learn obedience to be a lady. Remember our talk?"

"Yes," sulked Katie.

"Very well. Now, just a little look. What's her name?"

"It's Meg. And you can't hold her."

How surly! It was hard to believe that she was the product of her own bloodline. Mrs. Tuttle felt her blood pressure rise.

"Katie, I merely wish to see Meg because I can wash her, and make her neat again."

"I like her. She's pretty."

"She's pretty alright, pretty grubby. Has she lost an eye?"

"It fell off."

"If you ask nicely, I might find a button to match. Then Meg would have two eyes."

"I *want* her with one eye. It's how Meg is."

Sterner reasoning was required.

"Now *that* isn't very sensible, is it? Let's be grown up. Say please and I'll wash Meg. Then I'll do eye surgery. Meg would want to see properly, would she not?"

"I dunno."

"Believe me, she would. What is proper is always best, so I'll take Meg with me and find a matching eye."

"But I want her now."

"Katie!" Mrs. Tuttle had not meant her voice to carry so much severity, and she glanced around to see if anyone had heard. Outside, a sleazy young man whose face was festooned with piercings and pustules leaned on a lamppost. When Marjorie Tuttle was a girl, people of his sort would not have dared being seen in this neighborhood.

Mrs. Tuttle looked back to Katie and repeated with equal firmness, "Now, let me have Meg, please."

Katie's shoulders descended helplessly as she held out her doll.

"Thank you, my dear," lowered Mrs. Tuttle as she took the button before handing the doll back.

Katie gasped as she saw her beloved doll go blind.

"Pretend that Meg's sleeping with her eyes closed," reassured Mrs. Tuttle.

"But you took her eye," frowned Katie.

A half hour later Mrs. Tuttle smiled to herself as she pulled her old Ford out into traffic. Sasha had come by and she was free to go out while Katie napped. She blinked when sunlight glinted from the bumper of the red sports car that abruptly pulled in front of her. A dark frown crossed her face and marred the bright day when she met eyes with the other driver. He was a young man with midnight hair accompanied by a laughing blond. They were obviously enjoying her frustration.

Mrs. Tuttle scowled furiously and crept forward with all of the speed of an arthritic turtle. Behind her, a disgruntled motorist honked. When she looked towards the sound she saw a big man in cheap black sunglasses waving his fist from his perch high up in his four-wheel drive.

"Watch it, ya old bag!" he shouted.

"God bless you," croaked Marjorie in a hoarse whisper.

He replied by revving his engine and recklessly plowing ahead of her.

Looking in her rear view mirror, she saw it coming. She braced herself for impact and closed her eyes. Without realizing it she stepped on the brake.

"Oh God! Please help," she prayed.

The enormous truck roared like a wounded tiger as the driver frantically downshifted to avoid her.

"Damn it lady. Can't you stay in your own lane?"

"You drive too fast! I'm saving you a ticket!" she yelled, unheard above the din of the traffic.

Shaking her head, she muttered under her breath. "Hoodlums! I wish they'd slow down. They're going to get tickets, the lot of them!"

After making the driver of a Corvette swerve into the carpool lane with his third finger stretched towards the sky, Mrs. Tuttle sighed with relief and smoothed her hair with her left hand. She was unaware of both her flashing blinker and the line of cars behind her.

"What do I have to do now?" she asked herself, her eyes darting around her car for a clue.

A chorus of horns fell on her deaf ears as she continued driving, lost in thought. Most of the time *thought* for her was alien landscape.

Brakes squealed behind her. A carload of college girls who frothed with mirth appeared in her mirror. The driver was a young girl who wore a saucy ponytail and a simple sweatshirt emblazoned with a college logo.

Mrs. Tuttle's mind took her to her own youth for a moment. She was a girl once. But in those days girls dressed like ladies. They wore dainty sweaters and nice dresses and didn't look like tramps.

In her mirror she not only saw the young lady driving, she could also see the passengers as they goaded her on. The girl hesitated, then, with courage borrowed from her peers she shot ahead, nearly taking off Mrs. Tuttle's bumper.

An icicle of fear crystallized in her chest as she squeezed the wheel. It made her fingers ache and she nearly found herself in another lane. Moving in traffic with enough speed to make a caterpillar dizzy, Mrs. Tuttle began to feel a strange sensation growing within her. A prickling feeling burned its way up her back, and her hands began to sweat. Her neck tightened and she bit her lip with her dentures. She felt the spasm of righteous justification ache in her shoulder.

"Oops! I almost forgot. The button!" Mrs. Tuttle said as she careened to the right. She was still unaware that her left signal was on and oblivious to a bicyclist she sent sprawling onto a lawn.

"If the police can't stop these drivers, someone has to," she reminded herself. She noticed a slow moving lowered Impala filled with men in blue bandanas merge slowly in front of her. The throbbing beat of their loud music made her chest buzz.

"At least someone is driving sanely even if they listen to garbage," she muttered to herself.

Mrs. Tuttle thought again of her granddaughter. She had considered kissing her goodbye, but the thought of Katie's porridge streaked pinafore pressing against her clean, tan coat, amended her farewell to a pat on the head.

Mrs. Tuttle looked at her dash. The button she saw stimulated a softer memory. With her mind's eye she saw her granddaughter holding the ragged doll. She despised the fact that it was dirty, torn, and had only one eye which hung on by a lone thread.

Mrs. Tuttle recalled how her heart went out to her little granddaughter. The fact that the little girl's most prized possession was the doll was an unhappy one, but not nearly as troublesome as the fact that the little girl was a descendent of her own daughter. The consideration that her girl was the product of an obsessive compulsive and an alcoholic was not one that lived in her consciousness. Another chorus of honks brought Mrs. Tuttle out of her daydream.

"That's it! I'll have to go the yardage store, then on to St. Francis to deliver the bag of toys for the Helping Hand ladies," she said aloud.

The honks outside sounded like a gaggle of geese. Mrs. Tuttle glanced down at her speedometer. It read fifty-three miles per hour. Two miles an hour under the speed limit. Perfect, she thought. Surely they couldn't be honking at me, she mused. Only three miles per hour faster and I'd be breaking the law!

A car zipped by, and its driver grimaced at her like an angry monkey.

"You could get a ticket!" Mrs. Tuttle warned, under her breath.

The sun glinted off the shiny ebony button again and Marjorie Tuttle recalled the exit she needed for the sewing store. It was coming up.

"I'd better slow down," she mumbled to the button on the dash, finally realizing her left turn signal had been on all the while.

Across town, the Impala that had passed her earlier cruised to a stop. Paco turned up the rap music until the rhythm echoed off the graffiti covered walls of the alley. The cars three occupants bobbed their heads to the beat and slapped the aged leather seats like drums.

"Gimme a beer. I'm like dyin' man," barked the one they called El Guapo from the back seat.

"Juan, you heard the man," peeped Paco, the driver, as he smoothed back his hair. "Give."

"Like *chill*," responded Juan handing the can to the tall good-looking man in back. Although relatively new to the gang identified by blue bandanas, Juan understood gang authority. He knew that when the boss wanted something, it was to be delivered.

El Guapo downed the remainder of the frothing liquid and threw the empty can out of the window. It landed on the dead lawn of a house that leaned perceptibly to the right. A moment later a lady emerged and waved a broom at them. El Guapo blew her a kiss and the others in the Impala burst out laughing. To them he was a god.

An old man appeared and frantically tried to pull the woman back inside. She whacked him with the broom and the youth in the car cracked up again. He had seen their bandanas.

"OK *chicas,*" snarled El Guapo from the back seat, "Initiation time."

"In the daytime? Now?" asked Juan, the newest in the group. He swallowed hard.

"Look man, if you chicken, you *know* you can get out the car," said El Guapo sternly.

We'll slow down to, say, eighty. Just like we did for the last homey who wanted out the gang," smirked Paco.

Paco looked in his rear view mirror and swung the car across traffic in a big U. Horns abruptly stopped when the occupants of the other vehicles saw the headbands. The handsome boss in the back seat smiled and pulled out his weapon. It was a nickel plated .38 and reflected the sun like a mirror.

"Let's go check on our business men." The leader fingered his blue bandana, pointed the weapon at Juan's head and said instructionally, "You see, Juan, we're just like Visine. We gonna get the red out."

Paco hooted, in a moment Juan joined in with a deep belly laugh, followed by El Guapo's cackle. The mirth was silenced by the gang leader when he said, "Bang!" He was still holding the gun.

The fabric store was crisp and clean and smelled like new carpet. Row upon row of bolsters begged to be fondled. There was something wonderful about textiles that always excited Marjorie Tuttle. It was a magical place to her as a little girl and not far removed as an adult. And it was so orderly and neat.

Marjorie Tuttle had the rare gift of being able to visualize the appearance of a fabric, not as a roll of material, but as an item of clothing. The red chiffon in the corner wasn't a roll of crimson; it was an evening gown with ruffles. The black silk roll was a basic skirt, and the green gabardine could be pleated slacks. Marjorie paused to rub some velvet between her fingers. Now that's something for a high school girl, she thought, sighing heavily. She suddenly wished she were young and pretty again.

"That's lovely isn't it?" asked the sales girl.

"It is nice. I was just thinking..."

"It's on sale! Fifty percent off. It would make a lovely dress. A formal, maybe a ball gown. Are you shopping for yourself?"

"I think it's for a much younger woman," blushed Mrs. Tuttle.

"What can I help you with?"

Mrs. Tuttle opened her hand and the employee looked down and adjusted her glasses.

"Can you match this?" asked the older woman.

The girl picked up the button and examined it thoughtfully. She rolled it over and held it up to the light like a jeweler estimating the value of a stone.

"Hmmm," she wondered.

"I haven't much time," said Mrs. Tuttle, shifting her purse from one arm to the other. "The neighbor is watching my grandbaby while I'm out. I need to be back before she wakes up from her nap."

"I understand," nodded the sales girl.

"Do you have one?"

"I think we can come close. How many do you need?"

"One if you can find an exact mate, two if you can't."

"What did you say it was for?"

"Eye surgery."

The yardage clerk cocked her head to the side and raised her eyebrows a notch.

"For a doll," smiled Mrs. Tuttle.

"Granddaughter?"

"Of course."

"I love little girls! What does she look like?"

The little brown-haired girl with rich dark eyes a few miles away gave her blind doll a hug. Awake from her nap, and finding her sitter sleeping, she peered at the scraggly man still standing on the corner outside. She then glanced over at the couch across the room. Sasha, the babysitter slept the sleep of the just on the old sway back sofa and did not stir. She looked out again. Through the crooked screen, the little girl could just make out some dandelions poking through a half dead lawn.

"Flowers, Meg! Let's get some flowers for Grandma! Babysitter won't mind. She's sleeping. We big girls take short naps now, don't we?"

Katie quietly slid the cracked screen door open and crept outside. As she scampered down the steps she paid guarded attention to the thin pimple faced man leaning against a pole taking a drag on his cigarette.

He was even scarier up close. She didn't like his long curly hair and crooked goatee. His black leather jacket was covered with shiny studs and there was a tattoo of a teardrop at the corner of his right eye. Then she saw *IT* on his head, and stopped cold in her tracks. She gasped and held her breath as tightly as she held the doll.

She could feel her heart race and her hands freeze. If she ran now he might see her. The screen door, hanging by one hinge creaked behind her. The ten feet that separated her from the safety of the doorway seemed like a million miles.

Katie sat down on the concrete path and began to quiver. Suddenly she had to go potty so badly it hurt. Wishing she were inside, she squeezed Meg so hard that her stuffing began to burst through her seams. Seconds ticked into minutes. She covered her face with her toy. At least Meg would be with her to the end, she thought.

When nothing happened a few moments later, Katie slowly lifted the doll and peeked at the strange youth. He didn't look like a bad man, she thought. But he was a stranger. Not just a stranger, a stranger with *color* around his head.

She knew what it was but couldn't understand why it was called by the name of a fruit. It was one of those things that were so confusing to little girls. It didn't look like a banana, but then again the curb at the side of the roadway didn't look like a *curve* on a circle either – but grownups called both things '*curbs*' anyway.

The man looked in her direction and flicked his spent cigarette to the sidewalk. With a gasp she covered her face again. Silent tears began to flow down her cheeks, and she wiped them with her doll's torn dress. *Something* was going to happen, she just knew it.

Another minute of months silently passed, and a braver Katie peeked over her doll's moist outfit. She regarded the stranger once more when she realized it. She couldn't believe her eyes at first, but a second glance confirmed her hope. *IT was* red. *Red!*

The man in front of her home wasn't wearing a blue scarf tied like a banana around his head, he wore a red one. He was NOT a *BLUE banana-head*; he was a *RED banana-head.* The image of another man flashed across her mind. Mommy's last boyfriend always wore a red scarf around his head and mommy said he was a good guy. So this man must be OK too.

Katie gathered up all of her courage and started walking towards the man with the red bandana. She said to herself, "He has a red banana. He's a good guy."

Katie forgot all about the flowers she set out to collect. She decided to talk with the man. After all, he was wearing red, so he could not be a stranger.

"Hi," said Katie.

"Yeah?" replied the man, turning toward her.

"My name is Katie," she announced.

"So what?" he spat. Katie could see the pockmarks in his face now that she was closer and she started to get scared again.

"What's your name?"

"Dale."

"Dale what?"

"Just Dale."

"Whatcha doin' Dale? 'Sides smokin'. Grandma says it's bad to smoke."

"Yeah. Maybe I'm bad too, so just leave me alone, huh? Scram. I'm waiting for a deal."

Katie started to cry. But it was not just a little blubber. It was one of those little girl bawls where the lip starts to quiver then a silent trickle begins. After the quivering comes a tremor, and before long, the tremor becomes full-blown lip quake. That's when the trickle becomes a stream. In a moment there's a flashflood. Katie's flashflood quickly grew to Niagara proportions with the accompanying roar. She roared.

It was now Dale's turn to be scared. He looked around. No one was to be seen. Like most men he didn't know what to do when a woman cried. When a little girl sobbed he was lost, *especially when he was waiting for a deal.*

"Come on little girl. Don't cry. Where's your mamma?"

His answer: tears.

"Oh, man. Now they'll never bring the goods. Come on little girl. What's your name? Kay? Kaylin? That's it! *Katie*. What's the matter Katie?"

The girl continued to howl. Exasperated, he felt in his pocket.

"Katie! Katie, listen. I don't got no candy, but look here – I got a quarter! Nice and shiny. And there's a picture of a man on it!"

Katie stopped crying and wiped her runny nose with her doll's hair.

"I'll give it to you if you stop crying. Why are you crying anyway? I ain't done nothin'."

"Cause."

"Cause why?"

"Cause I'm scared," howled Katie.

"There ain't nothin' ta' be scared of little girl," laughed the man in the bandana as he gave her the quarter.

A frantic voice from inside the apartment startled them both. "Katie! Where are you?"

"That's my babysitter," said Katie, as she scampered towards the crooked screen. "I gotta go."

Sasha held the screen open and beckoned Katie inside. The babysitter was the only one who saw the lowered Impala creep around the corner. Guardian angels wept as the torrent of lead hail stormed. In seconds the fusillade was over and squealing tires conveyed the blue bandanas away, leaving behind a trail of smoking shells and crimson rivulets. One nickel plated handgun slid under a seat as two fell to the dust.

Mrs. Tuttle finished her business with her usual care in spite of the cell phone message she had just received while at the fabric shop. Sasha had called to say that her granddaughter was going to the City Heights Hospital Emergency Room. The message was hard to understand. Sasha seemed hysterical. But Mrs. Tuttle remembered that her daughter had left clear instructions that if Katie's cold worsened she should be taken to see the doctor.

Mrs. Tuttle would tolerate the inconvenience of meeting them at the emergency room, of course, but she made a mental note that the neighbor girl, Miss Sasha, was going to hear about calm correctness always being preferable to haste and frenzy in such situations. And she wouldn't speed on her way to the hospital. It wouldn't be proper.

Mrs. Tuttle was happy because she managed to find an exact match. Being correct, however, she bought two so that one eye wouldn't be shinier than the other. She whistled as she waddled over to the cash register. In the distance she could hear the wail of mournful sirens and dogs baying in response.

"I hope those police catch whoever they're after," she wished to the sales girl.

"Me too, but I think that might be an ambulance. City Heights is a full-on Trauma Hospital now, like the one on TV."

"Really?" answered Mrs. Tuttle absently, as the new inconvenience of driving to the hospital dawned on her.

City Heights Emergency Department was as chaotic as beehive on fire. Both the Trauma Surgeon and Pediatric Trauma Surgeons on call were in the operating room and the Emergency Physician was struggling to keep ahead of the flood of incoming wounded.

To Dr. Webster, it seemed like the ambulances were on some kind of supernatural bungee cord attached to the hospital. Each time they left – *boing*! They'd be back, dragging with them another victim of fate.

An eighty-nine year old with shortness of breath. A confused forty-five year old street person found under a bush with a cut on his head. A psychiatric patient as fat as a walrus insisting that she was the president's wife, informing everyone that if they would just call the White House, the president himself would clear things up.

Dr. Webster was informed that there were two more inbound ambulances. Each had a patient with gunshot wounds, but fortunately one had only minor extremity wounds. He knew he'd be busy because the other sustained multiple hits to the chest. The nurse relayed the information from the paramedics on the radio that the most severely injured was the adult.

A strange calm began to creep over Dr. Webster as he anticipated his next moves. He knew the decisions he would make in the next few minutes would determine the difference between life and death, disability and function. But the feeling didn't come from god-like power, or adrenaline pumping through his veins, it came from something else: dedication, purpose, training, and years of self-effacing service to the world.

In the small physician's study, Dr. Webster returned to a snack he was eating before the radio interrupted and informed him of the inbound patients with gunshot wounds. He had missed lunch and recalled that his last nutrition was ten hours ago. Dr. Webster was not briefly jittery as he finished his snack. It was *Josh* Webster, the little boy who resided deep inside of him who was nervous.

Josh Webster, the child within, would frequently anguish over patients like Katie, a doll-hugging, porridge-spilling, grace-scrambling child. It would be Doctor Webster, however, who calmly prepared to treat a female, Caucasian, about five years old; and a pockmarked male, age unknown, who had both been sprinkled with flying lead.

He knew he had only five minutes before the arrival of the traumas and he had to get some things done quickly before they arrived, so he called the charge nurse to join him as he took one more bite.

"What can I help you with?" she asked.

"OK, I know the trauma surgeons are in the OR, but let's do this: Call the senior surgical resident and see if he can break out to get down here and help. Also, check the blood refrigerator in the trauma room and make sure there are two units of O-negative. Page a 'Trauma Activation.' I want a respiratory therapist, an X-ray tech, and the lab people here waiting. And don't forget to get the chest tube and thoracotomy trays out."

The nurse frantically scribbled the doctor's instructions. She knew that each was important and she didn't want to go home with the guilt associated with missing something which made a difference in a life.

"A couple of more things: The guy in bed three needs an ultrasound of his abdomen; make it 'rule out cholecystitis' and the guy in bed six needs a CT of the head. Call and see if they can take him now. Oh, there's one more thing; the patient of Dr. Gilmore has an acute MI in the cardiac room, we're still waiting for his call back. If he answers and I can't talk on the phone, tell him to come on in and that I think we'll need the Cardiac Cath Team."

"Anything else?"

"Do a 'road test' on the drunk in nine. He can go if he can walk. I've already talked to him and written instructions. The laceration in eleven is going to have to wait."

"They're here, doc," announced a large male nurse by the door.

"Thanks, Jim. I'll see the adult first, he's the one with the major injuries."

"Think again, doc," said the paramedic as he wheeled in the first gurney. "The kid's the sick one."

In the hallway, Dr. Webster could see blood bubbling from twin wounds in a little girl's chest. In moments he had all the information that he needed and had her intubated and on life support. He deftly sutured a tube in each side of her chest, but it became quickly clear that the blood ran out of the tubes faster than fresh blood could be pumped into her veins.

"Get me Dr. Williams the pediatric chest surgeon. Tell him we've got a five-year-old with gunshot wounds to the chest. We need him down here stat to lend a hand. This girl's going to crash!" commanded the doctor.

"He was on last night!" countered the nurse.

"He'll come in," answered Dr. Webster. "There's no-one else, and at this point every second counts."

A few miles away, a grey haired man in a white coat briskly got into a long black Mercedes and screeched out of his driveway. Closer to the hospital another highway drama was being played out.

Mrs. Tuttle pulled ahead of a beat up Volkswagen Beetle as she left the parking lot of the yardage store. Like most other drivers on the road, the man behind the controls of the Bug was trying to go a little too fast for Marjorie Tuttle, self-appointed guardian of the rules.

Mrs. Tuttle glanced in her rear view mirror and sized up the speeder. He was young, couldn't be more than about thirty-five and his car was a mess. She could see a ripped portion of the headliner hanging down above his shoulders and a dent in the right front quarter panel. Her hands were sweating and she was getting that spasm of righteous justification in her shoulder again.

The man was disheveled, his hair was wild, and his face looked as if he hadn't shaved for three days. As he rode her bumper she was close enough to see the scar below his right eye and a gold chain around his neck. As she scrutinized him more closely, she could make out the frantic expression on his face. He was even more agitated than the other drivers on the road. He must be on drugs, she concluded.

She checked her speedometer. Twenty-seven miles per hour. *Perfect! A thirty miles per hour zone and three miles per hour under the posted limit. Just right.*

The man behind her gunned his engine and tried to pass. Mrs. Tuttle guided her trusted Ford to the left. The man honked and pounded his steering wheel.

"You'll thank me for this, you'll see," she said to herself, adjusting her scarf. "I'm keeping you from getting a ticket." The man waved his hand, frantically motioning for her to get over, but she smiled and waved back, and ignored his gesticulations.

"No, you don't my friend," she spewed, grinding her false teeth and guiding her car back into her lane. "Obviously you can't obey the rules of the road, so today I'm going to help you. You'll be glad I did," she said.

The man revved his engine and tried in vain to pass her again, nearly getting hit head on by a city bus. He moved closer to her bumper and laid on his horn, wildly indicating she should get out of his way at once.

"I wonder what kind of a guy you are to be in such a hurry?" she asked herself. "Probably just trying to make it to a liquor store before the shakes get too bad. You'd have to be an alcoholic to run around looking like that," she smirked to herself.

Mrs. Tuttle looked at her mirror and exclaimed, "Even though I'm going to a hospital I'm not going to hurry like that fellow behind me. No sir-e. Not me!" Marjorie always thought it was fun to be righteously indignant and go under the speed limit.

She watched the car behind her in her mirror. She could see the frantic man in the dented old VW edging out and trying to pass again and again. His horn yapped plaintively and begged for the right of way. He flashed his headlights in desperate attempt to get her attention.

"Heavens," said Marjorie Tuttle. "How *do* such people get a driving license?"

She reduced her speed to twenty-two miles per hour; she was now in a twenty-five miles per hour zone. From her example, the driver behind *might* learn responsibility – *and* patience she thought, ignoring his barking horn, and flashing lights.

A red light halted her lane of traffic and she was startled to see the VW driver leave his car and shout for her to please kindly let him pass. The man was tousle-haired and disheveled and wore what looked like an old wrinkled green leisure suit. His feet seemed wrapped in rags. Such eccentricity of apparel might be excusable in a great poet or in a scientist with a mind on higher planes perhaps. But in the driver of a rickety old ruin that probably should not even be on the road? Disgraceful!

Mrs. Tuttle swiftly made sure that her doors were locked and her windows closed. In the next instant she was relieved that the light changed to green and she could pull away from that flapping, pajama-clad nonconformist. He had almost reached her station wagon, probably with some profanity prepared for her, when she drove off.

In the next few blocks, the VW continued to follow closely behind. Mrs. Tuttle felt her own patience hardening to resolve. The driver persisted with his demand that she pull over and let him pass. Well, some people might be intimidated but not Marjorie L. Tuttle, she reflected.

She was now in a thirty miles per hour zone. Gripping the wheel more firmly, she was careful to proceed at four miles below the posted limit, still heading towards the hospital. "I could be saving a life by going this slow," she gloated.

Along the last two miles the congestion was horrible. Gridlock was the fashionable name for a traffic situation permitting Marjorie to creep forward at five miles an hour. Automobiles stretched ahead of her to infinity. She frowned at that absurd Bohemian behind her still maneuvering his repulsive old car in a hopeless struggle to pass.

Finally she was able to turn from the traffic lane into the parking lot of the hospital. No sooner was she beyond its gate when the Volkswagen clanked and clattered by. The bed-headed man wrestled its steering wheel and spared her not a glance. He drove right up to the hospital door and abandoned his car in a zone clearly marked NO PARKING. *The nerve of some people!*

The man disappeared into the building as if possessed.

More than a little perturbed now, Mrs. Tuttle parked nearly in the center of her spot. Then she too entered the hospital and asked directions to the emergency room.

In that strange cocoon of nerveless tension where calmness was imperative and the slightest movement keenly purposeful, the only one who disobeyed the mandated composure was the child within the Emergency Physician. After the arrival of the pediatric chest surgeon he left the resuscitation room to discipline his inner child.

At that moment, Mrs. Tuttle approached the admissions desk and asked where she might find her little granddaughter. She was sure that it would be in the area where they treat colds and coughs.

"Slow down a minute ma'am." replied the clerk. "If you could tell me who you are looking for, perhaps I could help."

"It's my grandbaby. I think she was brought in with a cold. Where is she?"

"I can help," said the clerk, "but what is her name?"

"Katie. Katie Simonds. She's five years old and stands about this tall." Mrs. Tuttle gestured

"Please wait here, someone will be with you in a moment."

Mrs. Tuttle waited impatiently at the desk. The poor girl, she thought. Sniffles becoming a chest cold! And that nervous wreck of a babysitter! I'll have a word with her about not waiting for me to get home.

So caught up in her own emotions, Mrs. Tuttle was shocked when a young, but tired-appearing doctor appeared in front of her. His eyes looked puffy but he maintained composure. He was flanked by a charge nurse and a social worker.

"Excuse me, are you here for the little girl who was injured?" asked the man in the white coat.

"Land sakes no! My granddaughter had the sniffles. The babysitter – "

"You said her name was Katie Simonds?" interrupted the doctor.

Mrs. Tuttle was at a loss for words for the first time in years.

"My name is Dr. Webster. I'm the Emergency Physician on duty. Why don't we have a seat in a place where we can talk?" The lady next to him, wearing a nametag introducing herself as a social worker, smiled weakly.

The doctor continued, "I didn't catch your name."

"I'm Marjorie Tuttle, Katie's grandmother. Her mother is . . . unavailable and not very responsible I might add. I won't go anywhere until you tell me where she is."

The doctor looked sad. Mrs. Tuttle noticed for the first time that his voice shook a little. He didn't like what he was about to say.

"When they brought your granddaughter–"

"Katie."

"Yes, when they brought Katie in, we found that she sustained two major gunshot wounds to the chest. Her blood pressure was very low and she was in shock."

"Oh my God! I thought she had a cold! You must be wrong. You're WRONG!" screeched Mrs. Tuttle.

"I wish I was. Let me explain," said the physician. "She was in extremis when she came in. Her chest was full of blood. That is to say she was bleeding internally. We had to put tubes in to drain the blood."

"So she's going to be OK isn't she? Isn't she?" Mrs. Tuttle was frantic. The church lady was evaporating and the scared little girl inside of her, who she had repressed many years ago, materialized.

The doctor put his hand on her shoulder. He looked even more serious. Dr. Webster had pushed the boy Josh deep inside a few minutes ago. "It isn't easy to explain. The only thing I can do is put it to you like this; shortly after she arrived, we not only had to put tubes into her chest, but we gave her blood and had to put her on a respirator, a machine to breathe for her. Then her heart stopped but we got it going again."

Dr. Webster's mind drifted to the hole in the little girl's heart he had rapidly stapled closed in heroic attempt to buy her a few more minutes.

"Oh no!" Mrs. Tuttle gasped. She looked as if she were going to crumble.

"I'm afraid there's more," said Dr. Webster. "While we were waiting for the surgeon to take her to the operating room, her heart stopped again and we could not restart it."

"Well what kept the surgeon? I want to talk with him, right now." Mrs. Tuttle, the exactly precise church lady was back.

"That's not possible."

"I know you doctors, always protecting one another. I'm going to have a word with him. A *proper* doctor would get to the hospital faster."

She looked at the stately gray haired man writing on a chart at the desk. He wore a long white coat and held a wad of keys with a Mercedes fob.

"Is that him?" she asked, starting towards older physician.

"No, he's a cardiologist."

She turned around, and saw the words "Trauma I" emblazoned on a doorway.

"He's in there, isn't he?" she asked.

Dr. Webster stood in front of her. You can't go in. We've started a bedside surgery. You see, a few minutes ago I had to open her chest to do open heart massage. The surgeon just arrived and can't be interrupted. He was kind enough to race in despite not having any sleep last night. He wasn't really on call, but he came in anyway."

"But," Mrs. Tuttle stopped short. Someone was coming out of the Trauma Room.

An unshaven man with a scar below his right eye appeared. He had dark unkempt hair and sported a familiar gold chain. He also wore green pajamas that Mrs. Tuttle could now identify as surgical attire.

He somberly shook his head and spoke. "If only I was here two minutes earlier I–."

A tear trickled down the cheek of Dr. Webster. The repressed child *Josh* Webster was finally out. And for one righteously indignant woman the room spun wildly and went black.

A nurse peeked out of the trauma room and said, "Doctors, we have a heartbeat again!"

Resigning my Commission
James Chandler

Today I resign my commission with the California Highway Vigilantes. I've given up my responsibility to keep the highways safe from dangerous drivers. There are just too many of them. I can't keep up. None of us can keep up.

It's not for lack of trying. The highways are strewn with the wreckage of cars, trucks and SUVs I've blasted to smithereens. You must have seen all those splinters of plastic, twisted pieces of metal and shards of glass along the side of the road. It's all that's left of the offenders, fallen as they have to my phasers and photon torpedoes. Still, they come, careening down the highway like pinballs gone astray.

I've turned in my weapons and, most of all, my sense of outrage. No longer will I fire phasers at reckless lane changers speeding about like players in a video game. Never again will I hear the satisfying <u>whoosh</u> of mortars being lobbed up ahead, the <u>kaboom</u> as they land on the rooftops of intruding line-crashers.

No more will I exercise the gratifying use of my extensible hammer, levering ahead to bonk the roof of a cell phone addicted driver. Not to get the attention of that idiot careening past me, merging at the last possible moment in a desperate attempt to be one car closer to his destination. Not even to rattle awake the woman tailgating in the fast lane, late for work, head buried in the rear view mirror as she puts on her mascara.

Sometimes I catch myself looking up the exit lane, past the half-mile line of patient drivers, feeling a sense of satisfaction as my blood rises to the gall of the inevitable lane-intruders. "Fire one!" I cry, reaching to launch rudeness-seeking missiles that pass over the innocent and utterly destroy these offenders. But I stop myself.

No more phaser blasts for me. Not even my favorite remote-detonation missile. I used to shoot them into the rear of cars that cruised past, hunting for a chance to cut in front of a truck, causing him to hit his brakes with a screech. On those rare occasions where the cruiser didn't barge in, I could release the missile and let him live another day. Most, however, were destroyed moments after their transgressions.

As I leave the Vigilante service, I cannot report the battle won. There seem to be just as many hyped-up lunatics behind the wheel as ever. They continue to jerk, dart, dive into and around us. For all our determined efforts, they still swarm over the roadways like insidious pests during a harvest season.

Perhaps these were the students who slept through physics class, believing that speed will warp the fabric of space and squeeze a GMC Yukon into a ten-foot space. These are the same scientists who tailgate in torrential rains and treat curve warnings as indicators of the minimum speed for best road traction. I cannot educate these intransigents. Instead, I must acknowledge my defeat.

I do not resign for the sake of California's worst drivers. Pity does not make me hang up my guns. Rather, I do this for my own sanity. For I have come to the realization that nothing – not all the summary and heroic efforts of our esteemed Vigilante Order – will dissuade these drivers from hurling themselves to their doom, and perhaps to ours. Attempts of law- and etiquette-abiding citizens to keep the lane crashers out only exposes us to greater danger. I am more likely to bump the car in front, now too close for my weary reflexes. Repeatedly I've been rear ended as I tried to maintain a tight formation.

The thing that gives me hope in all this is that mile-long line. There is nobility in the socially responsible majority, that eighty percent who DO wait in the exit lane. Well, maybe seventy percent, but still the majority! They – not the road-ragers or even my fellow Vigilantes – hold the fabric of civility together. So it is their example I follow. I will create passable spaces, loosening the warp and weave of the dense traffic, spreading peace and light on the highway.

I will miss, though, the intensity of the moment as a photon torpedo finds its target, exploding a fast lane tailgating car and its cell phone distracted driver to bits. Like that idiot who just … but no, I am relaxed. I am at peace with the road.

Author Biographies

James Chandler — James is a carpenter, map publisher, and writer living in the East Bay. Originally coming to attend college in the SF Bay Area, he is half-Minnesotan by birth, half-Cuban by marriage, and half something else yet to be discovered. Most of his work is non-fiction, as he concludes, "you just can't make this stuff up." He believes that a keen sense of observation will reveal life to be infinitely entertaining. Read more of his writing at www.bummermanual.com

Kinsley Earl — Kinsley is not a professional writer, but likes to pretend. She graduated from Stanford in 1996 with a BA, in a field unrelated to writing. She live in Los Angeles and has spent several years working in advertising, and wondering what to be when she grows up.

Nancy Earl — Nancy was born in Chattanooga, Tennessee in 1944. She graduated from Northwestern University in 1964 and married in 1973. She and her husband live in Sacramento and have two grown children. She keeps a sign on her bathroom mirror: "a few funny sentences do not an author make."

Gregg Garmisa   Gregg conceived and helped organize the first Stanford Alumni Creative Writing Retreat, now held annually at Stanford's Fallen Leaf Lake Camp. A published ultra-short storywriter, he is at work on his first novel. Separately, he is writing a collection of short, interlocking, stories from which "The Runner" is drawn.

Will Harrison, MD   Will (MD, to be distinguished from his nephew-author, who also writes as "Will Harrison") is a retired Navy infectious disease physician/medical school professor/bioterrorism expert. His pieces in the Fallen Leaf Anthology stem from his experiences in southern Sudan at the turn of the century. He spent the better part of two years there, behind rebel lines, working with a Non-Government Organization, "Samaritan's Purse." Some of the time he was at a partially-rebuilt hospital; the remainder was at a camp for demobilized child soldiers. It was one of the best times in his life. Stanford, Class of 1960. eyedeedoc@aol.com

Melanie Johnston   Melanie has worked as a professional writer in advertising and television. In 2007, Merriam Press published Melanie's book about the Holocaust, "What My Father Saw." It has been placed in the historical archives at the United States Holocaust Memorial Museum, Yad Vashem in Israel as well as Buchenwald Concentration Camp and The Berlin Library. She is currently working on a novel about the oceans. MelanieJohnstonwriter.com

Laura Kaufman Laura completed her undergraduate work at Stanford in Journalism and American Studies, and earned a Master's in Journalism at Columbia University in 1983. She has been a health and medical writer, editor and public relations consultant and has worked for health agencies including the American Heart Association and the March of Dimes, as well as California hospitals and research institutions. She contributes to magazines and newspapers on a wide variety of topics, and particularly enjoys cultural activities and humor. Laura, a Seattle native, lives in the East Bay with her teenage son. lbkaufman@comcast.net

Bernd Kutzscher, MD Bernd was an undergraduate in History, Stanford class of 1971. After graduation, he dedicated himself to outdoor adventuring including more than ten years

of working in the summers as a professional whitewater guide in Idaho, California and Montenegro. In 1981, he graduated from Stanford Medical School and now lives in San Francisco where he specializes in eye surgery and continues to go with his family on annual whitewater adventures. His three children are currently students at Stanford.
San Francisco, CA.
EyeMDBK@gmail.com

Petra LaVictoire — Petra has recently completed a play based on her trilogy "The Root of All Evil" and is currently composing her first novel. Writing short stories, cooking and traveling are some of her many passions in life. She also enjoys copyediting, having copyedited both volumes of "The Fallen Leaf Anthology" as well as a memoir which will be published by the end of this year. She is a Certified Identity Theft Risk Management Specialist; Group Benefits Specialist & Independent Associate with Pre-Paid Legal Services. She resides in Southern California.
www.prepaidlegal.com/hub/petralavictoire

Betty A. Luceigh — Betty earned her PhD in Organic Chemistry from Stanford University in 1970. She had a long career in organic

chemistry as researcher, administrator, and primarily, as her true love, teacher. She retired as a Senior Lecturer from the Dept. of Chemistry, UCLA, in 2004. She is an award-winning teacher and originator of CHEM TV instructional materials. She has continuing interests in classical piano, reflective creative writing, and inspirational speaking. She is a published author in chemistry, poetry, and philosophical essays.
luceigh@chem.ucla.edu

Lynette Kent

Lynette is a split nationality – both Californian and Parisian. She has split Stanford degrees – both Art and French, and both BA and MA. And she has split creativity. A writer, photographer, and artist, she has written eight books on Photoshop, Lightroom, and the Mac operating system, all published by Wiley. She often teaches art and computer graphics techniques, but prefers to draw, paint, or photograph her own images, or work on a novel she started during the Stanford Write Retreats. She can be reached at lynettekent@gmail.com Her images can be viewed at www.lynettekent.com

Neil McCabe	Neil did a lot of writing in his career as an attorney, and he enjoyed doing it. But he dreamed of writing just for the fun of it. Since 2002 he has been doing that, writing short stories and enjoying the freedom of fiction. Neil lives in Chico with his wife Susanne. nsmccabe@comcast.com
Frederick Michaud	Fred is a judge who has heard and decided 7000 disability cases, after his career as Deputy District Attorney prosecuting criminal cases, and then as a trial lawyer for injured people. A graduate of Stanford and Cal, he lives on the Peninsula with his wife, close to their three daughters and eight grandchildren. fredandbette@sbcglobal.net
Lila Perdue Naimark	Lila was born and raised in Indianapolis to unassimilated Tennessee parents with strong, restrictive Pentecostal beliefs. She is currently working on a memoir detailing how rock 'n roll aided and abetted her escape to the real world at age 25. Lila has a BA and an MBA from Boston University and has worked in high tech for 30 years in marketing and communications. Her two grown daughters are her best accomplishments, but she's also proud of the publication in a Tennessee newspaper of the story about

how strawberries brought her great-grandparents together.

Kathy (Chang) Nakamatsu	Kathy is a high school Chemistry teacher in Saratoga, California. She lives in Campbell with her husband, Jon, and their cat, Freddie. When she's not teaching, she loves to travel, hike, write and play word games. She has enjoyed writing ever since she won a contest in 5th grade with her first book "Mystery of the Dognapper." She is currently working on a memoir and has written some short stories for her writing group, the Saturday Writers Block. Heymoe755@aol.com
Robert Nielsen	Bob is a Carmel Valley writer, photographer, and performance poet. Australian-born, he is a graduate of Stanford University and Columbia Law School. To him a poem and a photograph are the same thing. Each reflects his perceptions, feelings and dreams, and his worldwide experience as an international lawyer. His poems and photographs can be read or seen on their own or with others as parts of a larger story. His poetry has appeared in various publications; his images have been exhibited and are included in public and private collections in the United States. Website: pilgrim-

"The Write Retreat" - Stanford Sierra Camp 2010

	arts.com Email: rrntae@redshift.com
Patricia Northlich	Patricia (Patty), born in New York City, has a BA in Political Science from Northwestern University. Patty was a long-time lobby Concierge at the Claremont Resort in Berkeley, CA. She is writing her Claremont memoirs, and a children's picture book set in the Claremont. Patty was in the Berkeley Friday Writers group. She is a member of the Stanford Women's Club of the East Bay, where she has been a book reviewer and chaired the annual Books on Review Program. Patty is an avid tap dancer. pnorthlich@yahoo.com
Karen Paluska	Karen is a freelance marketing consultant and graphic designer. She lives in the San Francisco Bay Area with her husband and two young children. She holds a BA from Stanford University and an MA from Georgetown University. karenpaluska@yahoo.com
Lorilyn Parmer	Lorilyn is a writer who also works as a mom, education reform advocate and life coach. Since graduating from Stanford, she has traveled the world and followed a meandering career path that included jobs as budget and policy analyst, international

aid worker, educational exchange tour leader, human resources director... and lifeguard, waitress and soup cook. She has recently unearthed old letters, notes and manuscripts, and is working on a book based on her experiences as a relief worker in Sudan. Lorilyn lives in Davis, California with her family, which includes a young black lab named Aqua. lorilynparmer@stanfordalumni.com

Kathleen O'Hanlon Peterson   Kathleen received a BA in English from Stanford and a law degree from UCLA after being told time and again (by her musician father) that it was not a good idea to try to make a living in the arts. She recently completed a memoir entitled "Standing Room," which details her experiences as a student at American Ballet Theatre in New York. Her "day job" is practicing family law in Orange County, California.

Tori Ritchie   Tori lives in San Francisco, where she's been writing about food for over 20 years. She's written four cookbooks, edited several more, and contributes regularly to "Bon Appetit" and other magazines. She also teaches cooking at Tante Marie's Cooking School and volunteers for Food Runners, a nonprofit that delivers food to the needy. www.tuesdayrecipe.com

Cynthia Roberts — Cynthia is an aspiring mystery writer. She won the Write on the Sound writing contest with her piece, "Widowhood Noises," and has just finished her first novel, a high-energy cozy entitled "Jack's Other Beanstalk." She is currently searching for an agent and starting the second book in the series. While she waits to become a bestseller author, she spends her days working at Microsoft in Finance. fpaconsulting@earthlink.net

Taly Rutenberg — Taly lives in Berkeley with her husband, two children (the first just left for college) and a puppy. She has been a psychotherapist in private practice for 20 years and has recently started to write fiction. Poems have occasionally flowed out of her since youth.

Jerry Thrush, MD — Jerry is a graduate of Stanford University School of Medicine and board certified in Emergency Medicine. He practices at a trauma center in San Diego and has served as an Emergency Medical Services Medical Director as well as the Medical Director of an ambulance service. His more than two decades of experience has led him to develop a lecture series entitled

"The Behavioral Basis of Disease." He is actively involved in the development of the Eden Clinic and Spa Resort in Oregon and is engaged in an Anti-Aging Medicine fellowship training program. In his spare time he enjoys sailing, water sports and playing the violin. Thrush@cox.net

Jeanne Verville	Jeanne has had careers in audiology, real estate and law. She is writing a memoir about the roles she played during years of cultural change. She also writes essays from a contrarian point of view. The initial draft of "The First Step" was written at The Write Retreat. Jeanne lives in Seattle. Her guiding principle is *carpe diem*. Stanford, MA 1964. jnnvrvll4@gmail.com